**REA**

ALLEN COUNTY PUBLIC LIBRARY
**ACPL ITEM**
3 1833 03967 5032
RELIGION **DISCARDED**

D0583755

APR 6 2001

# European Societies

*Series Editor:* Colin Crouch

Very few of the existing sociological texts which compare different European societies on specific topics are accessible to a broad range of scholars and students. The *European Societies* series will help fill this gap in the literature, and attempts to answer questions such as: Is there really such a thing as a 'European model' of society? Do the economic and political integration processes of the European Union also imply convergence in more general aspects of social life, like family or religious behaviour? What do the societies of Western Europe have in common with those further to the east?

The series will cover the main social institutions, although not every author will cover the full range of European countries. As well as surveying existing knowledge in a way that will be useful to students, each book will also seek to contribute to our growing knowledge of what remains in many respects a sociologically unknown continent.

*Forthcoming titles in the series:*

**Social Change in Western Europe**
Colin Crouch

**European Cities**
Patrick Le Galès

**Education in Europe**
Walter Müller, Reinhart Schneider, and Suzanne Steinmann

**Ethnic Minorities in Europe**
Carl-Ulrik Schierup

# Religion in Modern Europe

*A Memory Mutates*

Grace Davie

# OXFORD

UNIVERSITY PRESS

Great Clarendon Street, Oxford OX2 6DP

Oxford University Press is a department of the University of Oxford.
It furthers the University's objective of excellence in research, scholarship,
and education by publishing worldwide in

Oxford New York

Athens Auckland Bangkok Bogotá Buenos Aires Calcutta
Cape Town Chennai Dar es Salaam Delhi Florence Hong Kong Istanbul
Karachi Kuala Lumpur Madrid Melbourne Mexico City Mumbai
Nairobi Paris São Paulo Singapore Taipei Tokyo Toronto Warsaw

and associated companies in Berlin Ibadan

Oxford is a registered trade mark of Oxford University Press
in the UK and in certain other countries

Published in the United States
by Oxford University Press Inc., New York

© Grace Davie 2000

The moral rights of the author have been asserted

Database right Oxford University Press (maker)

First published 2000

All rights reserved. No part of this publication may be reproduced,
stored in a retrieval system, or transmitted, in any form or by any means,
without the prior permission in writing of Oxford University Press,
or as expressly permitted by law, or under terms agreed with the appropriate
reprographics rights organizations. Enquiries concerning reproduction
outside the scope of the above should be sent to the Rights Department,
Oxford University Press, at the address above

You must not circulate this book in any other binding or cover
and you must impose this same condition on any acquirer

British Library Cataloguing in Publication Data

Data available

Library of Congress Cataloging in Publication Data
Davie, Grace.
Religion in modern Europe: a memory mutates / Grace Davie.
p. cm.—(European societies)
Includes bibliographical references and index.
1. Europe—Religion—20th century. 2. Religion and sociology—Europe.
3. Memory. I. Title. II. Series.
BL695.D38 2000 306.6′094—dc21 00–029350
ISBN 0–19–828065–3
ISBN 0–19–924124–4

1 3 5 7 9 10 8 6 4 2

Typeset by Hope Services (Abingdon) Ltd.
Printed in Great Britain
on acid-free paper by
T. J. International Ltd
Padstow, Cornwall

For Mark

who has travelled with me
through much of Europe

# ACKNOWLEDGEMENTS

A great many people have helped me in the research for and writing of this book. The more formal thanks, first of all, must go to the Christendom Trust for their help in financing some of the travel involved and to the Department of Sociology in Exeter, who gave me two terms' study leave in 1998 to enable both the completion of the research and a significant part of the writing.

Equally important have been those—both institutions and individuals—who have given me hospitality all over Europe. I have taught on a short-term basis in the Universities of Uppsala and Vilnius, in the Jagiellonian University in Poland, and at both the École Pratique des Hautes Études and the École des Hautes Études en Sciences Sociales in Paris. I have given occasional seminars in many more institutions all over Europe (in, for example, the Universities of Aarhus, Louvain-la-Neuve, Strasbourg, Lausanne, and Padua). I was also invited to the European University Institute in Florence by Colin Crouch, the editor of this series of publications. In each of these places, teaching commitments have been combined with the gathering of data and have permitted detailed exchanges with both staff and students. More than this, each episode has been a great pleasure and has resulted in warm friendships all over the continent.

Colleagues in the Sociology of Religion Study Group of the British Sociological Association, in the International Society for the Sociology of Religion, and in the American Association for the Sociology of Religion have heard various chapters or parts of chapters in the form of papers offered at conferences, giving me valuable feedback on each occasion. Preliminary versions of Chapters 3, 5, and 6 were initially presented as the Drummond Lectures at the University of Stirling in March 1996, a particularly pleasurable occasion. I would like to express my thanks to the Trustees at this point for their invitation. Sections of Chapters 2 and 3 were presented in lecture form in September 1997 at the School of Advanced International Studies of Johns Hopkins University in Washington, DC; they have subsequently been published in Berger (1999). I was also grateful to take part in a more historically based conference on 'The Decline of Christendom in Western Europe c.1750–2000' held in Paris in May 1997.

Not for the first time, I must acknowledge the help of the European Values Study team in establishing the tables that appear in Chapter 1 (the figures are taken from the 1981 and 1990 EVS enquiries). I must also thank the Institut National d'Études Démographiques in Paris for permission to reproduce the maps appearing in Chapter 4 and David Higham Associates and Macmillan Press Ltd. for the tables and diagram that appear in Chapter 7.

There are, in addition, a number of more personal debts. David Martin has, as ever, been both guide and mentor from start to finish. Anders Bäckström (in Uppsala), Irena Borowik (in Krakow), and Miklos Tomka (in Budapest) have answered repeated requests for more information or for clarification of specific points regarding their own parts of Europe with the greatest possible patience. Among the very many French colleagues who have helped me, Danièle Hervieu-Léger (who also read the final typescript), Jean-Paul Willaime, and Jean Baubérot have made me especially welcome in France; the same goes for Karel Dobbelaere and Liliane Voyé in Belgium, Roland Campiche in Switzerland, and Enzo Pace in Italy. I am grateful to them all, as I am to the other readers of the typescript—Colin Crouch (the series editor) and John Kennedy at the Council of Churches for Britain and Ireland. The comments of all three readers were invariably pertinent, constructive, and gently put.

As ever, my own students have given me valuable feedback. I have been particularly glad to teach Rosalind Fane, Dominique MacNeill, Philip Thompson, Keith Williams, and Zoë Reidy—the latter three were pioneers in the exchange between the Department of Sociology in Exeter and the Jagiellonian University in Krakow. Stefanie Lotz (at the University of Lancaster) should also be mentioned. Finally, a former student from Exeter—Dominic Byatt—has been the anchorman at the Oxford University Press; invariably cheerful, he has held the whole thing together over several years.

Most of all, however, my thanks must go to my husband, who has frequently travelled with me in Europe. When this has not been possible, I have been assured not only of the warmest of welcomes home but of constant encouragement to complete the task.

# CONTENTS

# LIST OF FIGURES

# LIST OF TABLES

# INTRODUCTION

This book should not be considered in isolation; it is conceived as one item in a whole cluster of new writing in the field.[1] Together these publications represent an important undertaking: namely the reconsideration of European religion as the twentieth century gives way to the twenty-first. Such rethinking reflects a variety of factors. It is a response, first of all, to a rapidly changing European context, whether economic, social, or political; a context which remains as unpredictable as it is forceful, and in which the religious factor can operate in a bewildering variety of ways. Secondly, this series of publications forms part of a continuing reappraisal of the place of religion in the modern world, a discussion developed in some detail in Chapter 2. More specifically it calls into question at least some aspects of the process known as secularization, notably the assumption that secularization is a necessary part of modernization and that as the world modernized it would—all other things being equal—be likely to secularize. An alternative suggestion is increasingly gaining ground: the possibility that secularization is not a universal process, but belongs instead to a relatively short and particular period of European history which still assumed (amongst other things) that whatever characterized Europe's religious life today would characterize everyone else's tomorrow. If the revised view is correct (or even partially correct), Europe's religious life should not be considered in this way. It is not a prototype of global religiosity; it is, rather, one strand among many which make up what it means to be European. What then has been the nature of this strand in the latter part of the twentieth century and what will it be like in subsequent decades? It is this essentially *European* question that this book considers in more detail.

The approach is explicitly sociological in that the book looks at the subtle and elusive connections between religion, in all its bewildering manifestations, and the wider society; in this case a rapidly changing society but one whose history is inextricably bound up with the emergence and development of Christianity. It is not concerned with the relative truth-claims of the diverse religions that now compete on European soil. Empirically it draws on a variety of sociological sources, both quantitative—notably the European Values Study—and qualitative. Regarding the latter, particular attention is given to the historical dimension, without which there can be no understanding either of Europe's religion taken as a whole or of the religious life of Europe's constituent nations. Martin (1978) becomes a key text in this respect, recognizing

[1] For example Fulton and Gee (1994), Gill, D'Costa, and King (1994), Dierkens (1994), Davie and Hervieu-Léger (1996), Martin (1996*b*), Campiche (1997*a*).

the crucial importance of the tensions and partnerships between Caesar and God in the early modern period and their formative effect on the religious life of Europe's nation states. Martin's new book (Martin, forthcoming) both widens and deepens this discussion. Above all an exercise in sociological mapping, it includes a necessary update on Europe's tensions and partnerships in view of the sweeping changes that have overtaken the continent since the earlier publication; notably the relentless, if not always very steady, emergence of the European Union (including monetary union) and the extraordinarily rapid unravelling of post-war categorizations following the *annus mirabilis* of 1989.

The composition of this book complements that of Martin. Its approach is thematic rather than territorial. Its principal theme—the handing on of an authorized memory—reflects the work of Danièle Hervieu-Léger, a French sociologist of religion. Hervieu-Léger has been described by Peter Berger as one of the most original and productive scholars working in the sociology of religion today. Her book *La Religion pour mémoire* (Hervieu-Léger 1993)[2] attempts to break through some of the most difficult debates in the discipline, not least the question of how to define religion. Its themes are provocative, particularly the notion of an 'authorized memory'—in other words a tradition—which lies at the heart of religious belief. Applying such ideas to the European case generates a whole variety of questions. What, for example, is the nature of this 'authorized memory' in contemporary Europe and how is it maintained? How has it changed from the memory shared by earlier generations? What happens if such a memory ceases to exist at all? Can it—from a sociological point of view—be replaced, and if so by what? What are its likely mutations in a society increasingly dominated by consumerism? Do such mutations differ for men and for women? Can such a memory be maintained vicariously by a relatively small minority? If so, the understanding of secularization becomes very different indeed; so, too, does the focus of the enquiry. Through what institutional mechanisms, for example, might this minority be able to operate outside of the churches themselves? Who has access to such institutions (the education system, the mass media, and the law, to name but a few) and how, precisely, do they operate? These, it seems to me, are some of the crucial sociological questions to ask about the nature of European religiosity at the turn of this millennium. Their content is developed more fully in the following chapters.

A second—and related—point of departure comes from my own work on religion in Britain (see especially Davie 1994), for in many ways this asks a parallel set of questions about religion in modern Britain. It encompasses two themes in particular, both of which will be developed in the present book. First, it observes and reflects upon the profound mismatch in the religious statistics relating to contemporary Britain and indeed to contemporary Europe:

---

[2] An English translation has now been published (Hervieu-Léger 2000).

namely that statistics relating to 'soft' religious variables—general statements of belief, the notion of a religious disposition, and denominational self-ascription—remain relatively high, whilst those that pertain to regular religious practice or to the credal statements of Christian doctrine have dropped very markedly indeed. Hence the formula 'believing without belonging', which is explored in a variety of British contexts—both geographical and sociological—but which invites extension into the European framework. One example will suffice. On a superficial level the Scandinavians appear to reverse the British idea: they belong without believing. (To be more precise, almost all Scandinavians continue to pay tax to their state churches, but relatively few either attend their churches with any regularity or subscribe to conventional statements of belief.) On closer inspection, however, they behave like their fellow continentals; in other words they maintain a nominal rather than active allegiance to their churches and what they represent, but in a way provided for by their particular ecclesiastical history. Or, as one Swedish observer succinctly put it: what the Scandinavians believe in is, in fact, belonging. Membership of their respective national churches forms an important part of Nordic identity.

The second theme of my earlier book highlights the European—rather than English-speaking—nature of British religiosity, considering the different countries of the United Kingdom as four variations on the European theme. The book concludes by proposing a wider framework. It uses a citation from John Habgood, former Archbishop of York:

These conflicting pressures, manifesting themselves in local earthquake and continental drift, are shaping the new world. It is not about whether individual politicians like or dislike Europe. It is about the forces at work in an era of world-interdependence, easy communication and disorienting change. (*Independent*, 12 Mar. 1992: 11)

A theoretically informed observation of these pressures, and within this a sensitive awareness of the religious factor, sets a demanding agenda for the sociology of religion at the turn of the millennium. Exploring such themes for the European case is the intention of the following chapters.

It is necessary to make one further (rather extended) point at the outset. This book will deal with Western Europe—in the sense of Western Christianity—rather than a wider (or narrower) definition, or description, of the continent. The marker in question derives from the split between Roman Catholicism and Orthodoxy that divided the continent a millennium ago, a far more fundamental division in my view than the relatively recent opposition between communist and non-communist Europe in the post-war period. Indeed the terms 'East' and 'Central' Europe have significance in this respect, for East Europe (Romania, Bulgaria, and most of European Russia) belong to the Orthodox tradition, whereas the central European countries (Poland, the Czech Republic, Slovakia, Hungary, and what was East Germany) developed

within Western Catholicism. The position of the Baltic states is equally revealing. Roman Catholic Lithuania and Poland are closely linked historically; in
contrast, Latvia and Estonia belong essentially to Western (Lutheran) Europe.
None of them face East.

We would do well to remember these distinctions in discussions about the
future of Europe. The countries which shared the experience of post-war communist domination represent very different religious traditions (Walters
1988). These traditions are likely to have contemporary significance.
Countries that belonged, and continue to belong, to Western rather than
Orthodox Christianity may well find it easier to realize their political and economic aspirations. Despite their real economic difficulties, their aim is to re-
establish Western traditions; they are not learning something totally new.[3]
They have, for a start, been part of a continent which experienced the
Renaissance, the Reformation, the scientific revolution, the Enlightenment,
and the Romantic revival; countries further east have been through an equally
formative, but entirely different, historical evolution.

The continuing vicissitudes in the Balkans exemplify, albeit rather differently, the same point. The post-war entity known as Yugoslavia combined
within one country not only contrasting Christian traditions but a sizeable
Muslim presence as well. For a relatively short space of time (two generations,
perhaps) the country held together under the personal authority of Marshall
Tito. As that authority—and the creed that underpinned it—collapsed, it is
hardly surprising that Yugoslavia's pseudo-unity began to fall apart. Ethnic
nationalisms, bolstered by religious differences, interacted with a multiplicity
of factors (linguistic, historical, and economic) to create an explosive situation. At the same time, the presence of sizeable ethnic minorities within the
borders of each state rendered the dissolution of the country as problematic as
its retention. Long-term stability remains elusive. In more ways than one,
Europe reaches its limits in the Balkans; the essentially European patterns that
will emerge in the following chapters start to disintegrate at the margins of the
continent.

The first two chapters provide a framework for the rest of the book. The first
offers an empirical overview in the form of a profile of religion in West Europe;
the second initiates the theoretical discussion. The order and content of the
remaining chapters emerge from the theoretical discussion and can be found
in the final section of Chapter 2.[4]

---

[3] The situation is, however, far from predictable. Greece, for example (an Orthodox
country), has been a full member of the European Union since the early days of the
European Community. Austria, in contrast, joined as late as 1995.
[4] One further publication came to my notice when this book was at proof stage.
Rémond (1990), published simultaneously in five languages, provides an invaluable
overview of the shifts in European religion from 1789 to the present day. The process of
secularization becomes an organizing theme.

# ONE

# *Facts and Figures: A Profile of Religion in Modern Europe*

B ROADLY speaking this chapter falls into two sections. The first examines the characteristics of religious life in Western Europe taken as a whole. In other words, it concentrates on what Europe has in common, not least its shared religious heritage. The second section adopts a rather different focus. It looks at the way in which such common patterns have been differently refracted across a variety of European nations. A whole range of factors comes into play in this section, the differing combinations of which account for the religious diversities of Western Europe rather than its unity. The major theme of this chapter—balancing unity against diversity (across time as well as space)—begins to emerge as the two sections are drawn together.

## The European Framework

What, then, do the countries of Western Europe have in common from a religious point of view? There are several ways of looking at this question. There is, first, an historical perspective. O'Connell (1991), amongst others, identifies three formative factors or themes that come together in the creation and re-creation of the unity that we call Europe: these are Judaeo-Christian monotheism, Greek rationalism, and Roman organization. These factors shift and evolve over time, but their combinations can be seen forming and re-forming a way of life that we have come to recognize as European. The religious strand within such combinations is self-evident.

It is, however, equally important to grasp from the outset the historical complexity of European identity. O'Connell approaches this question by introducing a series of interlocking and overlapping, blocs which exist within the European whole. There are seven of these: the western islands, Western Europe, the Rhinelands, the Nordic/Baltic countries, the Mediterranean group, the former Ottoman territories, and the Slav peoples. Not all of these will concern us in this chapter, but the 'building bloc' approach underlies a crucial aspect of modern as well as historical Europe:

If I have taken this building bloc approach, it is to make clear, on the one hand, how closely knit Europe comes out of its history and how important it may be to make a future unity, and to suggest on the other hand, how complex Europe is and, in consequence, how varied might future unity mosaics prove to be. (O'Connell 1991: 9)

There is nothing deterministic about the future shape of Europe: several approaches are possible; so, too, are several outcomes.

For the time being, however, it is important to stress one point in particular: the shared religious heritage of Western Europe as one of the crucial factors in the continent's development—and, possibly, in its future—and the influence of this heritage on a whole range of cultural values. Other very different sources reinforce this conclusion. One of these, the European Values Study,[1] provides a principal source of data for this chapter. In contrast with O'Connell's primarily historical approach, the European Values Study exemplifies, for better or worse, sophisticated social science methodology.[2] Using careful sampling techniques, the EVSSG aims at an accurate mapping of social and moral values across Europe. It has generated very considerable data and will continue to do so. It is essential that we pay close, and at the same time critical, attention to its findings.

Two underlying themes run through the EVSSG study. The first concerns the substance of contemporary European values and asks, in particular, to what extent they are homogeneous; the second takes a more dynamic approach, asking to what extent such values are changing. Both themes involve, inevitably, a religious element. The first, for example, leads very quickly to questions about the origin of common value systems: 'If values in Western Europe are to any extent shared, if people from different countries share similar social perceptions on their world, how had any such joint cultural experience been created?' (Harding and Phillips 1986: 29) As the European Values Study indicates, the answer lies in deep-rooted cultural experiences which derive from pervasive social influences that have been part of our culture for generations, if not centuries. A shared religious heritage is one such influence:

---

[1] The European Values Study is a major cross-national survey of human values, first carried out in Europe in 1981 and then extended to other countries worldwide. It was designed by the European Values Systems Study Group (EVSSG). Analyses of the 1981 material can be found in Harding and Phillips (1986) and Stoetzel (1983). A second enquiry took place in 1990. Published material from this can be found in Timms (1992), Ashford and Timms (1992), Barker, Halman, and Vloet (1992), and Ester, Halman, and de Moor (1994). Barker *et al.* includes a useful bibliography of the whole enterprise. A further restudy is currently in process—the data gathering took place in 1999. The longitudinal aspects of the study enhance the data considerably.

[2] The European Values Study reveals both the advantages and limitations of survey methodology. These are discussed in the introductory sections of Abrams, Gerard, and Timms (1985). Particular difficulties for the religious material will be highlighted in this chapter.

Both in historical and geographical terms, religion—or more specifically, the Christian religion—provides an example of an agency which through the promulgation of a universal and exclusive faith sought to create a commonality of values and beliefs across Europe, and elsewhere. A shared religious heritage based on Christian values, therefore, may be seen as one formative cultural influence at the heart of and giving substance to 'European' civilisation. (ibid.)

So much is unproblematic and confirms O'Connell's historical conclusions. On the other hand, as soon as the idea of value change is introduced, the situation becomes more contentious. A series of unavoidable questions immediately presents itself. How far is the primacy given to the role of religion in the creation of values still appropriate? Has this role not been undermined by the process known as secularization? Can we really maintain at the turn of the millennium that religion remains the central element of our value system? Surely the influence of religion is becoming increasingly peripheral within contemporary European society. Or is it? These are the questions that will preoccupy us over and over again in the course of this book. In the mean time it is important to indicate the principal findings of the 1981 and 1990 EVSSG surveys for a variety of religious indicators.[3]

There are, broadly speaking, five religious indicators within the data: denominational allegiance, reported church attendance, attitudes towards the church, indicators of religious belief, and some measurement of subjective religious disposition. These variables have considerable potential: they can be correlated with one another and with a wide range of socio-demographic data. In this respect the survey shows commendable awareness of the complexity of religious phenomena and the need to bear in mind more than one dimension within an individual's (or indeed a nation's) religious life. What emerges in practice, however, with respect to these multiple indicators is a clustering of two types of variable: on the one hand, those concerned with feelings, experience, and the more numinous religious beliefs; on the other, those which measure religious orthodoxy, ritual participation, and institutional attachment. It is, moreover, the latter (the more orthodox indicators of religious attachment) which display, most obviously, an undeniable degree of secularization throughout Western Europe. In contrast, the former (the less institutional indicators) demonstrate considerable persistence in some aspects of religious life:

In particular, some form of 'religious disposition' and acceptance of the moral concepts of Christianity continues to be widespread among large numbers of Europeans, even among a proportion for whom the orthodox institution of the Church has no place. (Harding and Phillips 1986: 70)

---

[3] The findings from the 1999 survey are not yet available. For a fuller picture of the earlier data—essential for any detailed work—see Stoetzel (1983); Harding and Phillips (1986); Barker, Halman, and Vloet (1992); and Ester, Halman, and de Moor (1994), together with the individual analyses for each European country involved in the survey.

The essentials of this contrasting information are presented in Tables 1.1 and 1.2, reproduced from the EVSSG data. These tables can be used in two ways: either to indicate the overall picture of the continent or to exemplify some of the national differences to which we shall refer in the second section of this chapter.

It is necessary, first, to look at the trends common to the continent as a whole. We should start, perhaps, by echoing one conclusion of the European Values Study itself: that is, we should treat with caution statements about the secularization process—in particular unqualified ones—either within Europe or anywhere else. For the data are complex, contradictory even, and clear-cut conclusions become correspondingly difficult (Harding and Phillips 1986: 31–4). Bearing this in mind—together with the clustering of the variables that we have already mentioned—it seems to me more accurate to suggest that West Europeans remain, by and large, unchurched populations rather than simply secular. For a marked falling-off in religious attendance (especially in the Protestant North) has not yet resulted in a parallel abdication of religious belief. In short, many Europeans have ceased to belong to their religious institutions in any meaningful sense, but so far they have not abandoned many of their deep-seated religious aspirations.[4]

Two short parentheses are important in this connection. The first may seem obvious, but the situation of believing without belonging (if such we may call it) should not be taken for granted. This relatively widespread, though fluctuating, characteristic within European religion in the late twentieth century should not merely be assumed; it must be examined, probed, and questioned (precisely this is attempted in the later chapters of this book). The second point illustrates this need for questioning. It introduces two contrasting situations where believing without belonging is not the norm. Indeed, in East and Central Europe prior to 1989, the two variables were (in some places at least) reversed, for the non-believer quite consciously used Mass attendance as one way of expressing disapproval of an unpopular regime. The Polish case is the most obvious illustration of this tendency. The second contrast comes from the United States. Here religious attendance has maintained itself at levels far higher than those that prevail in most of Europe; approximately 40 per cent of the American population declare that they both believe and belong.[5] Once

---

[4] One of the crucial questions raised by the EVSSG material concerns the future of European religion. Are we on the brink of something very different indeed: a markedly more secular twenty-first century? It is, however, very difficult to tell how the relationship between believing and belonging will develop. Nominal belief could well become the norm for the foreseeable future; on the other hand, the two variables may gradually move closer together as nominal belief turns itself into no belief at all. At the moment we can only speculate.

[5] Some sociologists dispute the figures for the United States. But even if considerably lower estimates are accepted, the figures for North America are still much higher that those for most of West Europe (for a full discussion of this topic, see Bruce 1996: ch. 6).

TABLE 1.1. *Frequency of church attendance in Western Europe, 1990 (%)*

| | At least once a week | Once a month or more | Once a month | Christmas, Easter, etc. | Once a year | Never |
|---|---|---|---|---|---|---|
| European average | 29 | | 10 | 8 | 5 | 40 |
| **Catholic Countries** | | | | | | |
| Belgium | 23 | | 8 | 13 | 4 | 52 |
| France | 10 | | 7 | 17 | 7 | 59 |
| Ireland | 81 | | 7 | 6 | 1 | 5 |
| Italy | 40 | | 13 | 23 | 4 | 19 |
| Portugal | 33 | | 8 | 8 | 4 | 47 |
| Spain | 33 | | 10 | 15 | 4 | 38 |
| **Mixed Countries** | | | | | | |
| Great Britain | 13 | | 10 | 12 | 8 | 56 |
| Netherlands | 21 | | 10 | 16 | 5 | 47 |
| Northern Ireland | 49 | | 18 | 6 | 7 | 18 |
| West Germany | 19 | | 15 | 16 | 9 | 41 |
| **Lutheran Countries** | | | | | | |
| Denmark | | 11 | | | | |
| Finland | | — | | | | |
| Iceland | | 9 | | | | |
| Norway | | 10 | | | | |
| Sweden | | 10 | | | | |

*Source*: Adapted from Ashford and Timms (1992: 46); additional figures for the Lutheran countries from EVSSG data.

TABLE 1.2. *Extent of religious belief in Western Europe, 1990 (%)*

| | God | A soul | Life after death | Heaven | The Devil | Hell | Sin | Resurrection of the dead |
|---|---|---|---|---|---|---|---|---|
| European average | 70 | 61 | 43 | 41 | 25 | 23 | 57 | 33 |
| **Catholic Countries** | | | | | | | | |
| Belgium | 63 | 52 | 37 | 30 | 17 | 15 | 41 | 27 |
| France | 57 | 50 | 38 | 30 | 19 | 16 | 40 | 27 |
| Ireland | 96 | 84 | 77 | 85 | 52 | 50 | 84 | 70 |
| Italy | 83 | 67 | 54 | 45 | 35 | 35 | 66 | 44 |
| Portugal | 80 | 58 | 31 | 49 | 24 | 21 | 63 | 31 |
| Spain | 81 | 60 | 42 | 50 | 28 | 27 | 57 | 33 |
| **Mixed Countries** | | | | | | | | |
| Great Britain | 71 | 64 | 44 | 53 | 30 | 25 | 68 | 32 |
| Netherlands | 61 | 63 | 39 | 34 | 17 | 14 | 43 | 27 |
| Northern Ireland | 95 | 86 | 70 | 86 | 72 | 68 | 89 | 71 |
| West Germany | 63 | 62 | 38 | 31 | 15 | 13 | 55 | 31 |
| **Lutheran Countries** | | | | | | | | |
| Denmark | 64 | 47 | 34 | 19 | 10 | 8 | 24 | 23 |
| Finland | 76 | 73 | 60 | 55 | 31 | 27 | 66 | 49 |
| Iceland | 85 | 88 | 81 | 57 | 19 | 12 | 70 | 51 |
| Norway | 65 | 54 | 45 | 44 | 24 | 19 | 44 | 32 |
| Sweden | 45 | 58 | 38 | 31 | 12 | 8 | 31 | 21 |

*Source:* Adapted from Ashford and Timms (1992: 40); additional figures for the Lutheran countries from EVSSG data.

again the situation should not be taken for granted; it must be examined, sociologically as well as theologically.

If we return now to the West European data and begin to probe more deeply, we find further evidence of consistency in the shapes or profiles of religiosity which obtain across a wide variety of European countries. One very clear illustration of such profiling can be found in patterns of religious belief, about which Harding and Phillips make the following observation:

Varying levels of belief in each country are similar to those seen on other indicators. Interestingly, irrespective of level of belief, the rank order among items is almost identical across Europe. The one exception to a consistent pattern, paradoxically, is the higher ranking given by English speaking countries to heaven than to life after death. (Harding and Phillips 1986: 47)

This kind of consistency is persuasive, the more so in that it is not easily predictable.

Correlations between religious indices and socio-economic variables confirm the existence of socio-religious patterning across national boundaries. For throughout West Europe, it is clear that religious factors correlate—to varying degrees—with indices of occupation, gender, and age (social class as such is more problematic). The correlation with age is particularly striking, and raises once again the issue of the future shape of European religion (see note 3). Indeed, it prompts the most searching question of the study: are we, in West Europe, experiencing a permanent generational shift with respect to religious behaviour, rather than a manifestation of the normal life-cycle? The EVSSG findings seem to indicate that this might be so:

The survey data are consistent with the hypothesis that there has been a degree of secularisation in Western Europe. Markedly lower church attendance, institutional attachment, and adherence to traditional beliefs is found in younger compared with older respondents, and data from other sources support the notion that these are not life-cycle differences. (Harding and Phillips 1986: 69–70)

If this really is the case, the future shape of European religion may be very different indeed. The data from the 1990 restudy reinforce this point.

So much for the similarities across West Europe. What about the differences? The first, and most obvious, of these lies between the notably more religious, and Catholic, countries of Europe and the less religious countries of the Protestant North. This variation holds across almost every indicator; indeed, they are interrelated. Levels of practice, for example, are markedly higher in Italy, Spain, Belgium, and Ireland (closer in its religious life to continental Europe than to Britain) than they are elsewhere. Not surprisingly, one effect of regular Mass attendance is a corresponding strength in the traditional orthodoxies through most of Catholic Europe.[6]

---

[6] Protestant Europe is undoubtedly more secular. One question posed by the EVSSG data concerns, however, the extent to which Catholic Europe will follow suit a generation or so later. Such a conclusion seems increasingly likely.

There are, however, exceptions to this rule, and at this point it is necessary to anticipate the discussion of church and state later in this chapter. For France displays a very different profile from the other Catholic countries, a contrast that cannot be explained without reference to the particular history of the country in question. Other exceptions to a European pattern, or patterns, should be looked at in a similar light; notably, the countries which do not conform to the believing-without-belonging framework. Conspicuous here are the two Irelands. Once again, the particular and problematic nature of Irish history accounts for this; for religion has, regrettably, become entangled with questions of Irish identity on both sides of the border. The high levels of religious practice as well as belief in both the Republic and Northern Ireland are both cause and consequence of this situation. In the Republic especially, the statistics of religious practice remain disproportionately high. Within Central Europe, the Polish case reflects a similar pattern. As ever, there are historico-political reasons for these exceptions.

Before such particularities are explored in detail, one further variation within the overall framework is, however, important. In France, Belgium, the Netherlands, and, possibly, Britain (more especially England) there is a higher than average incidence of no religion, or at least no denominational affiliation. Indeed Stoetzel (1983: 89–91)—in the French version of the 1981 EVSSG analysis—distinguishes four European types in terms of religious affiliation rather than three:[7] the Catholic countries (Spain, Italy, and Eire); the predominantly Protestant countries (Denmark, Great Britain and Northern Ireland); the mixed variety (West Germany); and what he calls a 'région laïque' (that is, France, Belgium, the Netherlands, and, possibly, England), where those who recognize no religious label form a sizeable section of the population. In many ways this analysis is more satisfying than groupings suggested elsewhere in the European Values material, where countries which have very different religious profiles find themselves grouped together.

In anticipating the following sections, it is already possible to indicate one of the severest limitations of the EVSSG data. There is no way of telling from the data why a particular country should be similar to or different from its neighbours. Apparently similar statistical profiles can mask profound differences, a point that will resonate in the more detailed discussion of church and state below. A second drawback must also be mentioned. The EVSSG sample sizes for each country are too small to give any meaningful data about religious minorities. It would, however, be grossly misleading to present even an overview of European religion at the end of the twentieth century without any reference to these increasingly important sections of the European population.

---

[7] Halsey (1985), for example, places British attitudes in a European perspective, offering three categories: Scandinavia (Denmark, Sweden, Finland, and Norway); Northern Europe (Northern Ireland, Eire, West Germany, Holland, Belgium, and France); and Latin Europe (Italy and Spain). The Northern Europe category includes some very different religious profiles.

The significance of such minorities as alternative forms of religious memory will provide the central theme of Chapter 7.

## Europe's Religious Minorities

The first of these, the Jews, has been present in Europe for centuries; a presence, moreover, that has been inextricably bound up with the tragedies of recent European history.[8] Nor, regrettably, can it be said that anti-Semitism is a thing of the past. It continues to rear its ugly head from time to time right across Europe, itself an accurate indicator of wider insecurities. Estimations of numbers are always difficult, but there are, currently, around 1 million Jews in West Europe, the largest communities being the French (500–600,000) and the British (300,000). French Judaism has been transformed in the post-war period by the immigration of considerable numbers of Sephardim from North Africa;[9] it forms a notable exception within the overall pattern of declining numbers (Wasserstein 1996: p. viii).

Former colonial connections also account for other non-Christian immigrations into Europe. The Islamic communities are, probably, the most significant in this respect, though Britain also houses considerable numbers of Sikhs and Hindus. Islam is, however, the largest other-faith population in Europe, conservative estimates suggesting a figure of 6 million.[10] Muslims make up approximately 3 per cent of most West European populations (Clarke 1988; Lewis and Schnapper 1994; Nielsen 1995; Vertovec and Peach 1997a). More specifically, the links between France and North Africa account for the very sizeable French Muslim community (3–4 million). Britain's equivalent comes from the Indian subcontinent (1.2 million). Germany, on the other hand, has absorbed large numbers of migrant workers from the fringes of South-east Europe, and from Turkey and the former Yugoslavia in particular. The fate of these migrants in the face of growing numbers of ethnic Germans looking for work within the new Germany remains an open question.

Whatever the outcome of this particular situation, however, one fact remains increasingly clear: the Islamic presence in Europe is here to stay. It follows that Europeans can no longer distance themselves from the debates of

[8] On the advice of one attentive reader of the typescript, I have, however, avoided the term 'Judaeo-Christian', except where this is strictly appropriate. Used indiscriminately, this term does not describe European history accurately; it has more to do with modern 'political correctness'.

[9] Information (including statistics) about the Jewish communities in West Europe can be found in Lerman (1989), Webber (1994a), Azria (1996), and Wasserstein (1996).

[10] Estimates of the size of Europe's Muslim population are, inevitably, related to questions about immigration. Statistics relating to illegal immigration are particularly problematic. See Nielsen (1995: 170–1) for a discussion of the statistical question and related difficulties.

the Muslim world. Whether they like it or not, the issues are present on their own doorstep. Admitting that this is the case is not easy for many Europeans, for the Islamic factor undoubtedly challenges the assumptions of European life, both past and present. Peaceful coexistence between Islam and an historically Christian Europe cannot, and never could be, taken for granted.[11] Nor can Muslims accept unequivocally the live-and-let-live religious attitudes assumed by the majority of contemporary Europeans. This, surely, remains the problem at the heart of both the controversy surrounding the publication of Salman Rushdie's novel *The Satanic Verses* and its French equivalent, the *affaire du foulard*. Both episodes will be considered in more detail in Chapter 7; both are central to the understanding of European religion at the turn of the millennium.

One further source of diversity remains: the presence of new religious movements in all European societies. The significance of such movements remains controversial. There can be no doubt, on the one hand, that new religious movements attract considerable media attention (often negative in tone); the numbers involved are, however, tiny. Be that as it may, such movements fulfil an important function for the sociologist of religion. Inadvertently, they have become barometers of the changes taking place in contemporary society (Beckford 1985, 1986). New religious movements 'represent an "extreme situation" which, precisely because it is extreme, throws into sharp relief many of the assumptions hidden behind legal, cultural, and social structures' (Beckford 1985: 11).

We shall use this perspective to examine one of the most urgent questions facing Europe at the present time: the need to create and to sustain a truly tolerant and pluralist society, both in Europe as a whole, and in its constituent nations—a society, that is, which goes well beyond an individualized live-and-let-live philosophy; a society able to accommodate 'that unusual phenomenon' in contemporary Europe, the person (of whatever faith) who takes religion seriously (Leaman 1989). By examining the divergent attitudes displayed towards new religious movements in different European countries, it is possible to learn a great deal about underlying attitudes. After all, tolerance of religious differences in contemporary Europe must mean tolerance of all religious differences, not just the ones we happen to approve of. If a country fails in its tolerance of new religious movements, it is unlikely, or at least very much less likely, to succeed with respect to other religious minorities.

---

[11] The outstanding example of creative toleration comes from medieval Spain, where Jews, Muslims, and Christians lived harmoniously for four centuries. The forcible expulsion of both Jews and Muslims from a re-Catholicized Spain in 1492 rendered the 1992 celebration of this year a very ambivalent European anniversary.

# Church and State

A broad-brush profile of religion in West Europe provides the background for a more detailed discussion of church and state relationships; these in turn constitute the parameters within which religious life on a national level takes place. It is helpful to set a discussion of church–state relationships within the following framework, taken from Martin's seminal work on the evolution of secularization in the Western world, *A General Theory of Secularization* (1978). Follow Martin (1978: 100), Europe is a unity by virtue of having possessed one Caesar and one God (hence the commonalities of faith and culture set out above); it is a diversity by virtue of the existence of nations. The patterns of European religion derive from the tensions and partnerships between religion and the search for national integrity and identity. These tensions and partnerships are continuing processes which have dominated four centuries of European history and have resulted in a bewildering variety of church–state relationships within the continent as a whole.[12]

The first split within Christendom—the divergence of Catholic and Orthodox Europe in the eleventh century—has already been referred to in the Introduction to this book; it is a crucial factor in establishing one possible 'edge' to Europe. The subsequent divisions of the West into areas or nations which are primarily Catholic or Protestant (or combinations of the two) are inseparable historically from the emergence of the nation state as the dominant form of Europe's political life. The processes by which such divisions occurred are highly complex, involving economic, social, and political as well as religious issues. Which of these led to the others and how the whole thing was set in motion in the first place is the subject of a continuing debate among historians, themselves of different persuasions. What remains indisputable, however, is an unprecedented upheaval in the ordering of Christian society in the sixteenth century; an upheaval which included the emergence of separate political entities or nation states, some of which expressed their independence from papal interference in the form of a state church. These state churches were increasingly underpinned not only by Protestant understandings of theology but by corresponding changes in the ecclesiastical order.

A striking visual illustration of the extent of this upheaval, the unease that it provoked, and its consequences right across Europe can be found in Holbein's celebrated portrait of *The Ambassadors* (London, National Gallery). In the centre of the painting, between the two ambassadors themselves, are two shelves filled with assorted objects. On the top shelf there is a celestial globe and a series of instruments which depend on the sun for various types of measurement; on the lower shelf can be found a terrestrial globe, a variety

---

[12] It is interesting to note that Declaration 11 of the Treaty of Amsterdam (Oct. 1997) recognizes this diversity. Church–state relationships remain the preserve of the nation state, not of the European Union as a whole.

of mathematical instruments, a lute with a broken string, a case of flutes with one missing, a German hymnbook, and a mathematical textbook. The significance of these objects lies in the fact that every one of them depicts 'disorder' in some sense or other—in the incorrect settings of the instruments, in the broken lute string, in the absent flute, in the particular pages selected for display in the books, and so on. The times (the year in which Henry VIII precipitated the break with Rome—hence the presence of the two ambassadors in London) are clearly out of joint, quite apart from the even more disturbing symbol of the distorted skull at the bottom of the painting. Holbein captures a moment of profound unease in Europe's politico-religious evolution, counterbalanced only partially by the half-hidden crucifix in the top left-hand corner of the canvas.

Part of the ambiguity regarding the whole historical process lies in the understanding of the term 'Reformation'. Does this imply innovation and the breaking of new ground? Or does it involve a return to and rediscovery of primitive excellence? Were those who endorsed the theological changes taking place at this time looking primarily for radical change or for conservative independence? Motives were bound to be mixed. The more conservative interpretation, however, was bound to appeal to those political rulers anxious to establish independence from external authority, but with a careful eye on stability within. Both were possible within the Lutheran concept of a 'godly prince'. Sometimes the prince had jurisdiction over a whole kingdom or kingdoms. Such was the case in Scandinavia, where Lutheranism became embodied in the state churches of Northern Europe. Elsewhere the process was far more local and concerned relatively small patches of land. The German case exemplifies the latter, leading to patterns which are not only extant but highly influential some four hundred years later (François 1996).

The Reformation took different forms in different places. In addition to Lutheranism, parts of Europe—notably the Swiss, the Dutch, the Scots, some Germans, some Hungarians and Czechs, and a small but significant minority of French people—were attracted first by Zwingli, but then by Calvin, towards a more rigorous version of Protestantism. Calvinism was both more radical and more restrained: radical in the sense of a new kind of theology based on the doctrines of predestination and redemption, but restrained in terms of its stringent moral codes. The effect of this particular combination on the subsequent economic development of Europe has provided inexhaustible material for an ongoing debate amongst historians and sociologists alike.

Broadly speaking, West Europe divided itself into a Catholic South (Spain, Portugal, Italy, and France, but also including Belgium and Ireland) and a Protestant North (Scandinavia and Scotland), with a range of 'mixed' countries in between (England and Wales, Northern Ireland, the Netherlands, and Germany). Central Europe exemplifies similar categories, though the geography is rather more complicated. Lithuania, Poland, Slovakia, Slovenia, and Croatia are firmly Catholic; Estonia and Latvia are Lutheran and relate closely to their Scandinavian neighbours (a commonality strongly re-emphasized as the Baltic republics regained their political independence); Hungary and the Czech Republic, finally, are rather more mixed (primarily Catholic but with significant Protestant minorities). In other words, boundaries gradually emerged all over Europe dividing one nation from another, one region from another, and one kind of Christianity from another. Boundaries, moreover, imply dominance as well as difference. Majorities and minorities were, and still are, created depending on the precise location of the line in question. One of the most arbitrary in recent years has been the line that divides Northern Ireland from the Irish Republic. The consequences of this division compound rather than resolve the Irish question.

The previous paragraphs have introduced the confessional map of Western Europe which emerged in the early modern period and which has remained relatively stable ever since. It would be a mistake, however, to assume that church–state arrangements necessarily follow suit. What evolves in the latter respect is a bewildering variety of arrangements dictated for the most part by particular historical circumstances and which change over time as political necessity dictates or as economic or social shifts suggest. The following summary (and it is only a summary) moves from north to south and covers, first of all, the countries of the European Union together with Norway and Switzerland.[13] The countries of Central Europe follow and are considerably harder to deal with, as their church–state relationships are part of newly established relationships in nations where independence remains a relative novelty. The point to recognize in all of these countries, however, is the significance of church–state relationships in an emergent democratic order. Freedom of belief and freedom of conscience are universal aspirations, but how this works in practice, particularly for smaller, less recognized denominations, is much more problematic. The solutions are by no means self-evident and are frequently disputed.

The Nordic countries (Sweden, Norway, Denmark, Finland, and Iceland) are the most straightforward to deal with from a church–state perspective. Here are the Lutheran state churches of Northern Europe, which have high rates of membership though practice is universally low; so, too, is the acceptance of orthodox Christian beliefs. These, in other words, to use the contrast set out in the early part of this chapter, are the countries that appear to belong but not to believe.[14] It is worth noting, however, that in Sweden, the gradual unpicking of the church–state relationship has already begun: the idea of a privileged

---

[13] For an up-to-date account of church–state relationships in the European Union, see Robbers (1996); this text provides considerable detail for the countries of the Union. More recent changes for the same countries are documented in the annual publications of the European Consortium for Church-State Research—a group of ecclesiastical lawyers.

[14] Or, more subtly (and as referred to in the Introduction), what Scandinavians believe in is 'belonging'. They find their identity in membership.

church is no longer thought appropriate in an increasingly, if modestly, pluralist society (see Chapter 3 for a fuller discussion of this point).

The Netherlands and Belgium are rather different and exemplify a pillarized society: i.e. a society where the *vertical* divisions between Catholic, Protestant, and secular have, historically speaking, provided the parameters for daily living. The system permeated almost every aspect of life (from the cradle to the grave)—schools, hospitals, trades unions, employers' associations, broadcasting companies, and so on. Both the particular nature of the pillars and their recent evolutions vary in the two countries concerned, themselves very different from a confessional point of view. In each case, however, church and state are technically separate, though the understanding of these terms is nuanced. In neither case is the separation rigorous; it should be seen rather as a 'mutual independence' implying, at the same time, a considerable degree of mutual respect. The case of the Netherlands is a particularly interesting one with respect to Europe's recent religious evolution. In little more than a generation Dutch society has shifted from being one of the most Christian societies in Western Europe to one of the least so; it seems, moreover, that the system of 'pillarization' acted first as a resistor to secularization (in marked contrast to France for example), but then almost as its conduit.[15] Interestingly, a modest form of *re*-pillarization is now taking place as both Muslims and the more extreme evangelicals claim their own space within an increasingly secular society (see Chapter 6 on the religious media for an illustration of this point).

The United Kingdom is a complex case, embodying as it does four distinct nations, each with its own religious history and constitutional arrangements. England has an *established* church (which is Anglican) and Scotland a *national* church (which is Calvinist); Wales has neither and its historically important non-conformist congregations are cross-cut by linguistic differences. Northern Ireland exemplifies the most problematic case in the European Union, given its divisive religious history still unresolved at the end of the twentieth century despite renewed optimism following the recent moves towards power-sharing embodied in the 1998 Good Friday Agreement. The Irish Republic, in contrast, is technically a secular state, though the preamble to its constitution is heavily Catholic and practice (though falling sharply in recent years) remains unusually high compared with the European norm. In 1998 the Irish government formally renounced its claim to the six counties of the North.

The German case is complicated by the reunification of the country after 1989. The bi-confessionality of the country remains none the less the most significant feature of Germany's religious life, despite the growing presence of (1) those with no confessional allegiance (partly but not wholly explained by the population from the former East Germany) and (2) a sizeable Muslim com-

---

[15] The outcome of this situation is, however, complex. What has emerged is a society with strong convictions either way: i.e. relatively high levels of churchgoing but also of unbelief (see Tables 1.1 and 1.2). It is the middle ground that has shifted so dramatically.

munity. In terms of categories, Germany holds a middle position between a state church and the separation of church and state. The Weimar Constitution (1919) ensured a constitutionally secured form of co-operation between church and state, structured around three principles: neutrality, tolerance, and parity. Such principles make up the freedom of religion, which is conceived both positively and negatively: German people are free to follow or not to follow their chosen religion, a right recognized in action as well as belief. Austria also maintains an intermediate position between separation and a state church; it is different from Germany, however, in that the population—at least in terms of nominal allegiance—is overwhelmingly Catholic.

France is a hybrid case in a different way; it is culturally part of Catholic Europe but far more like the Protestant North in terms of religious practice or patterns of belief. It is, moreover, the country of Western Europe which embodies the strictest form of separation between church and state. The French state is rigorously secular—or 'laïque', to use the French term. It is conceived as a neutral space privileging no religion in particular and effecting this policy by excluding the discussion of religion from all state institutions, including the school system. The incapacity of the French to accommodate the demands of young Muslim girls who wish to wear their *foulard* in school exemplifies the limitations of this system in a rapidly changing Europe (see Chapter 7). Switzerland is entirely different. Not only is it made up of 26 independent cantons, but each of these has its separate arrangements regarding church and state; confessional (and indeed linguistic) boundaries cut across cantonal ones, resulting in a highly complex but ultimately stable set of checks and balances.

Italy, Spain, and Portugal remain solidly Catholic at least in culture. The presence of the papacy within Italy undoubtedly influences the evolution of Catholicism within the peninsula despite the fact that the Italian state came into being in 1870 at the expense of the temporal power of the Pope. Relationships have eased since then, giving the Catholic Church a privileged position in Italian society, followed by a number of 'recognized' denominations (including the Waldensians). A third category, which includes Muslims, Mormons, and Jehovah's Witnesses—frequently more numerous than many of the 'recognized' denominations—is excluded from significant privileges. The Spanish case exemplifies a rather different history, where the re-creation of democracy is relatively recent. Technically speaking there is no state church in Spain; *de facto*, however, the Catholic Church is privileged simply by its dominance in terms of numbers. Regional autonomy remains an important issue in Spain—it is not without relevance for the status of the churches. Portugal is in many ways similar to Spain, exemplifying once again a halfway stage between theoretical equality before the law and a certain degree of privilege for the dominant religion. The concordat status of the Catholic Church, for example, still exists in Portugal despite a certain amount of constitutional reform in the 1970s.

Greece, finally, is the only Orthodox country of the European Union—the exception that proves the rule. (Always a hybrid between East and West, Greece became part of the Union very early on for particular political reasons.) In modern Greece, Orthodoxy is almost identical with Greek identity; it is the official religion of the Greek state, inevitably (if not officially) disadvantaging the members of minority religions, particularly the other Christian groups. Observance of the major festivals and the rites of passage is almost universal. Orthodoxy, moreover, is able by its very nature to contain a greater degree of diversity within itself than is Catholicism; this is one reason for its relative success in a changing moral climate.

The desire to legitimate greater freedom for religious expression undoubtedly played an important part in the efforts of the Central European nations to form more rather than less stable democracies in the years following the collapse of communism as an effective political force. But what, prior to 1989, was seen as a common aspiration could become rather more contentious thereafter, in so far as religious majorities have been reluctant to extend to minorities the rights they had so recently gained for themselves (Barker 1997; Herbert forthcoming). It is also difficult to disentangle the political aspirations of both the state and the churches in this part of Europe from church–state issues per se. In many places, the constitutions themselves are subject to continuing and divisive political pressures (Luxmoore 1995, 1996, 1997).

The Baltic states display relative stability in this respect. Estonia and Latvia affirm their respective Lutheran churches whilst respecting freedom of belief for everyone. Latvia has in addition an important regionally based Catholic minority in the south of the country. Both countries, however, house significant Russian communities which remain attached to the Orthodox Church. The external allegiance of the Orthodox communities is problematic: should this be to Moscow or to Constantinople? (Keleher 1997) Lithuania's Catholic Church is a conservative force in a predominantly Catholic country. Here, as in Latvia, a central question concerns the constitutional positions of newer religious groups. Barker (1997: 51) produces a useful analytic scheme in this respect, which can be applied all over Central and Eastern Europe. Mother/National churches are contrasted with—in descending order—other historically present religions, foreign mainstream religions, nineteenth-century sects, and new religious movements. Framers of new constitutions are understandably bewildered by such diversity and unsure of how they should distinguish the acceptable from the unacceptable, the recognized from the unrecognized.[16]

The place of the Roman Catholic Church in Poland is particularly difficult to assess. On the one hand, the Polish church is the most privileged in this part

---

[16] During a visit to Lithuania in 1994, I spoke with individuals responsible for the religious clauses in the Constitution. It was quite clear that the Constitution came into being under pressure—decisions had to made quickly and in difficult political circumstances; they were not the fruit of long-term reflection.

of Europe—with the capacity (after five years of wrangling) to push through the Concordat in February 1998, to intervene successfully (if not always very democratically) in constitutional debates, and to defend an advantageous financial situation; on the other, its position in Polish society is increasingly ambivalent as significant numbers of Poles come to resent the church's disproportionate influence. Minority groups, moreover, find it hard to gain a purchase in Polish affairs, despite legal toleration, as Polishness continues to be equated with Catholicism (Nowicka 1997). The situation in the markedly more secular Hungary and Czech Republic resonates in a different way, as the law surrounding church and state reflects persistent disputes about property and finance, about educational issues, and about the existence of smaller religious communities. The interplay of ethnicity and religion is an important element in these discussions.

The creation of an independent and notably Catholic Slovakia in 1993 illustrates a number of these points. Despite some efforts to 'calm' a difficult situation the church still sees itself as a 'Slovak' Catholic Church—Hungarian Catholics are welcome to participate and to receive appropriate pastoral support provided they acknowledge the church's Slovak identity. Slovakia, moreover, has a number of advantages in this respect (theoretically speaking) given the relative unity of the country in confessional, if not ethnic, terms (Byrnes 1997). The same can hardly be said of the former Yugoslavia, where the explosive complexities of ethno-religious divisions remain pervasive. It is important, however, to distinguish between the moderately stable, democratic—though still disputatious—Slovenia (Flere 1999) and the more volatile elements further south. Here significant and vulnerable Muslim minorities are a further complicating factor. Church–state relationships in the Balkan peninsula mean something quite different from those in most of Western Europe.[17]

An overview of church–state relationships such as this can only scratch the surface, beneath which lie layers of legal complexity concerning the financial arrangements of different churches, differential access to both education systems and the mass media, questions about divorce, abortion, and family life, and the legal protection of both religious communities and religious minorities. A number of these themes form the starting points for the chapters which follow. Before embarking on these, however, one further general point requires amplification.

---

[17] The detail of the Balkan situation lies beyond the scope of this book. A useful source of information can be found, however, in the journal entitled *Facta Universitatis (series Philosophy and Sociology)*, published by the University of Nis, and in the work of the Yugoslav Society for the Scientific Study of Religion, convened by Dragoljub Dordevic and Bogdan Durovic.

# Europe and Ecumenism

If the emergence of the nation state, and the role of the religious factor within this process, has dominated European history from the early modern period until the late twentieth century, the possibility that the final decades of that century might indicate the beginnings of a reversal in that process requires serious consideration. In 1945 Europe had come close to self-destruction for the second time in less than thirty years. The idea of European unity was barely conceivable, as individual nations struggled to come to terms with what had happened and to rebuild their devastated societies. Surprisingly quickly, however, the seeds of a European Community began to germinate in the form of Coal and Steel Agreements, which embodied the principle that the weapons of war should themselves be subject to supranational if not international control. Since then (the mid-1950s) Europe has moved inexorably, if not always very steadily, towards a greater common identity.

Coincidentally, or perhaps not, the Christian churches have made significant progress towards greater unity—for example, in the work of the European Catholic Bishops' Conference (CCEE) and that of the Conference of European Churches (CEC), a grouping of the Orthodox and Protestant churches. A similar thrust can be found in the Meissen and Porvoo agreements between the Anglicans and the Lutherans (each named after their place of signing) and in the continuing, if at times rather faltering, conversations between Anglicans and Roman Catholics. Two pivotal moments arrived in 1989 and 1997 in the European Ecumenical Assemblies held respectively in Prague and Graz, events which brought all Europe's Christians together (the first just before, and not unrelated to, the astonishing events which culminated in the fall of the Berlin Wall). Indeed it could be argued that the building of a greater European identity and the growth of ecumenical endeavour are part and parcel of the same process. There is, once again, a greater (if by no means unanimous) emphasis on what Europe has in common rather than its differences. That some nations/churches find this easier than others is part of the complexity of European religion. The Scandinavian, British, and Greek examples are particularly interesting in this respect. All these countries have ambivalent attitudes towards the European Union for one reason or another: in all their hesitations the religious factor as an exemplar of particularity plays a significant role.

Indeed it is part of the sociological task to ask what 'use' might be made of the religious factor, either by the state or by any number of interested parties in different parts of Europe. For example, can the religious element be pressed into service by pro-Europeans to emphasize what Europe has in common, or will it be used by their opponents to provide support for discrete and independent nations each with their own, carefully circumscribed religious sphere, possibly a national or state church (as in the cases mentioned above)? Either scenario is possible. The argument, however, can be turned the other way round. For the churches (national or otherwise), religious individuals or a wide variety of religious organizations may themselves attempt to initiate—rather than reflect—shifts in public opinion. In other words, the religious factor may operate as an independent variable in bringing about a greater European consciousness, or, conversely, in resisting just such a move. A theoretically informed examination of contemporary events, bearing this framework (or these frameworks) in mind, is one of the most urgent empirical tasks for the sociology of religion at the turn of the millennium.[18] One point of entry to this debate might focus on the external boundaries of Europe; these are more consciously 'Christian' than might be supposed given the apparent indifference of most Europeans to the presence of their churches within these parameters.

The Europe that is emerging as the twenty-first century dawns is, however, a rapidly changing place. From a religious point of view, one of the most significant evolutions of the late twentieth century has been the increasing representation of non-Christian faiths. Analytical concepts will have to evolve accordingly. European religion, for example—the legacy of Christendom that was outlined at the beginning of this chapter—is giving way to the 'religions of Europe'; the continent now houses a significant representation of Muslims, Sikhs, Hindus, and Buddhists in addition to the Jewish communities which have played such a crucial role in Europe's recent history. It is paradoxical that at precisely the moment when Europe, and to some extent the Christian churches of the continent, are attempting to draw themselves back together again, new forms of demographic and religious diversity are appearing. The tension between unity and diversity *re*-presents itself all over again, though in forms that are peculiar to late modern rather than early modern European society. An up-to-date analysis of religion in Europe is obliged to accommodate new as well as old forms of religious diversity both within the continent as a whole and in its constituent nations.

---

[18] An excellent start in this respect has been made in the collection of papers brought together in Bastian and Collange (1999). The papers are divided into three sections: those concerned with religion and modernity in Europe; those concerned with the relationships between church and nation in the construction of Europe; and those concerned with the notion of a civil religion of Europe as a whole. All three themes are related to the central argument of this chapter.

# TWO

# *Theoretical Perspectives*

How, then, can we begin to interpret the mass of data presented so far? I would like to offer three possibilities, the last of which becomes the springboard for subsequent chapters in that it offers an innovative approach to European specificity. All three represent relatively recent sociological writing, though they draw on the more familiar texts that deal with the secularization issue (notably Martin 1978, Dobbelaere 1981, and Wilson 1982). Each of the three takes note of the changing nature of European religion, but draws very different conclusions in terms of their explanations for such findings. Unsurprisingly their predictions for the future are equally contrasting.

## The Secularization Thesis: Steve Bruce

Bruce (1996) offers a classic statement—or restatement—of what has become known as the secularization thesis. Building on the work of the founding fathers of sociology, and more recently on that of Talcott Parsons, Peter Berger (1967), David Martin (1978), and Bryan Wilson (1982), Bruce sets out with admirable clarity what he feels to be the necessary connections between the onset of modernity and the demise of traditional forms of religious life. The key is to be found in the Reformation, which hastened the rise of both individualism and rationality, currents which were to change fundamentally the nature of religion and its place in the modern world. Bruce expresses these essential connections, the basis of his argument, as follows: 'individualism threatened the communal basis of religious belief and behaviour, while rationality removed many of the purposes of religion and rendered many of its beliefs implausible' (1996: 230). The two, individualism and rationality, go together and epitomize the nature of modern cultural understanding.

The process should not be oversimplified; it is both complex and long term. An underlying pattern can none the less be discerned, which took four centuries to complete. For at least three of these, religious controversy dominated much of Europe's political, military, and cultural life; it took the form of competing convictions about the nature of God and his (*sic*) relationship to the individual believer, notably Catholic and Protestant understandings about the right (and only) way to salvation. It is, moreover, the period of time associated with the emergence of the nation state as the effective form of political organization in Europe, a process inseparable from the break-up of Christendom. Only very gradually did a *modus vivendi* emerge as greater toleration of difference became the norm both within and between the states of Europe. But toleration is itself two-edged; it implies, following Bruce, a lack of conviction, a capacity to live and let live which becomes not only dominant but pervasive. A further epistemological shift is, it seems, inevitable. In the late modern period the concept of God, *himself* or *her*self, becomes increasingly subjective; individuals simply 'pick and mix' from the diversity on offer. Religion, like so many other things, has entered the world of options, lifestyles, and preferences. For the great majority, serious convictions are not only rejected from a personal point of view, they become difficult to comprehend altogether. Religious institutions evolve accordingly: church and sect give way in Bruce's terminology to denomination and cult—forms of religious organization that reflect the increasing individualism of religious life. Notably absent is the overarching sacred canopy, an all-encompassing religious frame expressed organizationally as the universal church. This no longer makes sense in the modern world.

What, though, do we mean by this phrase 'modern world'? Bruce is concerned with modern societies in so far as these display basically egalitarian cultures and democratic politics (1996: 232). In other words, he is concerned with modern Western democracies, including Europe (for the most part West Europe), the United States, and the English-speaking dominions (Canada, Australia, and New Zealand). There is passing reference to Latin America. Even this relatively limited selection of societies, however, reveals widely different religious profiles. At one extreme can be found the Protestant cultures of Northern Europe, with their tolerant and well-funded state churches, co-existing with low levels of religious practice and only moderate levels of religious belief (Sweden especially epitomizes these characteristics). At the other extreme lies the United States, also Protestant in culture but with an astonishing range of vibrant churches alongside (from a European point of view) extraordinarily high levels of religious belief. In between can be found (1) the Catholic cultures of Southern Europe, rather more intact than their Protestant neighbours but with historically strong oppositional or anticlerical tendencies, and (2) the English-speaking dominions, which display a halfway position between Europe and the New World. It follows that even within modern Western democracies individualism and rationality appear to have different outcomes in different places; nor are they necessarily linked with each other.

A second question immediately presents itself. Is it possible that one theoretical approach can account for a range of outcomes as great as this, never mind the innovative hybrids which are currently emerging in Latin America, which is beginning to look more like the United States than Latin Europe? Indeed two of Bruce's mentors—Peter Berger (1992) and David Martin

(1991)—have posed just this question concerning the secularization thesis and have revised their opinions accordingly. For both, the question of 'exceptionalism' provides the focus of the argument.

The secularization thesis developed within a European framework. For certain stages in Europe's religious development, moreover, there is a convincing fit between the argument and the data. As Europe's economic and political life developed, it was evident that religion diminished in public significance; religious aspirations continued to exist, but were increasingly relegated to the private sphere.[1] Bit by bit, however, the thesis rather than the data began to dominate the agenda. The 'fit' became axiomatic, theoretically necessary rather than empirically founded—so much so that Europe's religious life was considered a prototype of global religiosity; what Europe did today everyone else would do tomorrow. Secularization was a necessary part of modernization and as the world modernized, it would automatically secularize. But if this was the case, how was it possible to accommodate the very different situation found in the United States within the same theoretical framework? The answer lay in trying to understand American exceptionalism; i.e. in accepting that America was different and in elucidating the specificities within American society which could account for the successful cohabitation of vibrant religiosity and developed modernity. So far, so good; the secularization thesis remains intact even if deviations from the norm can be found in the modern world.[2]

Not everyone, however, has continued down this path. Berger and Martin, for example, have suggested that the argument be reversed. Exceptionalism undoubtedly exists, but it is Europe rather than the United States which is exceptional. Not only, following Berger, is the *non*-Western world as 'furiously religious as ever' (1992: 32), but the United States itself continues by all conventional criteria to be an intensely religious country. So what happens to the argument about relativism breeding secularity? In the US it simply hasn't happened. What has emerged in its place has been a healthy and competitive market of religious institutions, some of which appear to be thriving more vigorously than others. Paradoxically, it is the more conservative religious groups which attract the greater numbers of religious adherents as the twentieth century draws to a close. It is, it seems, those who resist compromise most successfully that flourish in a culture of increasing uncertainty.

Where, though, does this leave the question of European—as opposed to American—forms of religion? They must be seen, surely, as one strand among many which make up what it means to be European. European religion is not a model for export; it is something distinct, peculiar to the European corner of

---

[1] Not all commentators agree with this interpretation. See, for example, the collection of papers gathered together in Bruce (1992).

[2] Indeed in Bruce's recent account, even American exceptionalism is hardly necessary, as the data are reconsidered to minimize the difference between Europe and the United States from this point of view (1996: 129–68).

the world. What then has been the nature of this strand in the latter part of the twentieth century and what will it be like in subsequent decades? It is precisely these issues which underpin this book.

## Religion in the Modern World: José Casanova

A second attempt to understand both the nature of secularization and its application to European society can be found in the work of José Casanova. Casanova (1994) agrees that the paradigm of secularization has been the main theoretical frame through which the social sciences have viewed the relationship of religion and modernity. Part of the confusion about the consequences of such analyses, however, lies within the concept itself. It follows that a clearer articulation of what is meant by secularization is essential before the debate can be taken any further. An attempt at conceptual clarification therefore provides the starting point for Casanova's approach to religion in the modern world:

A central thesis and main theoretical premise of this work has been that what usually passes for a single theory of secularization is actually made up of three very different, uneven and unintegrated propositions: secularization as differentiation of the secular spheres from religious institutions and norms, secularization as decline of religious beliefs and practices, and secularization as marginalization of religion to a privatized sphere. If the premise is correct, it should follow from the analytical distinction that the fruitless secularization debate can end only when sociologists of religion begin to examine and test the validity of each of the three propositions independently of each other. (1994: 211)

Secularization as a concept is not abandoned but refined, enabling a more accurate analysis of religion in different parts of the world.[3] Casanova elaborates five case studies; two of these are European, two are from the United States, and one is from Latin America.

Two points emerge from these case studies which are essential for our understanding of modern Europe. The first is that *secularization as differentiation* constitutes the essential core of the secularization thesis. 'The differentiation and emancipation of the secular spheres from religious institutions and norms remains a general modern structural trend' (Casanova 1994: 212). It is not the case, however, that modernity necessarily implies either a reduction in the level of religious belief or practice, or the relegation of religion to the private sphere. Indeed the intention of Casanova's book is not only to discover, but to affirm, a legitimate *public* role for religion in the modern world,

---

[3] In many respects Casanova is building on the seminal work of Karel Dobbelaere in discerning the different strands within the concept of secularization (see especially Dobbelaere 1981); in other ways, he is clearly a disciple of Martin (1978), a debt which is repeatedly acknowledged.

including modern Europe. The second point follows from this: it is precisely those churches which have resisted the structural differentiation of church and state—notably the state churches of Europe—which have had the greatest difficulty in coming to terms with the pressures of modern lifestyles. Hence the decline, relatively speaking, of religious vitality in much of modern Europe where state churches persist with the greatest frequency. This is not an inevitable outcome of modernity, but the consequence of the particular arrangements of church and state that predominate in European history. It is, to anticipate the central argument of this chapter, a European phenomenon with a European explanation; it is not an axiomatic connection between religion and the modern world taken as a whole.[4]

The two European case studies selected by Casanova provide contrasting illustrations of this approach. The first, Spain, supports Casanova's conclusion. Here the long, protracted, and indeed tragic resistance of the Catholic Church to modern forms of economic and political life has had inevitable and profoundly negative consequences for religious life in Spain; only now can the Spanish church begin to shake off the associations of its past and begin to come to terms with a modern democratic regime. The Spanish case is particularly instructive sociologically in that it constitutes an artificially delayed and therefore speeded-up version of modernity, in which the competing tensions display themselves with unusual clarity. What has taken a century in most parts of Europe has happened within a generation in Spain and can be analysed accordingly. The statistics tell the same story—the drop in religious practice between the 1981 and 1990 European Values Studies was larger in Spain than anywhere else, and so too was the fall in vocations to the priesthood (Pérez Vilariño 1997). A very significant generation gap is emerging.

In Poland, however, there has been a different juxtaposition altogether: here a powerful and increasingly monolithic church has been the focus of resistance to, rather than the ally of, a state which itself lacked legitimacy. In Poland resistance to secularization became associated with resistance to an illegitimate power: a combination which strengthened rather than diminished the position of the church in question and resulted in unusually high figures of religious practice throughout the communist period. But what of the future? Since 1989 the Polish church, like its Spanish counterpart, has had to come to terms with a very different situation and to find its place in a modern democracy where a monolithic, semi-political presence (even one that could take pride in its resistance to communism) is, quite clearly, no longer sustainable. Paradoxically the most powerful church in Central Europe is, it seems, the one least able to trust itself to the democratic process.

It is also worth pointing out that Casanova makes almost no reference to the state churches of Northern Europe in his analysis. Is it the case that these

---

[4] It is, of course, an argument strongly reminiscent of de Tocqueville, who made a similar observation following his own experiences in North America in the 19th century.

too exemplify resistance to the modern order and find themselves, by definition, ill-suited to the competitions of late capitalist society? Some would
argue that this is so, not least a section of those most active within such institutions (this is certainly the case within the Church of England). Casting cov-
etous eyes across the Atlantic, a vociferous minority of active Anglicans argue
that deregulation of religion in the United States is a principal reason for religious vitality in the New World, so why not try the same formula in Northern
Europe? From a sociological point of view, rational-choice theorists would
support such a notion.[5] I am not so sure, however, for the hypothesis requires
that all other things be equal, and all other things are clearly not so in this
case.

Indeed the thesis put forward by Gill (1993)—that the overprovision of
churches in parts of Britain was the *cause* rather than the consequence of religious decline—undermines rather than supports the assumptions of the rational-choice theorists. It is, moreover, a thesis based on persuasive empirical
evidence, both rural and urban. According to Gill, an increase in supply in certain situations does not lead to an increase in religious practice; on the contrary it simply overburdens the system as a whole and leads relatively quickly
to demoralization (these churches can never be filled so why bother trying?),
and subsequently to religious decline. With this in mind, there are those (Gill
among them) who demand a considerable degree of rationalization if the
churches are to function efficiently, indeed if they are to function at all, in
modern European society.

That is one possibility. Another lies in identifying—and indeed from the
point of view of the churches themselves in exploiting—the particularities of
existing arrangements in Northern Europe where Protestant state churches co-
exist alongside moderately secular, but far from oppositional, cultures. This is
a situation rather different from the clerical–anticlerical tensions of Latin
Europe (so well described by Casanova), a contrast that can be explained eccle-
siologically. In most of Northern Europe, Protestantism itself declericalized
the church; there was no need for an anticlerical alternative outside the institutional framework of religion. But how such churches should move forward
within a modern democracy is, again, an open question. It provides the starting point for Chapter 3.

---

[5] Rational-choice theory offers a supply-side analysis of religious activity: the greater
the choice of religious organizations, the greater the response will be. A lack of choice—
for example a dominant state church—leads to reduced religious activity. The outlines
of the rational-choice debate and a range of case studies (some for and some against the
analysis) can be found in Young (1997), and in 1990s issues of the *Journal for the Scientific
Study of Religion*.

## Religion as Collective Memory: Danièle Hervieu-Léger

My third theoretical approach borrows from a leading French sociologist of religion, Danièle Hervieu-Léger, whose point of departure (Hervieu-Léger 1993) lies in trying to identify and refine the conceptual tools necessary for the understanding of religion in the modern world. In responding to this challenge, Hervieu-Léger draws on an entirely different school of sociological thinking. The inspiration is notably French: Durkheimian in origin, it is mediated through the work of Maurice Halbwachs—a writer little known outside France—to offer Hervieu-Léger the key to her understanding of religion in the modern world (MacNeill 1998*a*; Hervieu-Léger forthcoming). This key lies in the concept of 'memory', through which Halbwachs analyses the bonds between individual and society. Following Halbwachs, an awareness of shared memory is an essential feature of both individual and social identity; without such an awareness a society (never mind an individual) will have difficulty facing its future.[6]

The link between Halbwachs and Hervieu-Léger's own thinking becomes evident in the latter's definition of religion as a specific mode of believing. The crucial points to grasp in this analysis are (1) the *chain* which makes the individual believer a member of a community—a community which gathers past, present, and future members—and (2) the tradition (or collective memory) which becomes the basis of that community's existence. Hervieu-Léger goes further than this: she argues that modern societies (and especially modern European societies) are not less religious because they are increasingly rational but because they are less and less capable of maintaining the memory which lies at the heart of their religious existence. They are, to use her own term, amnesic societies. This is a rather different situation from one which assumes, uncritically, that European societies have found satisfactory alternatives to the traditional forms of religion so crucial in their historical formation. Manifestly, they have not.

Indeed, Hervieu-Léger argues in a earlier text (1986) that modern societies are by their very nature corrosive of the traditional forms of religious life and supports this argument with the kind of data presented in the previous chapter, notably the fall in the hard indicators of religious activity. In this sense the argument is reminiscent of Bruce's presentation of the secularization thesis. But it is only half the story. Modern societies may well corrode their traditional religious base; at one and the same time, however, the same societies open up spaces or sectors that only religion can fill. These Hervieu-Léger refers to as 'utopian' spaces. Modern individuals are encouraged to seek answers, to find solutions, and to make progress; in other words to move forwards. Such aspirations become an increasingly normal part of human experience. But

---

[6] The trauma of World War I is evident in Halbwach's writing.

their realization is, and must remain, infinitely problematic, for the horizon will always recede. The image of utopia must always exceed reality and the more successful the projects of modernity, the greater the mismatch becomes. Hence the paradox of modernity, which in its historical forms removes the need for and sense of religion (the amnesia), but in its utopian forms cannot but stay in touch with the religious (the need for a religious future).

Through what mechanisms, then, can modern European societies overcome their amnesia and stay in touch with the forms of religion that are necessary to sustain their identity? That seems to me the challenge set by Hervieu-Léger's analysis.

## The Mechanics of Memory in the European Case: Building on Hervieu-Léger

*La Religion pour mémoire* is an exacting book to read—inevitably, for it struggles with conceptual issues within the sociology of religion that have, from the outset, proved impossibly difficult to resolve, notably the question of definitions of religion. It is equally inevitable, I think, that Hervieu-Léger's reconstruction of the definitional problem will please some scholars more than others, for difficulties arise, unavoidably, in the application of her new formulations. As we have seen, the proposed ideal type takes as its organizing axis some sort of reference to the legitimating authority of a tradition: a point of view which postulates the existence of a believing community, either concrete or imaginary, linking the individual believer to something beyond him- or herself. Such links become a chain of belief, the crucial focus of interest. But precisely which chains should be included in the definition of religion and which chains should not will depend, once again, on the judgements of the observer. There are bound to be differences of opinion as disputed and marginal cases catch the attention of sociologists.

The disputed and the marginal should not, however, detract from the wider issue. For there can be no doubt at all that Hervieu-Léger's analysis offers a major step forward in the sociology of religion, in that it provokes an important series of sociological questions. The concept of memory as a way of looking at religion opens up new and creative formulae, through which old questions can be looked at in different ways and altogether new questions can be assembled. Examples abound. One set of possibilities could, for instance, include systematic and empirical work on the classic sociological variables of class, gender, and race, in order to discover the crucial groups or individuals in society who take responsibility for the creation, maintenance, development, and control of a memory. This kind of approach becomes, in fact, a new look at an old debate; it reflects very directly Weber's preoccupation with the decisive social strata that were bearers of a particular religious ethic (Weber

1961). Rather more recent lines of sociological enquiry might, however, pick up the themes of age and gender rather than those of class or status, for men and women quite clearly behave differently with respect to a wide range of religious variables. Men and women are, in addition, differently responsible for the handing on of a tradition from one generation to another, a crucial task in the perpetuation of a memory. This kind of thinking introduces, inevitably, the concept of a generation, a critical unit of time in the understanding of religious change and one that both draws on and contributes to an analysis based on the concept of memory. For over and above the idea of time, a generation includes the sense of passing something on. A failure in this respect is noted; in other words it breaks a chain that should, it seems, be continued. But generations should also be seen collectively, for certain 'generations' have a greater tendency to belive than others. Why should this be so? What are the contingent factors that determine a greater or lesser sense of believing? The way is immediately open for a whole range of empirical studies that relate generational factors to wider sociological debate.

A more immediately relevant set of questions follows on; these concern larger memories—regional, national, or international in scale. The analysis in this case can proceed in any number of ways: historically, empirically, quantitatively, qualitatively, and so on. Two short illustrations from the European context will suffice to indicate the potential in this approach. One of these is quintessentially English; it concerns the reconsiderations of memory that are taking place in some circles with respect to the English Reformation (Collinson 1994). Prompted at least in part by the debate surrounding the ordination of women within the Church of England and by the associated uncertainties about the nature of Anglicanism, a clutch of books emerged with a common theme. They look again at a pivotal moment in English history, Henry VIII's break with Rome and the establishment of an English church. The author of one such publication, Christopher Haigh, encapsulates the underlying argument: 'It was the break with Rome which was to cause the decline in Catholicism, not the decline of Catholicism which led to the break with Rome' (quoted in Collinson 1994: 74). This 'new orthodoxy', as it has become known to the aficionados, arises from a series of ethnographic studies which have sought to rediscover the essence of British religiosity in the early sixteenth century. And if one concludes—as some of these authors do—that Britain was indeed a Catholic country at this time, how then was the Catholic memory lost so completely and for so long? And why now, at the end of the twentieth century, should a different version of the memory begin to assert itself? The answer depends on contemporary and sociological factors just as much as historical ones.[7]

---

[7] A rather similar argument occurred in connection with the supposedly 'Catholic' rituals that took place after the death of Princess Diana at the end of August 1997; they were thought to reveal the latent Catholicism of the British people as described in Duffy (1992).

A second example looks at some of the material presented in the last chapter and reformulates this in terms of Hervieu-Léger's theoretical approach. Once again the long-term historical view turns out to be crucial, for the religious factor has played a whole variety of roles in the creation and recreation of the entity that we have come to recognize as Europe. There have quite clearly been times when a common memory was a factor which moulded the continent into a unity in which secular and temporal power were barely distinguishable. Later centuries saw this common memory disintegrate into a whole variety of national and regional variations in which competing religious memories became a crucial variable in emphasizing difference rather than commonality. In the 1990s, as the Single European Act became, however tentatively, a reality, the situation altered once again, to one in which all sorts of possibilities present themselves regarding the potential influence of the churches (Bastian and Collange 1999). Examining these possibilities within the framework elaborated by Hervieu-Léger seems to me a self-evidently fruitful approach to some of the most crucial questions facing the European continent at the turn of the millennium.

As a preliminary to my own contribution to the debate I would like to stress once again the *specificities* of Europe's religious life. What I am suggesting in this book is not an analysis of religion in the modern world, or even in the Western world, but an attempt to grasp both the nature of European religion as it emerges from a complex past and the forms that this memory or memories are likely to take as the twentieth century gives way to the twenty-first. It is a part of the world characterized by unusually low levels of active religiousness, but with relatively high levels of nominal belief: or to put this into a convenient shorthand, Europe believes but it does not belong. The next task must be to examine the connections between these two variables and their implications for those institutions—both religious and secular—which find themselves responsible for maintaining in positive and constructive forms (or alternatively choosing not to maintain) the essence of Europe's religious traditions.

# Effecting the Task

The analysis which follows starts, inevitably, with the institutional churches themselves. Compared with previous generations, the institutional churches may be reduced both in size and in social significance; they remain, however, enormously influential as voluntary organizations (at both national and local level). Chapter 3 will start by fleshing out the church–state connections already outlined in different parts of Europe, with particular attention to finance. It will ask a crucial set of questions. How are the churches funded in different parts of Europe and what is the relationship, if any, between finance and 'success'? What is the likely future of Europe's churches from this point of view? Does money make a difference? It will also look at the internal life of at least some of these churches, concentrating first of all on the professional ministries of religious organizations. Profound changes have taken place in the post-war period in this respect, not least the inclusion of women in the ministries of most Protestant churches. And if women are markedly different from men in their religious sensitivities, what is the significance of such changes, both long- and short-term, for the maintenance of a religious memory? Placing the churches in the wider sphere of the voluntary sector or civil society will provide an extended conclusion to this discussion.

Chapter 4 concentrates not so much on the churches themselves but on the people inside them. It will, however, reflect on an entirely traditional task of the Christian churches within European history: namely their role as the guardians (both spiritual and secular) of the sacred moments of human existence—birth, death, and, up to a point, marriage. The chapter will examine the ways in which such activities have changed in the twentieth century in Europe, setting such changes against the demographic metamorphoses of Europe in the same period, notably the transformation in life expectancy. Europeans may indeed live longer than they used to, but they still die—an irreducible fact which introduces the section of the chapter relating to the continuing significance of religious organizations at the time of death. The funerals of two prominent Europeans in the late 1990s illustrate this point: those of Princess Diana and President Mitterand. In both cases the institutional churches played a crucial role in marking the end of a public life, but in unexpected ways and alongside a whole range of extra-church rituals many of which were improvised by largely unchurched populations. The relationship between formal and informal patterns of religion is, once again, central to these discussions.

Chapters 5, 6, and 7 introduce a range of institutional mechanisms outside the institutional churches themselves which have, for a variety of reasons, become important carriers of religious memory in the European context. Chapter 5 concentrates on education. Education itself is changing in its attempts to keep up with the demands of a post-industrial society. Within these changes, moreover, the churches continue to play an important role as owners/managers of significant numbers of schools in many European countries. An important focus of this debate concerns which religious communities may or may not have access to this privileged position. The gradual (and ultimately successful) attempts by the Muslim population to achieve parity with both Christians and Jews in Britain provides an interesting case study in this respect. The chapter will also consider moral, social, and religious education within the school system. This highly political issue is debated within the context of prolonged and often confused exchanges about the transmission of values in modern European societies. The place of religion in the lives of young people forms a background to this discussion; this in turn reveals the need to take into account ongoing and profound economic and social evolutions.

Chapter 6 looks at the role of religion in the media at a time when technology has permitted exponential growth in the number of broadcasting outlets. The relationships between religion and the public media are, moreover, complex, for what is portrayed either in print or on the screen both reflects the realities of modern religion and creates new and persuasive images (or memories). It is, in consequence, of crucial importance to discover who has access to broadcasting outlets and which categories of people are most likely to be influenced by them. For many Europeans a central question dominates the scene: will American-style televangelism make inroads into the European market? If it does, will this change the nature of European religion as a whole? If it doesn't, what are the likely forms of religious broadcasting in the foreseeable future in the European context? Is the relative popularity of traditional religious broadcasting in Britain, for example, typical or atypical of European reactions? Is it, moreover, an illustration of believing without belonging taken to the extreme and if so, what might be the consequences of this situation for the institutional churches themselves? Another very practical set of questions follows on: are these tensions similar to those experienced by the sponsors of organized sport and the networks who wish to broadcast such events on television? The *financial* consequences may well be similar in both cases.

Chapter 7 is concerned with pluralism and the law. It looks at legal definitions of religion and the diverse manner in which 'religious' cases come before the courts. Who brings these cases? How and by whom are the cases presented and in what kind of court? What is the role of the European (as opposed to national) courts in this respect? Such issues have, very often, been brought to public attention in connection with new religious movements and their efforts to gain public acceptance and recognition. It is becoming increasingly clear, however, that the emergent issues—notably those of pluralism and tolerance—have equal, if not greater, resonance with respect to Europe's other-faith communities. Both the Rushdie controversy in Britain and the *affaire du foulard* in France brought such issues centre stage but failed to resolve them. Both episodes will be looked at in some detail within a framework of alternative memories. As a postscript, the chapter will also look at this question in relation to ethical issues. In many respects the Christian basis for ethics seems out of place in an unchurched and partially pluralist culture. Alternative foundations (including secular ones) are, however, less easy to identify. How, then, should the making of law proceed? How can seemingly arbitrary decisions be justified?

Chapter 8 also examines new forms of religiosity in contemporary Europe, notably those associated with alternative therapies and healing. Many of these are closely related to green issues and the environmental debate. New Age religiosity is central to this discussion, though its importance should not be exaggerated; it is essentially a middle-class rather than a mass phenomenon. Of far greater significance is a more general awareness of religious innovation, an approach which incorporates new ways of responding to traditional forms of religion as well as innovations *per se*. Young people, for example, may well respond positively to certain kinds of religious experience *within* both Catholicism and Protestantism as well as outside these; they appear to be considerably less interested in the historical content or dogmatic teaching of the traditional faiths. Central to this chapter are two case studies: that of Opus Dei (of Spanish origin) and the Italian Communione e Liberazione. Both illustrate a point important for the understanding of religion at the turn of the millennium, namely that innovation can take conservative as well as radical forms.

The final substantive chapter will build on this discussion by considering the growing popularity of sacred places in contemporary Europe—whether these be traditional shrines (for example Santiago in northern Spain and Lourdes in the Pyrenees) or more recent places of pilgrimage (notably Iona on the west coast of Scotland and Taizé in eastern France). The argument leads naturally to the relationship between tourism and pilgrimage and the importance of the aesthetic (architecture, art, and music) as a carrier of the sacred. It is not an exaggeration to consider Europe's cathedrals as a form of European museum. But for the faithful, they are more than this—they are *embodiments* as well as carriers of memory. The relationship between cathedrals and secular museums is a significant if under-researched area of enquiry, and one that is central to the notion of religious memory. Liturgical changes are also part of this discussion; so, too, is the contemporary significance of Europe's religious festivals, many of which are able to draw significant numbers of young people together at least in the short term, even if regular churchgoing has all but disappeared in this generation.

Chapter 10 will reintroduce the conceptual framework. It will look at a whole range of European issues through the concept of memory and its variations, using—as a *fil conducteur*—the notions of:

- vicarious memory (through which a minority maintains the tradition on behalf of the majority);
- precarious memory (conceived in different ways);
- mediated memory (and the confusion between the medium and the message);
- alternative memories (disagreement within as well as between the major faith traditions; the gradual establishment of non-Christian faiths in modern Europe; the emergence of alternative foci for the sacred which replace or exist alongside more traditional forms of religion);
- symbolic memories (notably the significance of anniversaries, including the millennium);
- extinguished memory (is this likely and what might be the consequences for other aspects of European life if certain religious memories were to disappear altogether?);

- ruptured and/or rediscovered memory (chains of memory are from time to time broken or ruptured; they can, however, re-establish themselves given favourable or appropriate circumstances);
- conflicting memory/memories (European versus national memory and the role of religion in each; Balkan and Irish illustrations);
- and, finally, mutating memory (the continuing reconstructions of European religion/s as the twentieth century gives way to the twenty-first).

It will be obvious that the first five of these more or less follow the chapter titles of the book; the latter four, which will be used to expand the earlier points, demonstrate the wider potential in this type of analysis.

The approach as a whole is clearly thematic rather than geographical. Each chapter will, however, contain a number of case studies or illustrations taken from different parts of Europe—within the parameters outlined in the Introduction—in order to illustrate the theme in question or to evoke particular points of comparison. Not every country will appear in every chapter. Rather, the illustrations are selected for their pertinence to the point under discussion. It is, however, inevitable that their selection depends to some extent on the sociological material available.[8]

---

[8] I have made systematic use of the material available in both French and English. For publications in other European languages I have been more dependent on the good will of other scholars to bring this to my attention.

# THREE

# *Vicarious Memory 1: The Churches*

T HERE can be no doubt that the institutional churches of Europe play a considerably reduced role at the turn of the third millennium if this is compared with their counterparts at almost any point in European history. The churches are no longer able to command the active allegiance of anything but a small minority of European people (though passive allegiance remains high); nor are they able to direct the decision-making of European populations. The latter is almost as true in religious and moral issues as it is in areas of society less directly related to religious teaching, in that religious adherence (whether in terms of practice or in terms of belief) has—just like any other leisure activity—become a matter of preference or personal choice. No public sanctions exist to prevent the European citizen from opting out of the churches' teaching either partially or completely; indeed the very idea that this might be otherwise is looked upon with extreme distaste in almost every country in West Europe.[1]

The churches remain, however, highly significant players at a different level of social reality. As voluntary organizations they are both influential and effective and compete successfully with comparable institutions in European society. They are, for example, considerably more successful in terms of recruitment than most political parties or industrial organizations (trade unions) and continue to hold their own with a wide range of leisure activities, with the partial exception of sporting pursuits (if these are taken as a whole).[2] It is true that the churches appeal more to some sections of the population than to others (see Chapter 4), but those who feel their significance is diminished accordingly lay themselves open to criticism in terms of both ageism and sexism.

How, though, do the churches (be they reduced in significance or not) continue in existence in order to effect these roles? One aspect of this subject has already been tackled briefly in the overview of church–state issues (Chapter 1); churches, just like any other organizations, require both constitutional status

---

[1] Poland remains a partial exception in this respect, especially in its more rural areas.
[2] See Ashford and Timms (1992) for comparative figures.

and legal existence. This point can be seen with greatest clarity in the debates surrounding church and state in the newly established democracies of Central Europe, all of which have taken steps to legitimize (or re-legitimize) the churches within the new social order. Churches also require a source of finance and, normally, the presence of a professional ministry if they are to function effectively at any level of society. The first two sections of this chapter will consider each of these in turn, though they are closely related issues (a professional ministry has to be remunerated to some degree in order to exist at all). In the final section, the discussion will return to the voluntary sector and more broadly to the discussion of civil society, in order to assess the ongoing significance of the institutional churches as effective carriers of the religious memory in modern European society.

## Financial Arrangements

Just like the questions of church and state, sources of finance and funding for European churches are enormously diverse. They range from the relatively wealthy state churches of Northern Europe (mostly though not exclusively Lutheran) to the very meagre institutional resources found in other European societies. The effects on professional recruitment and the status of ministers are immediately apparent. It is, however, a great deal easier to discover material about the systems of church finance than it is about the sums of money themselves; both are complex and comprise indirect as well as direct sources of income. Exemption from tax, for example, is often as important as income itself. Similarly indirect help with buildings or with pensions requires careful consideration if the situation is to be fairly assessed overall. The following paragraphs offer selective examples of the types of system in existence in different parts of Europe; they do not pretend to be a comprehensive account.[3] The stress lies, moreover, on financial support from the state (or the lack of this). There has been no attempt at a comparative assessment of private generosity.[4]

In many ways the most straightforward system to describe is the church tax arrangements in the Nordic countries and in Germany, where church taxes are collected alongside other taxes and all citizens pay the prescribed contribution unless they contract out of the system. The most striking thing about the Nordic countries in this respect is the very small number of people who do in

[3] For more information on the question of church finance, at least in the European Union, see European Consortium for Church–State Research (1992) and Robbers (1996).

[4] There can be no doubt, however, that individual or corporate finance can be very considerable; churches which take the practice of tithing seriously are seldom short of money. Tithing is more often found in the 'independent churches' though it may include particular parishes within the dominant religious groups, be they state churches or otherwise.

fact contract out, given the very low levels of churchgoing and orthodox religious belief (see the tables in Chapter 1). In Denmark, for example, 88 per cent of the population belong to the state church (and so pay tax), a figure which is very similar in Sweden, with minimal practice (4 per cent or so) in each case. Compared with Britain the 'take-up' of the occasional offices also remains high (particularly in Finland) and church buildings, not to mention staffing levels, are maintained to a standard that British churches can only dream of. Given the reputations of both Sweden and Denmark as two of the world's most secular populations, such financial generosity is all the more remarkable. This may not turn itself into higher rates of churchgoing per se, but must, surely, say something about the role of the national churches in Scandinavian societies. No population would support to such an extent institutions of which they fundamentally disapproved.

It is true that the Swedish situation is on the point of changing and in ways that are symptomatic of European society as a whole. A parliamentary commission established in 1994 examined both the church–state links and the financial arrangements that go with these. The intention of the proposed legislation—to become law in 2000—is to give equal recognition to all religious denominations but 'with due consideration paid to their different circumstances' (Schött 1996: 301). The commission maintained that in a modern society the state has no reason to show special favour to any one denomination. The links with the state will, therefore, be loosened; tax arrangements will benefit denominations other than the state church and non-members will not be under any obligation to pay church tax at all. The Church of Sweden will, however, retain the property that it currently owns and the state will continue to finance certain church activities, not least the maintenance of historic buildings. It seems unlikely that the Church of Sweden will suffer serious financial loss in the immediate future; the long-term prospects are clearly causing some anxiety.[5]

A rather similar situation exists in Germany, where both the Protestant and the Catholic churches benefit from the church tax system—as indeed do a number of smaller churches (those with the status of public corporations, which include the Jewish community). In the German case, however, there has been significant leakage in membership, especially from the Protestant churches. It is also important to note the somewhat controversial decision to impose the church tax system on the former East Germany, given the very marked degree of secularization in that area (a significant proportion of German people declaring themselves to be of no religious confession come from the former communist *Länder*). Despite both these factors (leakage in the West and secularization in the East), the size of the German population over-

---

[5] The changing situation in Sweden is being carefully monitored by an extensive research project, 'Fran statskyrka till fri folkkyrka', under the direction of Anders Bäckström at the University of Uppsala (an English version of the proposal is available from Professor Bäckström).

all means that the budgets of the major German churches are very considerable indeed (in 1997, for example, their combined income was estimated at
15.4 billion DM).[6]

At the other end of the scale can be found the French case, where public
funding of the churches ceased definitively with the separation of church and
state in 1905. Thereafter the churches were dependent on private sources of
income for their ongoing work, though there is a certain amount of indirect
help from the state in, for example, the financing of prison and hospital chap-
laincies and in the tax deductions offered on gifts for certain kinds of religious
work. For the latter to be granted it is necessary for the churches in question
to have the status of *associations cultuelles*, inevitably coveted for precisely this
reason. Further complexities arise from the fact that the Concordat arrangements (which date from the Napoleonic period) remain in place in the three
*départements* of the east of France which were under German rule at the time
of the separation of church and state, a situation which renders their financial
position very much more favourable than that in the majority of France.

Britain, too, is a society in which state help to the churches in any direct
sense is very limited, despite, in the English case at least, close ties between
church and state from a constitutional point of view. Indeed an overview of
financial arrangements in European societies, such as that offered in Robbers
(1996), indicates the highly complex nature of the relationships between legal
agreements and state financial support; one does not necessarily lead to the
other. Spain and Portugal, for example, are different in this respect: Spain *de
facto* offers a church tax system, though one that operates in a rather different
way from those already described; Portugal on the other hand has no public
funding, though indirect help to the Catholic Church is generous. The
Spanish system, moreover, has been adopted, more or less, by the Italians in
their 1984 Villa Madama Treaty, which set up the current financial arrangements in Italy and which *de facto* favour the Catholic Church (Ferrari 1996).
The two pillarized societies in Northern Europe are also different from a financial point of view: the Belgian government pays the salaries and pensions of
professional ministers (including some secular equivalents), the Dutch government does not, though a certain amount of support may come in other
ways. In Greece (the only Orthodox Church represented in this discussion)
there is no church tax, but the state has almost entirely assumed the financing
of the Greek Orthodox Church by means of direct and indirect subventions,
salaries, and tax exemption (Papastathis 1996: 87). Each case has to be considered individually and reveals a complex mixture of historical deposit and
shifting legislation.

---

[6] Income levels, however, have dropped through the 1990s. This is particularly true
for the German Lutheran churches. For a variety of reasons income from tax has diminished—partly due to significant numbers of people leaving the Church, but also to rising unemployment and the fact that fewer people pay taxes of any kind. Paradoxically,
the situation is exacerbated by the relatively high levels of ordinations in recent decades.

There are, however, important cross-cutting themes which need careful articulation. The first pre-empts the discussion in the second section of this chapter in that it concerns pensions as well as salaries for clergy. It is a matter in which the changing nature of European society needs to be taken into account, as religious professionals, just like everyone else, are living longer and so require financial support in retirement for a significant period of time. The problem, if such it is, is exacerbated in the case of married clergy, in view of the obligation to maintain a dependent spouse after the death of his or her partner. The English church offers an interesting case study of the stages in this evolution. In the 1870s, a new priest appointed to a benefice where his predecessor was still alive received two-thirds of the stipend from that living (according to the Incumbents Resignation Act of 1871, modified in 1877). The retired priest had the other third until his death—a system which quite clearly assumed that death would follow reasonably soon after retirement. A rather more formal pension scheme was established in 1926 (in the form of the Church of England Pension Board), but a priest was not obliged to retire at a specified age until 1976 (and even then, those already in a post were exempt from the legislation). The pension scheme eased the lot of individual priests. From the point of view of the institution, however, the problem has only been partially solved: it is not an exaggeration to say that much of the current financial stress of the Church of England lies in the question of pensions just as much as in the provision of salaries.

The second theme concerns the range of religious organizations to which financial privileges will apply—in whatever form they exist. This is an issue which becomes increasingly problematic as European societies lose their religious homogeneity. Two things are happening at once in this respect: the historic churches are losing their resonance at precisely the same moment as increasing numbers of new religious groups are arriving. It is therefore becoming more and more difficult to justify the exclusive support given to the former, whilst denying any such help to the latter. With this in mind, it is hardly surprising that the question of 'scope' bedevils a whole range of legal and financial questions as religious organizations of different sorts compete for the coveted legal status which brings with it financial advantage. Or, to put the question in terms of the theoretical position adopted in the previous chapter, which religious memories in the European situation merit financial (not to say other) support from the state, and which do not? And who is to decide where the appropriate lines are to be drawn? The answers are inevitably contentious and turn on the unresolved question of definition. The issue will return again and again in the following pages and notably in the discussion of alternative memories in Chapters 7 and 8.

What is most striking, however, in looking at the European churches as a whole from the point of view of financial support, is the apparent *absence* of relationship between financial strength and the most obvious indicators of religious vitality. Or to put the point even more bluntly, some of the richest churches of Europe are the weakest in terms of religious participation, though it has already been hinted that support for the churches in Northern Europe may in fact lie in financial provision rather than in active participation. The churches are maintained in order to function on behalf of society as a whole, in which case there is no need to attend them on a regular basis. Conversely, however, the more penalized churches of Europe from a financial point of view also seem to struggle in terms of members. This is particularly true in the French case, at least in comparison with other Catholic cultures, but also to some extent in Britain.[7] The lack of a convincing relationship overall remains, none the less, a puzzle. It seems to imply the considerable strength of cultural factors in determining patterns of churchgoing quite apart from the financial advantages/disadvantages of the religious organizations in question. Money talks, but so, apparently, do other factors.[8]

If some of the churches of the European Union have significant financial difficulties, these pale into insignificance in most respects compared with the religious organizations that are emerging from more than forty years of communism in East and Central Europe. Here, church property was very often confiscated or given over to secular use; getting it and other assets back—never mind its maintenance thereafter—has proved to be a disputatious process in countries where the general economic situation is difficult and that of the churches even more so (see Luxmoore 1995, 1996, 1997 for a ongoing overview of the situation). Particularly problematic are the cases where the alternative use was a humanitarian one which is then disadvantaged by the church's claim. By insisting on its own rights the church in question appears to oppose the 'common good'.

In the early 1990s the opinion of the Czechoslovak population was sought on precisely these issues: i.e. the returning of property to the churches and the financing of church activities (Mišovič 1997; Winter 1998). The population was, it seems, happy for the churches to regain property that had to do with religious, educational, cultural, and social purposes, but less so if there was a commercial dimension to the undertaking. The motive in affirming the return of such assets was primarily to free the churches from political control, to enable financial security, and to encourage philanthropy (help for the disadvantaged)—not the acquisition of profit. Similar questions a year or so later indicated an even greater ambivalence with respect to church property, with

---

[7] Lack of practice in turn discourages the lack of voluntary giving—the downward cycle is likely to continue. Or to put the same point a little differently, money doesn't seem to solve the problem, but the lack of it makes things even worse.

[8] Interestingly, exactly the same point was noticed by Adam Smith in *The Wealth of Nations* (bk.V, ch. 1, pt. III, art. iii, 'Religious Instruction'). Smith is particularly careful to defend the Church of Scotland: 'The most opulent church in Christendom does not maintain better the uniformity of faith, the fervour of devotion, the spirit of order, regularity, and austere morals in the great body of the people, than this very poorly endowed Church of Scotland. All the good effects, both civil and religious, which an established church can be supposed to produce, are produced by it as completely as by any other' (Smith, 1976: 337).

an insistence that both sides need to be taken into account in disputes about difficult cases and a strong affirmation that the primary financial responsibility for the churches should lie with the church members or believers and not with the state. Economic realities were beginning to outweigh earlier generosity.

A rather similar situation occurred in Hungary, where the restitution of church property in general was one of the final acts of the communist parliament. 'Each building became, however, a source of conflict with the present users' (Tomka 1997: 216), a process through which the churches lost much of the credit that they had won in the preceding years. Or, to put the same point in a different way, 'the Church risks the loss of its role to preach freedom in exchange for the reacquisition of real estate and institutions' (Tomka 1993: 103); the logic of politics, bureaucracy, institutions, and power work in a particular direction. Preoccupied by their own reconstruction, it appears that religious organizations become increasingly limited in their capacity to play a prophetic role in the creation of a new democratic order.

A final illustration comes from Estonia, the smallest and most northerly country in the Baltics. Here the authorities have been slow to return church-owned property and there is a serious shortfall in funds amongst churches decimated by the experiences of war and communist occupation (Davie, Kingsbury, and Bäckström 1997). The critical question facing the Estonian people, however, goes deeper than this; it concerns the kind of organization the Estonian Lutheran Church aspires to be as their country re-emerges as a modern democracy. In 1996, an Anglo-Scandinavian Pastoral Conference took place in Tallinn and was made aware of impressive rebuilding programmes, financed by both Scandinavian and German church partners. Few English parishes could maintain the kind of facilities being provided. An inevitable question presented itself: was this a sensible way to use what are evidently scarce resources or will the Church of Estonia find itself overburdened by the upkeep of unnecessarily extensive and costly plant? Only time will tell.[9]

## The Professional Ministries of the European Churches

In 1995, an edited volume appeared in both Dutch and English with the arresting title *Europe without Priests* (Kerkhofs 1995). The implications of the title need a certain qualification, however, for the book is almost entirely concerned with Catholic Europe and Catholic priests; indeed some of the remarks about non-Catholic Europe are misleading in the extreme. The book none the

---

[9] The June 1999 issue of *Religion, State and Society* contains an interesting series of articles on the religious situation in the Baltic states. The freedom aspired to for so long under Soviet domination brings with it new challenges and difficult decisions.

less poses a central question for the Catholic Church in Europe. The numbers of priests in both East and West Europe are declining, the average age of priests all over Europe is rising, and tens of thousands of parishes are without a resident priest. What is to be done?

The first point to grasp is that the overall figures in Europe mask considerable variations. Unsurprisingly the greatest concentrations of Catholic priests are to be found in Italy, France, and Spain, followed by Poland and Germany—what might be termed the Catholic heartland of Europe (though even here the internal variations are considerable). The ratio of priests to Catholics in the population is, however, far more favourable in what Kerkhofs call the diaspora countries of Europe (mostly the North)—i.e. those where Catholics are in a minority. Weighing one situation against the other is clearly problematic, for there are no easy answers to the relative demands of these very different situations. Indeed from a sociological point of view the complexities of the issue lie well beneath the national statistics. The data reflect instead the kind of cultures discerned by the pioneers of Catholic sociology, Le Bras and Boulard, in their detailed mapping of French religious life in the mid-twentieth century (Le Bras 1955, 1956, 1976; Boulard 1954; Boulard and Rémy 1968). Their work revealed the persistence of long-term cultural patterns *both between and within* particular regions of France that continue to produce not only different levels of religious practice but also uneven numbers of vocations. Once again, however, demographic change may prove to be the crucial factor, as the rural (normally agricultural) families from which Catholic vocations have frequently come not only diminish in size, but increasingly disappear. Quite simply, the combination of economic and cultural factors which sustained a particularly pious section of the population in traditional forms of employment no longer exists; unsurprisingly the remaining members of such families look for work elsewhere, usually in the much less religious environment of the city (Harismendy 1999).

A second point is also striking. It may indeed be the case that vocations to the Catholic priesthood are declining, but in the Catholic countries of Southern Europe in particular, they are declining from an extraordinarily high base. Italy, for example, still has by far the largest number of priests of any European society, but in the mid-nineteenth century it had far more—three times the number that existed in the period immediately following World War II (the decline began in 1861). One consequence of this historical legacy (deeply embedded in much of Europe whether Catholic or Protestant) is the degree to which the dominant churches have come to rely on their ordained professionals to effect certain tasks. It is assumed, for instance, that each parish *should* have a resident pastor—a situation which is unthinkable in many parts of the world where the religious sector is vibrant.

The European decline is none the less considerable and—given the expectations of previous centuries—devastating in its consequences. France offers the extreme case:

The number of priests has been declining steadily from as long ago as 1938 . . . from 40,981 diocesan priests in 1965 to 28,629 in 1985 and about 19,700 in 1995 according to maximal estimates. In 1965 40% were under 44; in 1989 5% were under 40 and 60% over sixty. In 1989 the average age was 66. Ordinations of priests declined from 1,355 in 1938 to 1,028 in 1951 and 370 in 1969. During the past twenty years the annual number of ordinations has fluctuated between 100 and 150, whereas 600 are needed to keep things stable. (Kerkhofs 1995: 23)

There is no arguing with statistics such as these, which take their toll on the health of the priests who still remain, individuals who are already living on salaries which are barely viable. As ever, however, necessity becomes the mother of invention: it is in France that alternative systems have begun to take root. ADAP (*Assemblées Dominicales en l'Absence de Prêtre*), for example, permits the celebration of the mass without a priest; responsibility is taken by the laity—and in 70 per cent of the parishes involved women play a crucial role in the proceedings. The implications for both the continuation and mutation of memory are considerable, as the laity increasingly assume responsibility for tasks previously undertaken by priests. The trend towards lay involvement is spreading throughout Catholic (and indeed Anglican) Europe and clearly derives from pastoral necessity, rather than theological innovation.[10] Theological justifications of 'partnership' or 'collaborative ministry' abound, but they are, at bottom, reactive. These are solutions imposed by the statistics; they are seldom introduced for their own sake.

Not all Catholic Europe finds itself in this predicament. A very different scenario exists, for example, in Poland—by far the most Catholic country in Central and East Europe and one in which the evolution of the priesthood (like so many other things) is distinctive. In recent decades the number of ordinations steadily increased to a peak in 1991, after which the numbers decline. The most rapid increase appears to have been in the late 1980s, reflecting the extraordinary role of the Church in the events leading up to 1989, within which the election of a Polish pope is clearly an important factor both politically and symbolically  in attracting young men to the priesthood and both men and women to the religious orders. An obvious consequence of this situation is the fact that almost no parish in Poland is without a resident priest (and the associated pastoral discipline), and large numbers of priests ordained in Poland can be found elsewhere in Europe. In the mid-1990s, ordinations in Poland accounted for more than a quarter of the total in the whole of Europe.[11]

[10] Exactly the same point will emerge in Ch. 8 in relation to Opus Dei, itself a reaction to the decline in the number of priests and members of religious orders in Spain. An organization (or order) in which laypeople and their credentials are strongly affirmed, rather than marginalized, emerges in their place (Pérez Vilariño 1997).

[11] Not only is Poland a net exporter of priests; the Polish Church is able to maintain the standard of living of those who stay at home at a level significantly above that of the population as a whole (Thompson 1998, interview data).

Poland is clearly an exceptional case. In the remaining Central European countries with significant Catholic populations—where aggressive secularization policies were partially if not totally effective—the most likely combination will be an extremely elderly priesthood, with a small number of recently ordained. The generation in between (the group which would normally provide effective leadership) simply does not exist. In this part of Europe, the chain of memory came perilously close to breaking, at least in terms of designated religious professionals. Once again, however, improvised alternatives emerged to fill the gap, notably a small number of married priests in Czechoslovakia and the existence of underground organizations both in Czechoslovakia and elsewhere. Some of these gained partial recognition by the Catholic Church in difficult circumstances; their position subsequently remains highly ambiguous (Winter 1998).

Catholic Europe has, on the whole, held on to its habits of churchgoing for longer than the Protestant North despite the drop in ordinations to the priesthood. Paradoxically, and with some notable exceptions, a rather different relationship appears with respect to Europe's Protestant churches. The Lutheran and Anglican churches are easier to deal with than their Reformed equivalents in this respect, in that the statistics are more readily available at national level. Indeed it is the Protestant churches of Scandinavia and Germany that offer the most distinctive alternative to Catholic decline, the German case being of particular interest in that both Catholic and Protestant professionals are relatively well paid—a situation that inevitably raises the question of celibacy as a motivating, or demotivating, factor for Catholics. In Lutheran circles on the whole, it seems that a moderately well-paid and respected ordained ministry offers an attractive alternative to some professions, whose futures (for economic reasons) are rather less stable than they used to be. The figures speak for themselves: despite very low levels of religious practice, recruitment to the ministry has been rising, or is at least stable, in most Lutheran societies. In Germany, for example, the numbers of ordinands to the German Evangelical Church (EKD), according to published figures, have risen from 624 (in 1975) to 662 (in 1984) to 1,015 (in 1995). Whether or not this situation will maintain itself in the twenty-first century is, however, a much more difficult question.[12] In Sweden the trend is rather more stable, from 126 (in 1975) through 131 (in 1985) to 116 (in 1995). The drop in the 1990s is recent and due, at least in part, to an *oversupply* in candidates in the early 1990s.[13] In the Lutheran situation a further point is important: in addition to an adequate supply of ordained ministers these churches employ large numbers of lay professionals. As yet, there is little space for the unpaid volunteer.

---

[12] Very recently, there has been a fall in the number of ordinations in the EKD—mainly for financial reasons (see n. 6). The financial situation and the number of ordinations are inevitably related.

[13] Information from Anders Bäckström (Dec. 1998).

For the Anglicans sandwiched in between, there has quite clearly been a degree of decline—notably in the *full-time* ordained ministry. This is, however, less severe than in many Catholic countries. Ordinations run at about 300 per year (they have been rising in the late 1990s) and if there is strain in the system, it lies as much in the financial difficulties raised in the previous section as it does in the question of recruitment *per se*. The emergence of part-time (non-stipendiary) and lay ministries, moreover, has compensated for this loss to a considerable degree. In the Church of England in the late 1990s, for example, there are as many 'readers' (licensed laypeople exercising a primarily preaching ministry) as there are full-time priests—a good example of a shift from clerical to lay responsibility. It is worth noting the high level of academic qualification of many of these lay volunteers.

A second shift in Protestant circles is crucial to the argument of this chapter, indeed to the book as a whole. That is the gradual opening up of the full-time ministry in almost all Protestant churches to women as well as to men in the later post-war decades. The reasons for this shift are complex and involve both sociological and theological arguments. There can be no doubt, however, that the debate occurred in view of the changing nature of European society. This was not a change initiated by the churches; rather, they were responding to profound economic and social transformations which have brought women to positions of responsibility in most professions in modern Europe (as indeed in the modern West as a whole). Increasingly, it is the professions which have no representation of women that have to justify their maintenance of the status quo, not the other way round. What then were the Christian churches to do given their insistence on an exclusively male priesthood since the time of the early church?

The Christian churches have responded differently to this challenge. The majority (the Catholics and the Orthodox) have rejected the idea of change and have reaffirmed the tradition of the male priesthood. Nor is there any indication that anything different is likely to happen in the foreseeable future, despite the increasingly significant role of women in the lay activities of the Catholic Church (not least in those areas where Catholic priests are thin on the ground). In the Protestant churches, the reaction has been different, for understandable theological and ecclesiological reasons. In churches where the professional minister is seen as representative of the people, rather than representative of Christ, it is easier to envisage a change, the more so, perhaps, in view of the predominance of women as active members in almost all the churches in question. Each Protestant denomination moreover, has, taken the decision unilaterally; it has been a piecemeal process, but cumulative in its effects. The decision, finally (in 1992), of the Church of England—the mother church of the Anglican Communion—to follow suit was a significant marker. Here a church which is both Catholic and Reformed voted democratically (and after much procrastination) to admit women to the priesthood. It was a decision that underscored the Protestant nature of the English church.

What, though, are the implications of this shift for the Christian tradition in Western Europe? If the churches are envisaged not only as carriers of religious memory, but an embodiment as well, the change must be significant. At the very least the visual impact will be different as women assume positions of prominence in the public dimensions of ministry (and notably in liturgy); so probably will patterns of pastoral care. More profoundly, however, the mediation of the message is likely to mutate in view of the difference between men and women in their interpretation of Christian teaching. Women, it seems, are more likely to believe in a God of love, comfort, and forgiveness than they are in a God of power, planning, and control, sentiments which may shift the manner in which the message is presented to a wider public (Walter and Davie 1998). Such influence, moreover, will be increasingly evident as women gradually move to positions of leadership within the Protestant churches, a situation that is unlikely to become fully apparent for some time yet.

A final, more general point about the professional ministry is evidenced from the British case but its implications are likely to extend to other parts of Europe (notably the state churches of Lutheran Europe); it concerns the vicarious nature of much of modern religion. With reference to British patterns of life, it is strange that in a society which even by European standards is more rather than less secular, considerable attention is paid in public discussion to the beliefs and behaviour of church leaders. Evidence for such a statement can frequently be found in the popular press, which contains an odd mixture of sentiments. At one and the same time, the popular press both castigates church leaders for their theological imprecision and for their failures to live up to exacting moral standards *and* indulges its readers with considerable details about a society which in its own ways of living clearly pays little attention to either the theology or the morality of the Christian churches. How can these apparent incompatibilities be reconciled? It seems that the population as a whole does not see any need to maintain for themselves either the disciplines of churchgoing or the observance of particular moral codes. It does, however, care that such standards are maintained by someone and seeks to impose this obligation on the senior professionals of the major religions and notably those of the state church. The memory, and the behaviour that goes with it, should indeed be maintained, but vicariously. The press is judgemental (sometimes fiercely so) towards those that fail in this duty.

In this respect the contrast with the United States is at its most marked, despite the seductions of language (in the British case) or denominational allegiance. Americans are anything but vicarious in their religious life (as indeed in almost every aspect of corporate living). Or to put the same point in a different way, Americans are inclined to articulate what British (and perhaps Europeans) are content to assume. With this in mind it is hardly surprising that depending upon a state church to do the job for them runs counter to the cultural as well as constitutional heritage of a country for whom the First

Amendment is of central importance to national understanding, a fact which is true symbolically as well as politically.

## The Voluntary Sector: The Effective Level of Operation

How, then, should the churches of Europe operate given their historical past as state churches, which is still in evidence in most European countries in terms of legal existence and financial privilege, if not always in terms of direct financial support? Where such privileges are no longer the case, moreover, the historical patterns continue to resonate, albeit in a different way. Connections which once existed but have been removed for political reasons—often with considerable bitterness—bequeath a situation quite different from that in those parts of the world where the churches were never permitted a constitutional role in the first place. The question that poses itself at the turn of the millennium therefore becomes the following: how is it possible for previously privileged churches to move forwards where religion ceases on the whole to be an affair of state, but figures significantly in the debates about civil society and in the establishment of an effective non-governmental sector?

There are schools of thought which imply that it simply cannot be done. There are those, for example, who consider that Europe has become secularized to such a degree that religion is simply vestigial. It may continue in existence in privatized forms—in personal belief or voluntary activity—but neither have significant public resonance at any level of society. This is the logical conclusion of Bruce's approach (1996), in which not only is religion dominated by the world of options and lifestyles in terms of belief systems, but the forms of organization themselves effectively become the denomination and the cult rather than the church or sect (see Chapter 2). Conspicuously absent is the notion of an overarching religious frame, the organizational expression of the universal church. If this point of view is pushed to its logical conclusion, the state or historic churches, in so far as they exist at all, are simply redundant in terms of the realities of modern European societies.

Two possibilities follow, both of which need careful articulation. The first stresses the fact that if this is so for the churches, it must also be so for a whole range of other institutions which struggle for organizational existence in modern Europe. It is quite clear, for instance, that churches are not the only institutions which have lost members in the post-war period and which now seek alternative forms of organization. Obvious examples of this situation can be found in the political parties and in the associations of organized labour. The first of these, the political parties, have to a considerable extent given way to a wide range of social movements or pressure groups, which come and go with a greater flexibility than parties and whose interests cut across the conventional party lines; this transformation has become commonplace in modern political analysis. Likewise, trade unions have not adapted well to the employ-ment uncertainties of late modernity and look increasingly out of place in a flexible labour market, in which short-term contract work has become the norm for those who are lucky enough to have a job at all. The insecurities of employment and the shifting nature of the labour market have, in turn, had an irreversible influence on the organization of pensions, welfare, and house purchase. Very little can be structured in the way that it was in the immediate post-war period and the state, *just like the churches*, is no longer able to func-tion as the confident provider of education, health, and welfare services from the cradle to the grave.[14]

Parallel shifts have taken place in attitudes towards authority. The European Values Study, for example, reveals that changing attitudes towards the churches reflect the general decline in confidence in major public institutions across Europe between 1981 and 1990; and, relatively speaking, parliament, the trades unions, and above all the press fare worse than the churches in terms of public confidence. The authors add, however, that feelings towards the churches are markedly different in older rather than younger age groups. For those under 35 the churches appear to have lost their credibility altogether (Barker, Halman, and Vloet 1992: 11–13). Indeed the main conclusion of the 1990 EVSSG study is that the Christian churches are gradually losing their place as the keystone in the arch of European value structures, but that noth-ing is emerging to replace them. The sociological consequences of this situ-ation are considerable. Clearly it is incorrect to isolate the churches from other institutions in terms of the structural changes of modern European societies. It follows that the partial collapse of European state churches is due not only to religious causes (pervasive religious indifference, for example, or the emer-gence of alternative creeds); it is part of the renegotiation of European society as a whole.

A rather similar situation can be found in the cultural sphere. Overarching value systems other than religious ones have collapsed, and some spectacu-larly so. The dramatic ending of communism as an effective political ideology in East and Central Europe cannot simply be ignored in this respect. Its demise is far more dramatic than that of the theologies of the Christian churches, which may indeed be reduced in significance but still exist. Likewise the receding confidence of rationalism (the West European version of the Enlightenment) as an all-embracing creed is permitting more rather than less space in certain areas of society for world-views which incorporate a religious element. Alternative medicine, for example, with its essentially holistic approach, insists on the need to take into account the health of body, mind, and spirit—it explicitly rejects the isolation of the physical symptom from the individual (the undivided) who is unwell. Similar shifts can be seen in

---

[14] In coming to terms with these changes, European societies are at very different stages of development. They involve painful transformations and difficult decisions about priorities—debates about modern health care epitomize these processes.

attitudes towards the environment. Gone are the carefree assumptions of previous decades as humanity is increasingly seen as part (and a very uncertain part) of nature itself, not as its manipulative and confident master (Davie 1994).

In short, if the state churches and the creeds that they stand for are reduced in both their institutional capacities and their cultural influence, this is equally true of many other areas in modern European societies. The consequences for the state churches are none the less severe in that they become less and less able to influence the society as a whole and to operate in any sense as a sacred canopy—*just like their secular counterparts*. In this sense they are, indeed, redundant. This, however, is not the whole story (and herein lies the second of the two possibilities that follow from Bruce's analysis), for even weakened state churches can operate effectively if they take account of what is happening and grasp their opportunities in an innovative way. Indeed, following Casanova's approach to religion in the modern world, religious organizations of all kinds not only could, but should, operate in the public sphere. The discussion therefore becomes normative as well as descriptive.

Casanova's approach lies in distinguishing the different strands within the term 'secularization'. These were outlined in Chapter 2, together with the assertion that one reason for the relative secularization of Europe lies precisely in the in-built resistance of state churches to structural differentiation. The thesis presents a rather different question from Bruce's analysis. It is this. Do the state, or former state churches, have the capacity to adapt to a changing situation and to play an effective role in the formation of civil society in different parts of Europe? The implication is that they will, indeed, become redundant if they perpetuate patterns of previous centuries, but that it could be otherwise if such churches have both the will and the energy to appreciate the demands of late modernity and to move forwards rather than cling to the past. A second element is equally important: the necessity for European religion to avoid the alternative of excessive privatization, just as much as total control or domination. It is, precisely, the 'deprivatization' of religion that Casanova is looking for, but in forms compatible with modern democracy.

Can it be done in Europe? Here, my own analysis would differ a little from that of Casanova. It may indeed be the case that European churches have declined in vitality in view of their failure to appreciate the need for structural separation between the religious sector and the rest of society. One obvious reason for this is the historical association between religion and power in the European case. As the democratization of power became a reality, religion discovered itself on the 'wrong' side, associated with forms of authority which, quite rightly, are unacceptable in a democratic order. I am not convinced, however, that a belated and rather artificial legal separation between church and state, especially in Northern Europe, is likely to put the situation right. Indeed it may only make things worse as the churches lose both the advantages of structural separation (in the North American sense) and the capacity to act vicariously which, despite everything, they appear to have maintained at least in parts of Europe.[15]

I would argue, instead, for a *de facto* rather than *de jure* separation of powers, at least in the Protestant cultures of the North, where state churches exist alongside secularized but largely tolerant cultures. Indeed, careful analysis reveals distinct advantages to a *weak* state church, which can operate as the representative of 'faith' in a way that hegemonic or overbearing churches cannot, whether that faith be the historic Christian community, other Christian churches, or other faith congregations. State churches no longer have the power to dominate (that has been made abundantly clear by the data presented in Chapter 1); they may, however, have retained the capacity to represent, to speak on behalf of the religious sector of modern societies, an important if reduced element. A belated, and possibly contentious, separation of church and state could well end in the state churches being able to do neither. A great deal depends, however, on the particular circumstances within each nation state—on the specificities of the historical deposit, the degree of religious pluralism, and the relativities of power and wealth. These, we have seen, are very different even within Northern Europe. (In terms of wealth, for example, the Church of England and the Church of Sweden lie at opposite ends of the spectrum; it is the latter, moreover, that is likely to lose its established status first). The essential point to grasp is the need to look for a European solution to a European problem, not to import unthinkingly the American pattern into an entirely different context.

The Catholic case is rather different. First, in Casanova's terms, there is the more positive point: the Catholic Church is less prone that the Protestant churches to excessive privatization, for the corporate sense of identity is stronger. There is, however, a corresponding downside. In Catholic Europe, the dominant churches resisted secularization from within; they withstood or rejected the Reformation, which in a very literal sense declericalized the Church. An obvious result of this resistance was the emergence and evolution of powerful anticlerical movements *outside* the Church which embraced secular rather than alternative Christian ideologies. One consequence of this situation is the relative incapacity of the Catholic Church to act on behalf of others—its situation has been too confrontational for this to be realistic. There are, however, signs of change in the post-Vatican II period. A clear, though controversial, example can be found in France at the time of the Rushdie controversy, in the protestations of Cardinal Decourtray of Lyons against *The Satanic Verses*. Effectively the cardinal defended the point of view of the believer—in this case the Muslim believer—stressing the parallel between *The Satanic Verses* and Martin Scorsese's film *The Last Temptation of Christ*.

---

[15] Indeed Casanova admits that the state church dimension of Northern European Protestantism is simply an anachronism and poses no real threat to the democratic order. I would go further and say that this residual characteristic can be positively exploited (see Davie 1994: 141–9).

Predictably enough, both book and film were equally strongly defended by the advocates of freedom of speech. Indeed the Rushdie episode revealed the traditional split in France between Catholic and free-thinker in a highly visible way. Since then, however, there have been hints of reconciliation in this respect as well: in, for example, the bicentennial celebrations of the French Revolution, when the Rights of Man (affirmed by the church) became the dominant theme rather than the revolutionary mood of anticlericalism (Willaime 1996), and in the gradual recognition of private schools as an accepted part of the French education system rather than the enemy within (see Chapter 5). The most striking illustration of all, however, can be found in the delegation sent from France to mediate in the New Caledonian crisis of 1988, a modest group of people which included representation on an equal footing of the 'spiritual families' present in New Caledonia—Catholic, Protestant, and Freemason.[16]

In terms of an effective way forward in Europe as a whole, the answer possibly lies in exploiting the historical networks of *all* churches, or all faith groups, at local rather than national level. It is at this level, normally, that effective action and maximum co-operation are possible in the form of practical rather than organic ecumenism (the exceptions, notably Northern Ireland, need not detract from the general argument). It is at this level, moreover, that the debate about civil society gains a certain purchase in view of the requirement to establish effective organizations that close the gap between the increasingly remote centre and the individual citizen. The aim, both direct and indirect, is the generation of 'social capital' as this is described by Putnam (1993, 1995) and in a growing socio-political literature (both theoretical and applied). Such capital is to be found in the networks of neighbourliness and reciprocity; that is, in the face-to-face human contacts and the myriad of voluntary organizations which resist the impersonalities of late modernity—rampant in both financial and cultural markets, and in the influence of television in particular.[17] The capacities of European churches—both state and free, Christian and non-Christian—are impressive in this respect; far more so, for example, than their political equivalents.[18] There are, however, unintended consequences. Resistance to the excesses of the market may well be reassuring; it may, on the other hand, prevent the churches from operating effectively

[16] For a full account of this episode in terms of ongoing debate about *laïcité* in French society, see Hervieu-Léger (1998: 70–7).

[17] A series of interesting case studies exemplify the Belgian situation; the most recent of these (Billiet 1998) revolves around the following question: 'does active participation in religious-philosophical or value-oriented organisations have a favourable influence on the development of attitudes that are conducive to social integration?' (233) The connection is tested empirically.

[18] An interesting—though theoretically rather different—approach to churches as voluntary organizations can be found in Harris (1998), who analyses both churches and synagogues as a form of voluntary activity, noting the special characteristics and problems that arise from this type of organization.

within the markets themselves (see Davie, forthcoming for a fuller discussion of this point).

The churches' capacity to create social capital can be seen in other ways as well. Gill, in both *Moral Communities* (1992) and *Churchgoing and Christian Ethics* (1999), offers an excellent empirical example. He analyses churchgoing as an independent rather than dependent variable, though at a micro rather than macro level. Churchgoing, though considerably reduced in modern Britain, does, it seems, have an effect on the way that people behave; it is not simply a reflection of other variables. One measurable influence, for instance, which resonates powerfully in the British context lies in the disproportionate numbers of the religiously active that can be found in the unpaid but highly trained voluntary sector—advice workers, prison visitors, charity workers, bereavement counsellors, etc.—whose contributions become increasingly valuable in a society where state provision, relatively speaking, is reducing rather than increasing. This is an army of people whose activities touch the most vulnerable groups in British society; without it the common good would, quite clearly, be diminished.

Two points follow on. The first asks how such a finding can be explained; the second looks at its capacity to take root in other parts of Europe. The first can be approached sociologically as well as theologically. If the latter concerns an ethic of altruism, the former undoubtedly resides in the local network. Groups of volunteers do not spontaneously present themselves for training as individuals; they emerge as the result of encouragement, knowledge, and con-tact, themselves the consequence of regular meeting and informal networks, activities in which the churches remain second to none.

How far, though, can unpaid but trained work offer a contribution outside Britain, where it has become a well-established way of working and one that resonates particularly well in a situation where state provision is seen to be inadequate? In some ways it is less easy to see a place for this in continental Europe, where welfare provision is more developed both in the social demo-cratic tradition of the Nordic countries (on a high-wage, high-tax, high-wel-fare basis), and in the corporatist tradition of continental Europe (where the feeling is strong that if something is worth doing it should be paid for, nor-mally by the state). Both alternatives are, however, under threat from the eco-nomic pressures of modern capitalism (epitomised in the entry requirements of European Monetary Union) and from the demographic pressures of mod-ern society. Equations of work, tax, and welfare, which balanced well in the immediate post-war period, do not offer viable solutions where the dependent and independent sections of the population have altered drastically. The Nordic countries are beginning to grasp this reality and look for solutions beyond the state welfare system. In the Catholic countries of continental Europe similar tendencies can be seen but in rather different ways. First, they are evident in the concept of 'personalism' (as opposed to individualism)—a Christian Democrat idea which persists in Catholic social teaching, despite the fact that some (if not all) Christian Democrat parties no longer resonate in a political sense. (This is so for a whole variety of reasons, only one of which is relative secularization.) Secondly, the developed emphasis on the state as the effective provider of welfare is not the only model that exists in Catholic Europe. Catholic charities—champions *par excellence* of the voluntary sector—continue to play an important part in the lives of many Europeans.[19] Interestingly, in their negotiations with the state in the nineteenth century, such organizations provided the initial focus for discussion of the concept of 'subsidiarity'—few ideas have been as influential as this one in the evolution of the European Union.

One point must be made abundantly clear before completing this discussion. It is very unlikely that any of these adjustments will result in a significant increase in churchgoing in modern Europe. The point lies elsewhere: that is, in the realization that the historic churches, though statistically reduced, still have an effective role to play—the more so if they are prepared to maximize their co-operation with other religious communities and use constructively the legacy of the past (notably the local network). It remains the case, however, that if the churches have retained the capacity to operate at all, they may—theoretically at least—be equally able to mobilize both themselves and others in ways which erode rather than build an effective civil society (see below). The sociologist can point out the functional capacity; others are responsible for the way that this is used.

## A Variation on the Theme: Central Europe

Much of the analysis so far rests on the assumption that a partial collapse of the centre in modern European societies has taken place, understanding the decline in influence of the historic churches—who bound themselves too closely to the political centre—as part of the decomposing process. In Central and East Europe, the alignments are different (Martin 1996*a*). Here the centre did indeed implode, dramatically so in 1989; it was, however, an aggressively secular centre with its own areligious ideology. As a consequence the churches (Christian and other) were pushed to the margin and effectively became the carriers of an alternative or unauthorized memory. In so doing the churches avoided the negative connotations of a discredited government and a collapsing centre, but—for the most part—paid a very high price in terms of the confiscation of buildings, loss of income and manpower, restriction of activities,

---

[19] The European Values Study gives a certain amount of support to these hypotheses. Churchgoers are disproportionately active in the voluntary sector all over West Europe, but in very varied ways, and depending on the particular characteristics of each European society (Ashford and Timms 1992). The place of the volunteer in the changing circumstances of Swedish society constitutes an important theme in the research project outlined in n. 5, a part of the study in which the comparisons with Germany form an significant element.

and at times aggressive persecution. Such churches emerge therefore on the eve of the millennium with a different set of advantages and disadvantages compared with their Western counterparts and with a different set of priorities.

Like the churches in the West—and perhaps even more so—they are called upon to fill the void of civil society in the 1990s. If the Western version of this derives from the exigencies of capitalism, the post-communist version is vastly more apparent and results from the abrupt removal of both the structures of communist society and the creed that underpinned them at every level of society. The churches, moreover, played a crucial part in bringing about this disintegration. In some places (notably Poland) the Catholic Church became the primary focus of effective opposition to communism, a story that is both well documented and frequently told. The capacity for the more depleted churches of Central Europe to operate in a similar fashion at crucial moments in the drama is less well known but they offer a valuable reminder that size and numbers are not the only variables to be taken into account. It is these churches, moreover, that face the reconstruction process with limited resources and little experience of democratic practice.

How, then, should these churches proceed? Once again there are choices to be made and one of the profoundest ironies of the present situation is the case of Polish Catholicism. Historically powerful, relatively well endowed, with no shortage of priests and close links with the Vatican, this Church repeatedly tries to dominate the democratic process rather than participate as one partner among many. Analyses of this situation are multiplying (Michel 1991; Casanova 1994; Rygidzki 1996; Sadowski 1997); they concern the constitutional order, the 1998 Concordat, religious education, the imposition of 'Christian' moral values, and the attempted control of the mass media, examples which will reappear in subsequent chapters. Given the lack of willingness to compromise, there is a real risk of a belated rerun of the clerical–anticlerical battles that dominated Western Europe in the late nineteenth century (Casanova 1994).

The Estonian contrast is striking. Here a tiny church very nearly collapsed in the communist period, illustrating amongst other things the relative incapacity of the Protestant churches (as churches) to withstand persecution, which is not to deny the extraordinary courage of many individual believers (a similar case can be found in East Germany). The struggle to re-establish any kind of institutional normality, moreover, will be both long and uncertain. Despite everything, however, both Lutheran and Orthodox churches in Estonia have emerged as accepted partners of the state and are considered crucial elements in the reconstruction of democracy (Davie, Kingsbury, and Bäckström 1997: 19). Here again the examples are many but concern above all the creation of norms, or an ethic, on which democracy and the rule of law can rest. The democratic legal process cannot even begin without this underpinning.

## The Possibility of Reverse Flows

A final question remains before drawing the threads of the chapter together: how far are the European patterns immutable? Or to put the question in a different way, is it possible to see reverse flows that run counter to the traditional assumptions? I have already argued against the artificial adoption of North American answers to European questions. It is not possible to create the kind of market found in the United States within the European context and probably foolish to try. It is possible, however, to see European 'spaces' previously occupied by hegemonic national churches (and their alter egos) filling up with new forms of religion.

Martin (1996*b*), for example, has meticulously observed the European scene for many decades, and comes to the following conclusion with respect to Latin Europe:

Initially, about a quarter of a century ago, I asked myself why the voluntary denominations of Anglo-American culture had not taken off in Latin America as they had in the U.S.A., and concluded that Latin America must be too similar to Latin Europe for that to happen. But now I am inclined to reverse the question and ask why the burgeoning denominations of Latin America have not taken off in Latin Europe . . . There are new spaces being cleared in which a competitive denominational culture can flourish. (1996*b*: 41–2; citation taken from the English original)

The essence of Martin's argument lies in the observation that the factors which encouraged European secularization in the first place—a fortress Catholicism, buttressed by political power and opposed by militant secularity—are themselves beginning to erode. There is no reason, therefore, why the voluntary denominationalism of the New World should not find a place in the Old, alongside if not replacing a weakened Catholic Church. And if that is true in Latin Europe, how much more spectacular are the spaces in much of the former communist world, which, quite clearly, are attracting sustained attention from the evangelical constituency all over the West, to the dismay at times of the historic churches.

Subsequent chapters will consider these innovations in more detail and will include considerable attention to Europe's other-faith communities, whose arrival is for economic rather than evangelistic reasons. The point to grasp here is that all such minorities arrive in a Europe deeply coloured by its Christian history and in which the state churches have played a dominant part. I have argued that the role of these churches is still significant though in ways rather different from those of previous centuries. Legal and financial issues remain crucial and pose difficult questions in terms of inclusion and exclusion. Patterns of leadership evolve but remain a significant issue, in that it will be the leaders of such churches (both lay and ordained) who are responsible for the manner in which these institutions contribute or fail to contribute to civil society. Compared with other voluntary organizations their potential remains high; whether or not they rise to the challenge is a matter of empirical enquiry, not theoretical foreclosure.

## Vicarious Memory

It is at this point that the idea of vicarious memory needs further articulation. It has already been referred to briefly with reference to British religion in paragraphs which suggested that one way of understanding patterns of religion, at least in Northern Europe, was to grasp the willingness of the population to delegate the religious sphere to the professional ministries of the state churches and, as a way of policing this delegation, to be profoundly critical of such elites when things go wrong (in the form of deviant beliefs or inappropriate forms of behaviour). Whether or not this can be extrapolated to the Catholic countries of Europe remains a difficult question given the confrontational nature of the past in much of Catholic Europe and a rather different attitude to public morality. But a similar resonance lies, perhaps, in the notion of Catholic identity—in that a sense of being Catholic appears to endure even when practice has ceased to be anything except spasmodic (far more so, in fact, than in Protestantism). Whatever the case it seems that significant numbers of Europeans remain grateful to rather than resentful of their churches at the turn of the millennium, recognizing that these churches perform, vicariously, a number of tasks on behalf of the population as a whole. From time to time they are asked to articulate the sacred in the life-cycle of individuals or families or at times of national crisis or celebration. It is significant that a refusal to carry out these tasks would violate both individual and collective expectations (see Chapter 4).

In many respects this pattern is hardly new, though the proportions of active and nominal members have changed markedly in the post-war period. It is, moreover, legitimate to enquire whether there is a minimum size below which the minority must not drop if it is to be effective at all (indeed there are some, following Bruce, who would argue that this limit has been reached already). These are questions that will be addressed in more detail in the concluding theoretical discussion (Chapter 10). In the mean time, it is important to grasp the continuing significance of the institutional churches as one of the carriers of Europe's religious memory, but to begin to discern the mutations in the manner in which this can be done in the present period. One of these concerns a shift in some of the traditional dividing lines. The contrast between laity and priest, for example, appears to be giving way to a contrast between inactive laity and the actively faithful (both lay and ordained), for both the latter become, effectively, the responsible professionals, especially where the number of priests is declining. The social composition of this group is a further factor to be taken into consideration (see Chapter 4) in that its influence will depend not only on the numbers involved but on who such people are and their access to channels of influence outside as well as inside the churches. A parallel mutation (noted once again in the sections above) concerns the changing gender patterns of the Protestant ministry, as increasing numbers of women emerge to take positions of responsibility in Europe's Protestant churches. In this respect, the ordained ministry looks once again more rather than less like the active laity with whom it is called to work.

Central to all these equations are the relationships between active and passive groups. On the eve of the twenty-first century, sufficient numbers of the religiously inactive in Europe appear to have retained a nominal, if vicarious, attachment to their churches in order for the representative role to be possible; indeed in many respects it is encouraged. Whether or not this will be the case for much longer remains an open question, in that one of the very obvious risks of operating vicariously is the lack of direct contact between the institutional churches and the population as a whole. This may not result in an immediate loss of religious sensitivity (the data suggest otherwise); it does, however, lead to a dramatic generation-by-generation drop in religious *knowledge*. Ignorance of even the basic understandings of Christian teaching is the norm in modern Europe. Indeed in younger generations in some parts of Europe, the knowledge of other faiths may be more developed than that of Christianity, a result of religious education in schools, itself a source of memory and the focus of Chapter 5.

# FOUR

# *Vicarious Memory 2: The Churchgoers*

I F the previous chapter was primarily concerned with the relocation of Europe's state churches within the voluntary or non-governmental sector, the first two sections of this one have as their principal focus the people or populations that inhabit these changing organizations. Conversely they are also concerned with those people or groups of people who are now out of touch with institutional religion (whatever form this might take) and why such choices have been made. In order to understand the complex nature of what is happening in this respect, it is necessary to take into account not only the changing nature of European religion but the shifting nature of Europe's demography as a whole.[1] This, moreover, is the context in which to consider the complex relationships between religion and family life. The family is indeed a crucial place of religious socialization, but is itself changing—responding necessarily to profound economic, social, and demographic transformations.

The historic role of the Christian churches as the institutions responsible for both recording and legitimating key moments in the life-cycle—and in the forming and re-forming of families—needs to be seen against this background. In some European countries, this role is still largely intact; in others it has shifted dramatically and appears increasingly irrelevant to many sections of the population. The comparative statistics of baptisms, marriages, and funerals provide an entry into this topic; so, too, does the shifting nature of the life-cycle itself and its implications for Christian teaching. Both concern the occasional offices, events which bring together the regular and the nominal churchgoer—and nowhere more so than in the attempts of a community or a nation to come to terms with death. With this in mind, the chapter concludes with case studies of two remarkable deaths in the late 1990s: those of Princess Diana and President Mitterand. Both epitomize amongst other things the deeply complex relationships between formal and informal patterns of

[1] Indeed a remarkably similar demographic profile is one of the factors that binds European countries together, particularly if these are compared with the patterns to be discovered, for example, on the southern rather than the northern shore of the Mediterranean.

religion. To a considerable extent each depends on the other but is at the same time in tension with it. Scrutinizing this tension enables a more nuanced understanding of the notion of vicarious religion.

# Europe's Demographic Profile

Shifts in the composition of populations are notoriously difficult either to predict or to understand. No sooner, for example, had Europeans begun to take the post-war baby boom for granted than the notion of zero population growth began to dominate the agenda, accompanied by increasing anxieties about the ratios of working and dependent populations. Why one trend gives way to another remains, however, as elusive as ever, as deeply personal decisions (concerning childbirth, marriage, divorce, illness, death, and migration) turn themselves into trends which have crucial implications for multiple aspects of public policy. They are equally significant for the understanding of religious change and patterns of religious activity.

Europe now enjoys, if that is the right word, low birth and low death rates. Population growth has slowed to unprecedented levels as a result of a dramatic improvement in life expectancy and a decline in fertility to replacement level or less. The relationship between reduced fertility levels and a complex web of economic, political, social, and cultural factors requires skilled analysis in order to discern the subtleties of cause and effect. What is clear, however, is that economic factors on their own do not provide an adequate explanation for the shifts that are taking place. The connections between low birth rates and the changing place of women in modern Western societies are a case in point; plainly the two are linked but the relationship does not always operate in the expected direction.

Why, for example, do Swedish women have markedly more children than their Italian sisters, given the predilection of the former for professional careers and the far more relaxed attitude of the Lutheran Church to contraception compared with official Catholic teaching? The illustration is all the more pertinent in that it immediately raises the question of the significance of the religious factor within these complex equations. It seems, in fact, that Swedish women are able 'to have their cake and eat it' given both the attitudes of the Lutheran Church towards changing gender roles and a considerable degree of state support for the working mother (itself a sign of cultural acceptance). Italian women, on the other hand, are obliged to make more difficult choices; and given such they are inclined to opt for their careers rather than a larger family. Catholic social policy is clearly a significant factor in this respect in that it discourages women from working when they have a family, but with unexpected consequences. Many women, it seems, choose 'wrongly', at least as far as the Catholic Church is concerned.

The most obvious effect of the change in both fertility and mortality rates in European societies is the 'ageing' of European societies (Giarchi and Abbott 1997). This is true in three senses: there will be an increase in the proportion of older people in the population, an increase in the actual number of older people, and an increase in the average age of populations. The proportional growth is indeed considerable but whether or not this amounts to a demographic disaster or 'time-bomb' is difficult to say, particularly as many of these elderly continue to enjoy good health for longer than their predecessors and might, if necessary, continue working if the pool of labour proved insufficient. In the mean time, the relative religiousness of older as opposed to younger people has an obvious effect on patterns of religiosity; it is likely to maintain levels of practice and belief at higher levels than might otherwise be the case (see below)—the more so in that women, who are more religious than men, tend also to live longer.

A second cluster of demographic factors relates to the changing nature of marriage, the rapid increase in the divorce rate, and an increasing tendency for Europeans to live in single-person households. In order to understand such questions fully, they should be linked to parallel evolutions in economic life, notably the shift from an industrial to a post-industrial society. The transition between adolescence and adulthood provides a pertinent illustration, introducing once again the significance of the religious factor in relation to demographic change. In the immediate post-war period—and in some parts of Europe for considerably longer—a young man became an adult when he left full-time education and entered the labour market, probably in his mid-teens. A young woman attained a similar status when she married and left the household in which she grew up to begin a new stage in life as a wife, and very soon as a mother. Once again this happened relatively soon after leaving school. At the turn of the millennium, in contrast, both young men and young women are likely to prolong both their education and their adolescence for anything up to a decade, during which their financial existence may be precarious (involving continual support from their parents) and their questioning of authority, including religious authority, considerable. What started as a natural moment in the life-cycle to rebel becomes almost a way of life (Fulton 1996; Campiche 1997*a*; Abela *et al*. 2000). Nor is this generation likely to delay sexual activity until they are married (in many cases well after their thirtieth birthdays) or to confine such activity to one partner during this period of waiting. The widespread availability of contraceptives all over Europe is both cause and consequence of these changes, in which sexual satisfaction has become less and less related to procreation (either can now take place without the other), a shift so widespread that the continuing protestations of the Catholic Church look not only out of place, but increasingly bizarre.

Not only is marriage delayed, it is itself changing in nature. A major factor in these changes is the growth in life expectancy. In the middle years of the twentieth century an innovative pattern emerged: that of relatively early marriage to one partner lasting for most of a lifetime (itself extending as the decades passed), as a consequence of which marriages of thirty, forty, or fifty years became commonplace. This pattern—increasingly thought of as 'normal' rather than innovative—gradually replaced the serial monogamy of previous centuries, brought about by the death of either partner relatively early in life, but very frequently of the woman in view of the dangers of childbirth. As long life has become the norm, however, it is clear that the notion of a prolonged marriage to one partner has come under increasing strain all over Europe. In the 1960s and 1970s, almost every European nation looked again at its divorce law in order to accommodate the growing need to bring some marriages to an end.[2] Serial monogamy began to assert itself all over again, this time through the mechanism of the divorce law rather than the early death of one or the other partner.

Changes in longevity are, of course, only one factor among many in the complex and at times extremely painful social evolution of marriage; others concern the expectations of the couple, the possibilities for independent living (especially for women), and the sense that a marriage (or equivalent relationship) should last only as long as it is mutually satisfying for both partners (Giddens 1992). And if mutual satisfaction is the key to the enterprise, rather than a life-long partnership centred on the procreation of children, why should partners be limited only to those of the opposite sex? The gradual acceptance of homosexuality as an integral part of modern living—still more developed in Northern Europe than in the Latin South—is a further factor to be taken into account as partnerships form and reform through the course of lengthening lifetimes in which child-bearing (itself an increasingly efficient process) plays a significant but more limited part.

Where, though, does this leave a church (or churches) whose traditional teachings have underpinned particular moral codes associated with one form of marriage rather than any other, and which have assumed that sexual activity should be limited to one partner within marriage and exists largely, if not solely, for the procreation of children? 'In difficulty' is the only answer. But the corollaries need careful interpretation. It is incorrect, for example, to assume that those—especially young people—who reject the teaching of the church (notably the Catholic Church) on questions of sexual ethics are necessarily rejecting religion, even the Christian religion, *per se*. Other, more subtle formulations are not only possible, but widespread. The tendency to bracket out certain aspects of its teaching is, however, far more damaging to the authority of the church than is sometimes realized, in that it becomes an

---

[2] The British law on divorce was revised in 1969 (the revisions coming into force two years later); the French went through a similar process in 1975, accepting divorce by consent. Consultations in other European states (Italy, for example, in 1974) took the form of a referendum; opinion changed faster in some places than in others—differences accounted for at least in part by the relative influence of the Catholic Church.

ongoing process. If some formulations can be bracketed out for particular reasons, so too can others—the slippery slope is difficult to resist.

It is also the case that in solving one set of problems (the need to bring some marriages to an end through the mechanisms of the courts), European societies have created others. It is becoming increasingly clear, for example, that instability in family life does have a damaging effect on children, the more so if partnerships come to an end more than once during a particular individual's childhood or adolescence. The delicate balancing of the needs or rights of children against the aspirations of their parents perplexes all European societies; it is, moreover, an area in which the pastoral care of the churches can be crucial.[3] Indeed the churches themselves are faced with an increasingly difficult tension: how is it possible to maintain the principle of marriage, as this is understood in Judaeo-Christian teaching, with the demand for pastoral generosity in the circumstances of a late modern society? The tension of being in the world but not of it is hardly new in Christian theology; it does, however, require painful rethinking in the shifting demographic circumstances of European society at the turn of the millennium.

The final demographic shift to be taken into account with reference to religious understanding concerns the changing nature of the European population as a result of immigration. Many, if not all, European societies were, in the late fifties and sixties, looking for alternative sources of labour (mostly unskilled labour) for rapidly expanding economies. Unsurprisingly each country turned to its former colonies, leading to significant immigrations into Britain from both the Caribbean and the Indian sub-continent, into France from the Maghreb and French West Africa, into Belgium from the Congo, and into the Netherlands from the East Indies and Surinam. Germany found equivalent sources of labour in South-east Europe (notably the former Yugoslavia) and in Turkey (see Chapter 7 for a more detailed presentation of these figures and their implications for religious change).

The relationship between immigration and religious diversity is to some extent obvious; European societies would not have changed in this respect but for the demands of the post-war economy. It is, however, a highly complex issue and requires considerable sensitivity, as much from sociologists of religion as from policy-makers. Racial differences, it is clear, are not co-terminous with religious differences; nor is it possible to jump to conclusions about the evolving needs and requirements of other-faith populations in a part of the world dominated for centuries by a Christian tradition. The patient working-out of policy both in Europe as a whole and in its constituent nations for a wide variety of racial and religious minorities is a painstaking process, which demands consideration on all sides. Such qualities are, however, increasingly

---

[3] An interesting example can be found in Britain, where the churches are frequently involved in offering both plant and personnel for the provision of 'Access Centres' (often in the centre of urban areas), where the non-custodial parent in a divorce case can have access to his or her child in safe and neutral circumstances.

difficult to come by in times of economic stringency, when jobs and the privileges that go with them are in short supply. It is once again a situation in which the representatives of the historic churches can, if they so wish, make a significant contribution.[4]

A crucial point arrives in this respect when both incomers and the host society become aware that those who came with an initial intention to return home relatively quickly are, in fact, here to stay. It is at this point that wives and other dependants arrive in Europe in significant numbers and when organizations associated with community life begin to burgeon. One manifestation is the emergence all over Europe of religious buildings other than Christian ones, an immediately visible sign of the presence of other faiths. In France, for example, the number of mosques grew from a handful in the early 1970s to more than a thousand by 1990 (Davie 1999a). The equivalent figures for Britain go from similar beginnings in the early 1960s to 850 in the mid-1990s, bearing in mind the difficulties in obtaining accurate and comparable statistics (Vertovec and Peach 1997a). A second challenge lies in the need to find acceptable solutions for the education of a new and increasingly diverse generation of Europeans; how this should be done is not at all self-evident and varies from country to country (see Chapter 5). Europeans are becoming aware of customs other than their own, and quite clearly vary in their capacities to accommodate such differences.

## Europe's Churchgoers

How then do Europe's churchgoers fit into this overall pattern of demographic change? They are, first of all, an elderly population, relatively speaking, a point easily observed in Europe's churches and in any opinion poll that includes questions relating to religious belief. The data put forward in Chapter 1 left no room for doubt that the actively religious in Europe were a shrinking constituency; it is quite possible that this proportion might well have shrunk still further but for the relative growth of older people within the population as a whole. A crucial question lies beneath these statements: will future generations of older people have a similar attachment to their churches as those who grew up in Europe before the Second World War? If they do, then the future of the churches as an institution well placed to cater for this expanding age-group looks rather more assured. It may not be the case, however. It is quite possible that the relative popularity of churches among older people in the late 1990s is simply a temporary phenomenon, reflecting patterns of previous generations, which are unlikely to perpetuate themselves into the next cen-

---

[4] In, for example, the protection of 'faith' as such, as opposed to the protection of an exclusively Christian faith (see the examples in Ch. 3).

tury despite the relative ageing of the population as a whole. The question is closely linked to the sociological interpretation of different levels of religiousness between different European generations: are these to be explained in terms of the life-cycle or in terms of age-cohorts? (Davie and Vincent 1998). If it is the former, the patterns are likely to continue; if the latter, it may well not be so. The most likely interpretation is a combination of the two.

A second, almost universal, factor relates to gender. It is indisputable that there are more women than men in European (and indeed in all Western) churches and that this difference holds across a variety of theological types and across all age-groups. It is, for example, equally present in the one-off gatherings of young people (at Taizé or at a youth meeting in the presence of the Pope) as it is in both smaller and larger parishes of the traditional churches. It is mirrored in the greater number of women (just like the greater number of older people) who assent to belief in God, a point picked up in every enquiry which addresses the subject. Why this should be so is a rather more difficult question and involves the complex interaction of explanations based on nurture with those that evoke the nature of women as the crucial explanatory variable (Campiche 1996; Walter and Davie 1998). Predictions about the future, just like those concerning age, vary accordingly. If women are more religious than men because of their socialization and their obligations within society, it is quite possible that their religiousness may alter as societies evolve (and sometimes very rapidly indeed). If women, on the other hand, are more religious than men because of what they *are*, rather than what they *do*, the difference may be more difficult to eradicate—always assuming that eradication is what the churches are after.

Two interrelated questions follow from this. This first pursues the issue of value judgements, and probes more fully the assumption that the over-representation of women in European churches is in some way a 'problem'; a problem often expressed, revealingly, as an under-representation of men. If in secular society there is constant effort to ensure an adequate representation of women, it is paradoxical that their presence in the churches should be seen in a negative rather than a positive light. The second question involves the mismatch between men and women depending on whether the focus of attention is on those who are active in the chancels of Europe's various churches or on those who are present in the pews. It is the latter not the former where women are to be found in relative abundance, though the gradual changes in ministry in the Protestant churches of Europe (already noted in the previous chapter) are likely to be of considerable significance in these complex evolutions.

Whatever the case, for the time being it is clear that women form a crucial group in both the maintenance and handing on of religious memory in modern European societies. This is even more the case in the more privatized aspects of religious life, which are, it seems, growing in importance (Walter and Davie 1998). Campiche (1996), for example, stresses the persistence of a marked difference between men and women in the matter of private prayer, a contrast that maintains itself even when a number of external factors are taken into account. Campiche's primary emphasis on the salience of nurture as the crucial explanatory variable is derived from a Swiss enquiry, in which many of the differences in the religiosity of men and women disappear once presence in the labour force, or different family structures, are controlled for (see also Steggarda 1993 and 1994 for similar findings in the Netherlands). Private prayer, in contrast, persists and remains very largely the preserve of women whatever the intermediate variables. Why this should be so inevitably provokes a renewed set of questions about the relative religiousness of women and the complexity of the reasons for this persistent phenomenon.

One explanation lies in the responsibility that women take for the nurture of the next generation, a possibility reinforced by the greater religiousness of parents (both male and female) as opposed to couples (married or otherwise) without children (Walter and Davie 1998). A double line of reasoning emerges from this statement: first, that parenting appears to encourage religious responses; second, that the family itself becomes an important site for the handing on of religious memory, the more so in its traditional forms (the full-time wife and mother is a crucial figure). Levitt (1996) has looked at a small, provincial community in South-west England from this point of view. The likelihood of successful religious transmission is at its highest when both parents are actively engaged in religious activity. It is, however, the women (the mothers) who take responsibility for this aspect of upbringing in the vast majority of cases. Bringing gender and generation together, the predominance of women shows in each generation despite the overall decline in religious engagement in each successive generation. Women do return to religious organizations when they become mothers, but in smaller numbers than they used to.

Compared with age or gender, the interrelationships between religion and, social class are rather more complicated; they also vary in different parts of Europe. In the West, for example, it is clear that churchgoing attracts disproportionate numbers of the relatively well educated and the professional classes rather than those with limited education, conventionally—if no longer very appropriately—known as the working classes (the European Values Study provides ample evidence for this statement). In Central Europe the pattern is very largely reversed, as the less-educated, rural populations are those most likely to be found in churches on a regular basis, a pattern which has persisted beyond 1989.[5] Patterns of *belief*, however, are rather different, especially in the West, where higher levels of education are more (not less) likely to be associated with unbelief or the espousal of alternative ideologies (though more so in some professions than in others). In other words, for Western populations, the higher the level of education the closer the association between patterns of belief and patterns of activity; amongst the more modestly educated, the phe-

[5] See Tomka (1992) for a discussion of the Hungarian case.

nomenon of believing without belonging is at its most marked. For many amongst Western populations, regular churchgoing is seen as at best unnecessary and at worst hypocritical, reactions which derive partly from the historical associations of religion and power, but also (and increasingly) from the capacity of Europeans to operate vicariously.

In those parts of Europe formerly under communist domination, the associations between religion and power were clearly different (so, too, was the notion of a representative role), encouraging an alternative form of social distribution in terms of churchgoing. There is also the phenomenon of the unbelieving intellectual (Michel 1996), who especially in Poland made use of churchgoing as a form of social protest—not only for him- or herself, but for the children in addition. The church offered space in which ideologies other than communist might be kept in place and for this reason, if no other, should be publicly endorsed. With this in mind, a careful tracking of the religious intellectual both before and after 1989 and in different parts of Europe would be a revealing comparative study, in view of the particular capacities of this social group to articulate a memory.[6] Be that as it may, it remains the case that a disproportionate number of more- rather than less-educated people are to be found in the churchgoing constituency of much of modern Europe; those, in other words, at the centre of activity rather than the periphery and those, frequently, with considerable influence at different levels of society.[7]

So far we have considered the Christian populations of Europe in terms of age, gender, and social class. The analysis could continue almost indefinitely with reference to spatial rather than sociological variables—concentrating, for example, on the differences between urban and rural communities and on the significance of different types of settlement and population density. The task would, however, become ever more complicated in that all these factors are themselves in flux, inevitably confusing any attempt to assess their influence on religious activities of different kinds. The point is clearly illustrated with respect to regional development within the new Europe. Until recently, major provincial cities often represented their regions—in terms of both economic and cultural life (some, for example, were noted centres of piety, others played host to secular alternatives). As modern transportation systems (notably high-speed trains and the motorway network) exert their influence over much of Europe, such cities 'move' nearer their capitals and become divorced from their hinterland and their representative role (see Le Galès 1999 for a fuller discussion of this point within the French context). Traditional regional cultures give way to a far more intricate pattern. Enduring deposits of centuries still

---

[6] Post-graduate work in this field is now beginning in the Centre d'Études Interdisciplinaires des Faits Religieux at the École des Hautes Études en Sciences Sociales in Paris.

[7] This point will be developed in connection with both education systems and the mass media (Chs. 5 and 6); it also relates to the influence of local church networks, already discussed in Ch. 3.

remain, however; visible to the discerning eye—though grossly distorted by average figures—they are sought after for their distinctiveness. Late modern Europeans are free to choose a regional identity (and all that goes with it) if they so wish; they are, conversely, less and less obliged to live with a historically defined region if they prefer to do otherwise.

## A Variation on the Theme: The Other-Faith Communities

In terms of social patterning the other-faith constituencies demonstrate a very different evolution. With the notable exception of Judaism, these communities are relatively recent arrivals in Europe and suffer the multiple disadvantages of marginal populations. This, in itself, is one reason for the importance of religion in both the individual and collective identities of many other-faith groups, an insistence which at times provokes unease in the host society, dominated for the most part by relative indifference. Practice, for example, remains high as other-faith communities must depend on themselves to maintain traditions in societies where the mainstream cannot help them. A second factor is equally important. On the whole it is relatively rare (but not impossible) for Europeans to convert to Islam or (in Britain) to Hinduism or Sikhism, though the apparent attractiveness of Buddhism to well-educated Western populations is a partial exception to this rule, placing this particular community in a different position from the others in terms of its social composition.

Generational change, however, may significantly modify this situation. At the turn of the millennium it is the third generation of the post-war arrivals which is reaching adulthood, posing questions rather different from those of their parents or grandparents (a fact which is true for girls as well as boys). One manifestation of this evolution is the arrival of other-faith representation in institutions of higher education and the adequacy of provision for their needs therein (Gilliat-Ray 1999). Higher education, moreover, may eradicate differences, leading perhaps to greater assimilation. But is this necessarily advantageous? The Jewish case is pertinent in this respect and will be considered further in Chapter 7. At this point it is sufficient to note that the 1990s have seen a number of publications (notably Wasserstein 1996) suggesting that the over-assimilation of Jews into post-war European society—itself an understandable, and in many ways welcome, reaction to the excesses of earlier decades—is a more dangerous threat to Jewish identity than the persecution that preceded it. But what in such circumstances is an appropriate course of action? It is one thing to identify the problem; quite another to find a solution that guarantees a future.

# The Occasional Offices: The Markers of the Life-Cycle

The role of the churches, indeed of all religious communities, in marking the turning points of life is a familiar theme in both the anthropological and sociological literature. It is, moreover, one that remains widespread in modern Europe—though more in some places than in others and with greater salience with respect to ceremonies concerned with the end of life rather than the beginning. Understanding the changes that are taking place in this respect requires that the data be set against the demographic shifts outlined in the first two sections of this chapter. Markers of the life-cycle cannot be considered apart from the life-cycle itself.

## *Baptism*

Rates of baptism vary greatly across different European countries. In some places, baptism remains almost universal—in the Lutheran North, for example (reflecting the importance of membership for the great majority of Scandinavians), and in the Latin South, where traditional Catholic practice persists. It is important to note that the statistics in Greece are particularly high, underlining the very close connection between Greek nationality and membership of the Orthodox Church. In between—in Britain, France, Belgium, and the Netherlands (to cite the most striking illustrations)[8]—there is an increasing mismatch in these variables. The assumption that baptism in the dominant church or churches is a necessary part of citizenship is increasingly being discarded; it becomes instead a conscious request for membership in a particular religious community. Such changes are provoked by a complex interaction of push and pull factors. At one and the same time, there is (1) a partial withdrawal on the part of the population—fewer parents see baptism as a necessary prerequisite to a good start in life—and (2) a 'tightening' of theology on the part of the church concerned. Both take place unevenly, resulting in piecemeal and inconsistent policies. Some parishes, for example, continue to offer indiscriminate baptism; others are considerably more demanding, requiring particular actions on the part of the parent(s) as proof of sincerity in their request.

The outcome of this process is a marked fall in the proportion of infants receiving baptism in the majority churches of these countries. Only 25 per cent of babies in Britain, for example, are now baptized in the Church of England, though another 25 per cent are baptized in either the Catholic or the Free Churches;[9] the figure for Catholic baptisms in France in 1993 was 58 per

---

[8] Voyé (1996) offers an excellent discussion of the Belgian case in this respect; it is equally relevant to the section on the changing nature of marriage. Religious marriages are chosen for a bewildering variety of reasons (see also Voyé 1991).

[9] The proportion of infant baptisms in the Church of England has dropped from two-thirds of all live births to one-third in the post-war period; this represents a considerable shift in cultural practice (Davie 1994).

cent (falling progressively in post-war decades from 92 per cent in 1958 to 82 per cent in 1968 and 66 per cent in 1984). Up to a point, however, such trends are offset by a corresponding—though by no means compensating—growth in the number of adult baptisms. Once again the equivalence between the Church of England and the Catholic Church in France is striking. In the Church of England, the number of adult baptisms in 1996 had reached 8,000 per year (*The Church of England Today: A summary of current statistics*, Feb. 1998); in France the figure for the same year was just over 11,000 (Service national du Catechumenat, Communiqué de Press, 5 mars 1996). Both figures are growing year on year. Even more noticeable was the proportion of adults (i.e. those over 20) confirmed in the Church of England—this has now reached 40 per cent of the total number. Adult baptism in Catholic France and adult confirmation in England are far from nominal procedures; both demand time and public commitment from the individuals concerned. They are, perhaps, indicators of a rather different future for religion in Europe. Churches that once operated as the *de facto* registrars of births are now reverting to a different (earlier) model of church membership. Voluntarism is necessarily, if not legally, asserting itself.

One further factor is possibly important. No longer is an infant life as vulnerable as it used to be. Almost all babies born in modern Europe live to maturity, a situation that could not be assumed until the early decades of this century, and even then confidence came gradually. Intimations of mortality quite clearly concentrate the mind, the more so in circumstances where pastoral discipline is strong (culminating, historically at least, in the exclusion from sanctified ground for infants who were not baptized). For the newly born at the end of the twentieth century, such intimations can safely be suspended in the vast majority of cases. Indeed, with this in mind, the question should, perhaps, be turned around the other way. Given the successes of both antenatal and neo-natal care, and the relatively low levels of religious practice in Europe as a whole, why do so many parents continue to ask for baptism for their children? In many ways, it is easier to explain the falling figures than those that remain stable.

## *Marriage*

The legitimation of marriage by religious institutions raises rather different issues, many of which reflect the shifting nature of marriage itself. For a start, large numbers of couples choose, at least initially, to cohabit rather than to marry. Traditional Christian (or indeed other-faith) congregations may not endorse this particular solution but cannot, realistically, do anything about it—it is part of European life whether the churches like it or not. The trend is largely a prolongation of the period of life traditionally known as adolescence; it can, however, become a long-term (if not always permanent) feature of many European lives. In terms of statistics relating to marriage itself, a further factor should also be kept in mind. In interpreting the proportion of couples still asking for legitimation for their marriage by a religious institution, it is necessary to know whether these are first or second marriages. In the case of second marriages, the Christian churches vary in their pastoral responses (as indeed do others): some are happy to conduct a second (or even third) marriage; others refuse altogether (still recognizing the permanence of the first union); yet others find a middle way between a full ceremony and no ceremony at all—and bless a civil marriage.

A revealing overview of the current state of affairs in Europe, which bears all these points in mind, can be found in Dittgen (1994, 1997); these publications are particularly useful in that they cover a wide variety of European countries. The patterns that emerge are both intriguing and significant—they are summarized in Figures 4.1 and 4.2.

Figure 4.1 reveals the proportion of marriages in different European societies which took place or were legitimated by a religious institution in 1990. With the exception of Finland, the difference between the Protestant North and Catholic (and Orthodox) South is striking, but with France, once again, looking more like her Protestant neighbours than a truly Latin country. It is also possible to see the great variety in the Central European countries in terms of marriage practice, remembering that these data need very careful interpretation in view of the rapid evolution of such nations since 1990—almost anything may happen to the religious sector of the former communist societies with respect to the occasional offices.

Figure 4.2 reinforces the need for caution in interpretation; it is clear that the statistics do not always move in the anticipated direction. In many parts of Europe, for example, there is an expected degree of decline, though more in some countries than in others. Some of these are Catholic (France, Belgium, and Austria), some are Protestant (the former East Germany), and some are confessionally mixed (the Netherlands and Switzerland). It is equally apparent, moreover, that a different set of pressures is operating in each of these places—the decline is not always brought about for similar reasons. By and large the evolutions can be summarized as follows: a gradual decline in the proportion of 'religious' marriages in most of Catholic Europe; reasonable stability in the British Isles and Denmark, but a noticeable rise in the figures that pertain to most of Scandinavia and to parts of South-eastern Europe. Once again the reasons are contingent and cannot be generalized to the continent as a whole.

Dittgen raises a number of interesting points in this connection. The proportion of religious ceremonies is, of course, related to the number of marriages per se, but the relationship is complex and which variable moves first cannot always be predicted (1994: 363). There is a similar complexity with respect to rates of religious practice—not all that predictable themselves, especially in the question of timing (in different parts of Europe they fall in different generations). It appears to be the case, however, that in those parts of

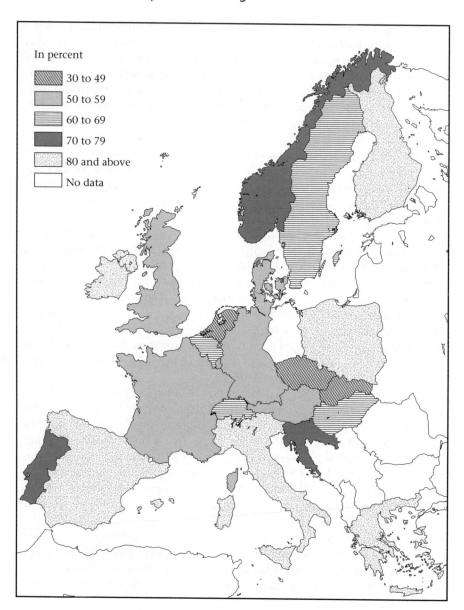

Fɪɢ. 4.1. Proportions of religious marriages or marriages followed by a religious ceremony, Europe, 1990

*Source*: Dittgen (1994: 364–5).

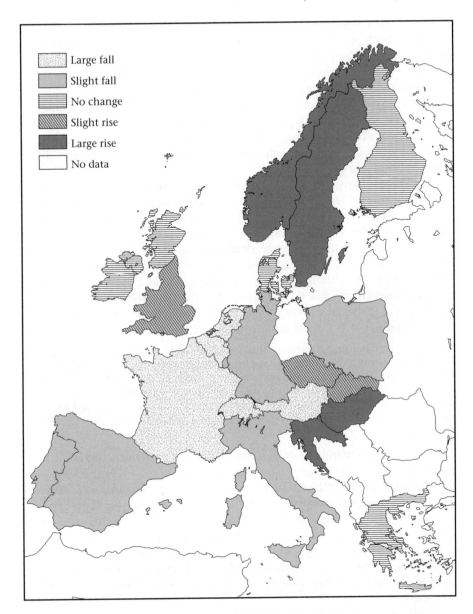

F𝐈𝐆. 4.2. Evolution in the proportions of religious marriage or marriages followed by a religious ceremony, Europe, 1975–1990

*Source*: Dittgen (1994: 364–5).

Europe which 'secularized' relatively early, a reasonable stability has emerged in terms of both practice and the proportion of marriages that are legitimated by the churches. Countries which followed suit a generation or so later have not yet reached this point of stability. The Scandinavian figures are none the less a reminder that patterns can and do go into reverse, and sometimes noticeably so (though not necessarily for religious reasons). With this in mind, there can be no alternative to careful empirical enquiry in order to reveal the complexity of what is going on, noting that theological currents interact with economic and social evolutions all over Europe, but bearing in mind very different political and cultural deposits.

Marriage, moreover, raises additional questions for the churches, one of which concerns the legitimation of their own status rather than the marriages they conduct. In those parts of Europe where the churches themselves take legal responsibility for the ceremony, the question of 'scope' (already discussed in some detail in the previous chapter) is immediately apparent. Which religious institutions are able and which are not able to solemnize a marriage? Dittgen (1994, 1997) covers this issue to some extent as a background to his statistical analysis (see also Robbers 1996), but the Danish example (Warburg 1998) offers a particularly interesting illustration of how the question of scope may be interpreted in a member state of the European Union:

My reason for choosing to discuss this particular right is because according to Danish administrative tradition the granting of permission to perform legally binding marriages is the basic criterion for granting tax reductions, as well as other benefits. A study of this administrative procedure of granting the authority to perform marriages thereby becomes a study of how the Danish State has developed a practice for distinguishing between religious and non-religious associations. (Warburg 1998: 268)

More specifically, Warburg analyses the claims of two Danish communities who both applied for the right to conduct marriages in the 1970s and 1980s—the Danish Baha'is and the Church of Scientology. The outcomes were different in each case (only the Baha'is were successful); so too were the motives that resulted in the different decisions. It seemed that the Danish state was reluctant to have as its representative at a marriage a member of the controversial Church of Scientology, whereas it had no problem with the 'decent and unprovocative Baha'is', though it was difficult to find a substantive difference in the cases put forward by either group. The decision was, it seems, essentially subjective.

Scope, moreover, can be considered in other ways as well. Which unions, for example, are the churches prepared to bless? Not only does this raise the question of the theological interpretation of marriage in terms of divorce and possible remarriage, it inevitably introduces the notion of a homosexual couple. The drive for legalization in this respect derives from a multiplicity of factors, not least—in terms of civil marriage—from the need for recognition with respect to pensions, adoptions, or inheritance (it has important economic con-

sequences). It is equally the case that amongst the actively Christian populations of modern Europe, there is a proportion (albeit small) who desire the
Church's recognition for a homosexual union for primarily spiritual reasons.
The churches remain understandably reticent in their reaction to such
requests. A further innovation reflects a second evolution of European societies: the creation of a liturgy to mark the end as well as the beginning of a
marriage. As yet informal, such ceremonies are growing, sought by those
(again the practising minority) who wish to place a marker on the turning
points in life. Divorce, a form of ending for a significant number of European
couples, is increasingly seen as one such episode.

## Funerals

Of all the occasional offices, the churches' role is recognized most widely in
the conducting of a ceremony to mark the death of an individual, whether
they be a member of a religious constituency or not (a fact endorsed by the
European Values Study). Once again, however, it is legitimate to ask whether
such requests will continue into the next century in view of the changing
nature of European societies and the apparent fall in religiosity in younger
generations. But fall in religiosity or not, death remains the unresolved mys-
tery of modern just as much as traditional societies. Something, moreover, has
to be done at this point, whether by the churches or by someone else—hence,
to a certain extent, a marked revival of sociological interest in the management of death and the processes that surround this in the circumstances of late
modern (and supposedly rational) societies.[10]

One factor is interesting in terms of changes in religious practice. In parts of
modern Europe—and particularly in the Protestant North—cremation as a
mode of disposal has grown dramatically in popularity. From an extremely
small percentage in the immediate post-war period, it has become the norm in
Britain and parts of Scandinavia—here the proportion of cremations is currently 70 per cent or more. Why this change should have taken place, and in
some places but not in others, continues to provoke considerable sociological
speculation (Davies 1990; Jupp 1990); rightly so in fact, for it amounts to a revolution in religious practice. An inevitable question follows: does a change in
religious practice necessarily imply a change in religious belief, notably a
mutation in the understanding of the afterlife? It certainly requires rethinking
in terms of the liturgy that accompanies the ritual.

A second, far more modest evolution should also be noted; that is, the
option of an entirely secular funeral. This certainly exists as a legal possibility
in most of modern Europe; uptake remains limited, however, though more so
in some places than in others and likely to increase rather than decrease.
Another possibility lies in the gradual evolution of the religious ceremony to

---

[10] See Walter (1994, 1996) for a discussion of the British case in particular.

contain elements that are both specific to the individual who has died and lie outside the religious tradition which takes responsibility for the ceremony. The late modern funeral in European society does not become so much secular as differently religious. Such tendencies can be seen in two remarkable ceremonies which took place in the closing years of the century. Each of them reflects the lives of the particular individual and the religious currents of the country involved; both, however, draw together elements of popular as well as institutional religion, but in innovative ways.

## Two Public Funerals on the Eve of the Millennium

François Mitterrand died from cancer in January 1996; he had been President of France for fifteen years and leader of the Parti Socialiste since 1972. In many ways he epitomized the aspirations of the French left and represented in his person (supposedly agnostic) as well as his beliefs the desire of the French state to be free of religion in the public sphere. Among his papers assembled after his death, however, the following decidedly ambiguous phrase was found: 'une messe est possible'. What in fact took place was not one Mass, but two: the first in Notre-Dame, which was effectively the state funeral to which both national and international representatives were invited; the second (a strictly private ritual) took place in Jarnac, the President's birthplace. The capacities of modern technology to bring these together on the television screen (they took place simultaneously) will be discussed in more detail in the chapter concerned with the media. Here it is sufficient to stress the need for a formal liturgy at the time of a death, even for someone as enigmatically attached to the Catholic Church as François Mitterrand (Hervieu-Léger 1996, 1999b).

Hervieu-Léger analyses both these events in some detail, stressing the discomfort of (1) certain types of Catholics and (2) certain kinds of *laïques* to the decision by the Church, not only to host but to legitimate these occasions. The first group (representing a particular understanding of Catholicism) felt that the President's life-style was not such as to merit a Mass at his death (a point underlined by the presence of both Mitterrand's wife and his mistress at the funeral in Jarnac); the second group (the *laïques*) resented the notion of anything Catholic at all. A third reaction—that of the small community of French Protestants—took the form of regretting that the official occasion was not more ecumenical, with at least some participation by the non-Catholic communities. The crucial point to remember is that an additional, entirely different ceremony took place on the evening before the Catholic funerals. This was the gathering of the French Left at the Place de la Bastille in Paris. It was here, moreover, that the greatest sense of continuity was felt—the continuity of French socialism to which the President had formally linked himself at the time of his inauguration in 1981 (visiting the tombs of his predecessors in the

Panthéon). And it was at the Bastille that extracts from Mitterrand's own writings were broadcast to the assembled crowd. Why, then, were the religious ceremonies necessary at all? The question isn't easy to answer. Hervieu-Léger concludes (1996: 29–30) that the Republic was simply not able to rise to the occasion; in the last analysis the church still has the edge when it comes to the most solemn occasions associated with human living—a point that will be repeated more than once in the pages that follow.

Diana, Princess of Wales, died in very different circumstances; she was the victim of a road accident in a tunnel close to the Seine in Paris—an accident brought about at least in part by the attention of the press, a fact that had dominated her life, never mind her death, since her engagement to the Prince of Wales. This is not the place to dwell on the circumstances of the accident (itself a continuing controversy), but rather to stress the nature of the reaction that its announcement provoked, not only in the whole of modern Britain, or indeed in most of Europe, but in very many parts of the world. The role of the media in permitting such participation is clearly a dominant factor (see Chapter 6); in itself, however, it could not initiate the reaction.

British, and indeed other people, responded to the news in several ways. There were, first of all, multiple examples of individual mourning. Endless individuals of every age and social type wanted to express something of their loss and found innovative ways of doing this. Individual 'shrines' appeared in unexpected places containing a bewildering variety of elements—some of these were Christian (in a generous sense of the term), others clearly were not, but it did not seem to matter. The juxtaposition of different types of symbol was an essential part of what was happening. It became increasingly clear, moreover, that people were coming together to make these various offerings. Not all could come to London, but many came to a particular place within their own village, town, or city. How such sites were designated remains a semi-conscious process; sometimes they were associated with a particular event in the Princess's own life, sometimes they were not. What is clear, however, is that many people congregated naturally, if not exclusively, in the buildings of the established church.[11] It was here that people signed the countless books of condolence, sometimes queuing for many hours to do so; it was here that people lit candles and laid flowers in unprecedented numbers. In the messages they wrote, the blend of formal and informal religion is immediately apparent—affirming strongly a belief in an afterlife, untroubled by the fact that Dodi al-Fayed (Diana's current partner) was a Muslim, rather than a Christian and with no element of judgement whatsoever.

From the point of view of this chapter, however, the crucial point to realize is the incompleteness of this process without the formal liturgies of mourning.

---

[11] This was especially the case in villages and cathedral cities; there was more variety in other urban areas, where supermarkets became a significant option for signing books of condolence. How this fact should be interpreted remains a difficult question: was it a sign of secularization or, conversely, of a re-sacralization of the market-place?

Here is a clear example of the need for the religious institution—in this case the state church (despite the markedly ambivalent position of Diana herself)—to provide a public marker for her death and a liturgy through which the communal loss could be expressed. It is equally evident that the refusal of the church to comply with this request would have caused a public outcry. What emerged in fact was a whole series of liturgies at every level of society and in almost every locality (Davie and Martin 1999). These culminated in the state funeral on the morning of Saturday 7 September, an event which became the most widely broadcast event of all time. It was a liturgy, moreover, framed by Christian thinking, but in which a number of innovative elements found their place. The first of these was Elton John's singing of 'Candle in the Wind' (a song initially written for Marilyn Monroe); the second was the provocative eulogy delivered by Princess Diana's brother, Earl Spencer. The responses to the former were mixed: for some it was an inspired choice reflecting the personality of Diana herself, for others it was a sell-out to sentimentality and to the exigencies of popular culture. Whatever the case, the song was executed with complete professionalism and became an instant best-seller. The eulogy was more difficult to categorize. On the one hand it was sharply critical of the royal family and their incapacity to understand Diana, but it was delivered by one whose own marital mistakes undermined the credibility of much of what he said[12] It was acclaimed, undoubtedly, in the short term; but less so, possibly, as the months and years go by.

The ambiguity of it all is the crucial point to grasp. Diana herself was a seeker.[13] Christian in her upbringing and institutionally in her funeral, she was, in between, an individual dissatisfied with both herself and much of modern living. Difficult to place in terms of her religious affiliations, she epitomizes the religiosity of European societies (revealing amongst other things the paucity of statistical analysis). The need for a liturgy to mark the end of her life on earth was, however, undisputed and for the time being it falls to the Christian churches to fulfil this need, unless the individual concerned has an affiliation elsewhere. At the time of their death, if not before, Europeans are, it seems, obliged to contract out of, not to contract into, institutional—and for the most part Christian—religion.

## Conclusion: A Return to Vicarious Memory

If the previous chapter ended by noting that religious institutions cannot flourish without the passive acceptance of larger numbers in the population

---

[12] Three months after the funeral service, Earl Spencer's own divorce case was heard in the South African courts; he was clearly guilty of adultery on a significant scale.

[13] In Hervieu-Léger's analysis, Princess Diana fits neatly into the 'pilgrim' type (Hervieu-Léger 1999a); her religious explorations outside the Church of England are not only well documented, but are typical of many British people.

and that the future of religion in Europe will depend very largely on the complex relations between the two, this chapter concludes, at least in part, the other way round. In many ways informal patterns of religion cannot continue without the institutional churches, for it is these that provide the liturgies which frame so much of human living. Partially dispensable as the circumstances of modernity render birth rather safer than it used to be, and as patterns of marriage alter, they remain—for the time being—of considerable significance when a human life comes to an end. The funerals of public figures simply amplify the picture, which is the same at every level of society. The liturgy is enacted *on behalf of* both the individual and the community; it is essentially vicarious religion.

A final point in this connection returns to the question of memory and the need to guarantee a future. If the Jewish communities of modern Europe are under strain in this respect, it is clear that one reason for their discomfort is the tendency for the younger generation to marry out of their community. Endogamy is a safer route in this respect, for it guarantees a further generation of membership if not always of commitment, a point that is well understood by any religious minority. Paradoxically, endogamy does, it seems, persist in some parts of Europe within the Christian population even though religious practice has rapidly diminished. This was a major finding of a detailed study of the Swiss population in 1988–89 (Campiche *et al.* 1992); religion remained, despite everything, a framer of identity and expressed itself—amongst other ways—in the choosing of a marriage partner. A form of pillarization was still in place.

How far the same is true elsewhere (in Germany or in the Netherlands for example) is not an easy question to answer. On the surface, young Europeans are likely to disregard the religious factor with respect to their choice of marriage partner, at least in theory. Mixed marriages are, moreover, increasingly common. But dig a little deeper, and it is striking how enduring the older patterns are, the more so if thought has been given to the upbringing of children (the perpetuation of a memory). Marriage partners are chosen from similar rather than contrasting socio-economic groups (proximities that can be measured in various ways). An awareness (even if only implicit) of similar rather than contrasting world-views—a wider term than religious membership—is a further factor to be taken into account. Significant change has occurred in the post-war generations, but in ways more subtle than are indicated simply by the statistics.

But what in Switzerland (or elsewhere) is relatively benign, indeed almost reassuring, has been very much less so in Northern Ireland, where endogamy not only guarantees a future, but perpetuates a dangerous divide. In terms of social well-being, there are—it seems—no easy answers to these complex and continuing questions.

# FIVE

# Precarious Memory: Religion in the Education Systems of Europe

## Education in a Post-Industrial Society

THE education systems of all European societies—as indeed of all Western societies—are under considerable strain as the demands of an industrial economy give way to a post-industrial one. In the former, large numbers of workers, particularly male ones, were able to gain employment in industries where manual labour was in demand (indeed in the early post-war decades it was often in short supply) and where educational qualifications were of less significance than good health and strong shoulders. It is, however, precisely these sections of the economy which have found themselves at the sharp end of economic change and giving way to an entirely different sort of activity—forms of employment which not only give preference to the more highly educated, but also treat men and women alike.

If one function of the education system is to equip an appropriately skilled work-force, this implies that students be sufficiently stimulated to gain the necessary qualifications and that they stay in the education system long enough to do this. It also requires that the curriculum be adapted to suit the needs of the late-modern world. And if it is moderately easy to decide what new skills should be learnt in order for a young person to function efficiently in a late-industrial economy (information technology being but the most obvious), it is very much harder to discern what subject areas should be removed in order to make room for the new, the more so as soon as the second function of the education system is introduced—that is, the obligation to pass on the norms and values of any given society to the next generation.

Here the mutation of European religion into the religions of Europe has an immediate resonance in that one of the traditional sources of norms and values within Europe has undoubtedly been a shared Christian inheritance, a statement strongly underpinned by both the historical and empirical findings set out in Chapter 1. It is also clear that the evident decline of Christian values as one of the cornerstones of European culture has not so far been matched by the emergence of an alternative value system which can be unequivocally adopted in its place. It is hardly surprising in consequence that those who take responsibility for the educational task in Europe are confused not only about what to teach in the way of values but also about who should teach it and with what authority.

Conspicuous ambiguities emerge if the two aims of education are run alongside each other, the more so if the transitional nature of the European economy is kept in mind. For if the industrial economy required large numbers of male workers, mainly concentrated in urban centres of employment, it also required a particular kind of family structure to go with this—notably a traditional division of domestic labour with a sharp separation between the workplace and family life (an idea already hinted at in Chapter 4). Both were underpinned by a firm articulation of associated values, often thought to be Christian, in which the work ethic figured prominently—an outlook which assumed amongst other things that work would be in plentiful supply. In the final decades of the twentieth century, workplace, family life, associated ethic, and employment expectations have all changed beyond recognition. How, then, is the education system in general to respond to such changes, never mind the sector which takes responsibility for articulating the value system and passing it on to the next generation? That is the demanding context within which to consider the role of education in the maintenance or otherwise of the religious memory of modern Europe.

That the education system is considered a crucial place for this kind of activity can be judged once again from the attitudes of the interested parties in the countries of Central Europe in the years immediately after 1989 (Luxmoore 1995, 1996, 1997). Indeed the point had already been made in a negative sense in the previous decades as religious education was eliminated more or less systematically from the communist curriculum and alternative ideologies were put in its place. The teaching profession in general is under particular strain in such circumstances precisely because of its recognized role in the formation of young people; doubly so in the post-1989 situation when the ideology changes once again. The controversies surrounding the restoration of religious education in Hungary provide an excellent illustration of the complexities of the issue. Religious education did not entirely disappear under the communist regime—it varied considerably from place to place, depending on the local situation and on individual teachers. And since 1989 both the form and the content of the new programmes have been highly controversial: clearly a return to the pre-war system is inappropriate but what exactly is 'right' for a country which is emerging from forty years of communist domination into a modern democracy is not entirely clear. In the late 1990s just over 30 per cent of young people received some sort of (voluntary) religious instruction—in classes held in school buildings but out of school hours. Teachers of religious education are considered marginal to the teaching profession; so too is the subject matter in terms of student reports (attendance is recorded but not the results achieved). Alternatives to religious instruction (i.e. classes in morality or ethics) are under discussion, with no very clear outcome—the suggestion is vehemently opposed by some sections of the Hungarian population.[1]

The ambiguities of the Polish case have already been mentioned in Chapter 3. The debate about religious education provides a telling illustration of the rather overbearing attitude of the Polish Catholic Church in the post-1989 period. The church, it is clear, imposed its will in terms of religious (i.e. Catholic) education in schools without permitting an adequate public discussion to take place beforehand. It behaved as if it knew what the people wanted, but declined to listen to attempts by the people to articulate such sentiments themselves—the democratic process was effectively sidelined, notably with reference to the role of the ombudsman. The issue of religious education became an important factor in the evolution of public opinion *vis-à-vis* the role of the Catholic Church in Polish society (Sadowski 1991; Rygidzki 1996).

## The Churches as Owners/Managers of a Significant Number of Schools

The provision of adequate educational facilities for the population as a whole is the responsibility of the state in all European societies. The gradual emergence of a discrete and autonomous educational sector is an almost universal characteristic of modernization; it is part of the undisputed structural differentiation of modern societies so well described by Casanova. In this respect the evolution of education is similar to the developments in health care and welfare. All three, however, were part of the churches' domain for many centuries. Unsurprisingly their emergence as autonomous sectors took place in different ways in different European societies and the process was more easily accomplished in some places than in others (Martin 1978; Willaime 1990, 1993*a*). More to the point at the turn of the millennium, the gradual disentangling leaves noticeably different arrangements in different national contexts. In large parts of West Europe, the churches remain influential in the educational field as the owners and managers of significant numbers of schools, but the ways in which these schools operate vary from one place to another. All of them, however, are subject to the regulation of the state in terms of their care for pupils and their educational facilities. The French and English educational systems offer contrasting case studies in this respect, each starting from the opposite extreme, but gradually working towards each other in practical terms; the two cases will be used to illustrate some of the key points in the argument.

[1] Information from Miklós Tomka of the Hungarian Religious Research Centre.

## England and Wales

Denominational schools in England and Wales[2] are of two different types (aided and controlled schools), each type depending upon the specificities of the financial arrangements and the degree of control that goes with these.[3] Taking both together, the number of children being educated in such schools is considerable; it involves nearly a quarter of all pupils in the state system. In terms of institutions rather than pupils, the proportion is higher still, in that the churches have some sort of control over more than 25 per cent of the non-fee-paying schools of England and Wales. Most of these schools belong to the Church of England, but a number (especially in the secondary sector) are Roman Catholic. There is, however, an important difference between the two denominations with respect to educational policies. The Catholic schools in England and Wales have kept a much closer link with their church—a link which assumes that most staff and pupils will be Catholics and will be looked after as such. This is not the case for most Church of England schools, which are often the only schools in the neighbourhood, attended by all children whatever the religious preferences of the families involved. Some of these contrasts derive from theological differences between the two denominations; others result from the minority status of Catholics in British society and a desire to be self-sufficient in educational terms.[4]

Both, however, are very largely funded by the state and form a significant part of the public education system.[5] Denominational schools, moreover, are popular schools—they are frequently sought after by parents who have no particular denominational allegiance but simply want a good education for their children. A further question follows on: why are church schools associated with a good education (recognizing, of course, that many other schools also fall into this category)? It appears to be a combination of the two functions of

[2] It is important to remember that the Scottish system is separate and operates independently from that in England and Wales.

[3] 'Controlled' schools have rather more financial support from the state than their 'aided' equivalents, in return for which they have less independence in terms of policy-making and in the appointment of staff.

[4] Or in terms of the principal argument of this book, Catholic schools are regarded as a source of Catholic memory—a habit that dies hard. Catholics who have ceased to practise in any regular sense often seek out a Catholic education for their children and expect from this that their children will acquire some knowledge of the faith.

[5] There are, in addition, denominational schools in the fee-paying sector of the educational system. Once again it is possible to see the historical evolution of each denomination in the characteristics of their schools even in the private sector. Such characteristics are, however, changing as Catholicism becomes increasingly an integral part of British society and Catholic children attend the same schools as their peers of a similar social class. In these social groups the tendency to seek a specifically Catholic education—often in schools whose geographical location reflects the historical positioning of Catholics in British society (for example Lancashire or Yorkshire)—appears to be declining. The presence of a Roman Catholic chaplain at Eton (the most prestigious of all the private schools) is once again a sign of changing times—the other side of the same equation.

education outlined at the beginning of this chapter. For church schools not only produce creditable examination results (due maybe to the disproportionate presence of a churchgoing and so middle-class population), they are also noted for the value systems which they promote and the working-out of such systems in the form of pastoral care for both pupils and their families. Children, it seems, are well prepared for the demands of the modern economy and for the vicissitudes of modern living—or so their parents perceive.[6] For this reason alone it is very likely that church schools will continue as a significant section of the education system of England and Wales for the foreseeable future.

So far the discussion has involved Church of England and Catholic schools, but the system extends further than this. For some time the Jewish population of England and Wales, though modest in terms of overall numbers, has maintained a small number of voluntary aided schools (some of which have a noted reputation for excellence). And if this is the case for one religious minority in Britain, why should it not be so for others? Precisely this question has bedevilled the political debate about church schools in recent decades in the British context; once again it reflects very directly the debates about 'scope' raised in Chapter 3 with respect to the legal and financial privileges of religious organizations. It is, moreover, an exceedingly difficult question to resolve given the historical legacies of each European nation and the changing nature of European society as a whole.

In England and Wales, for example, there is a strong argument, at least in terms of logic, in favour of the abolition of church schools altogether, on the grounds that children will receive a better preparation for life in an evidently pluralist society if they are educated together and learn to accept one another's differences (including religious differences) at an early age—children should not be categorized by the education that they receive and least of all in religious terms. But for the reasons articulated in previous paragraphs, notably the success and popularity of most church schools, such a solution is politically non-viable; no political party is going to risk the negative consequences of a policy which recommends the abolition of schools favoured by their constituents (indeed, very often favoured by the politicians themselves).[7] So what is to be done? Here an alternative logic takes hold, for if it is permissible for certain denominations to possess their own school and, to a large extent, have these financially supported by the state, it is difficult to exclude other significant religious minorities (often the newly arrived) from such privilege without

---

[6] The relative success of church schools is easily quantified in the league tables published by the government (in 1997 and 1998, for example, the trend was clear). Whether or not such schools will perform as well in league tables in which intermediate variables are controlled for (the relative deprivation of the school population, for example) remains to be seen.

[7] The historic connection between the British Labour Party and the Catholic community should be noted in this respect: support for denominational schools crosses the political divide in England and Wales.

appearing discriminatory—the more so if such minorities can prove that their schools are educationally sound and pastorally responsible.

The campaign by the Muslim community in England and Wales finally came to a successful conclusion in 1998. Until then, each application for voluntary aided status made by a Muslim school was turned down by the Secretary of State for Education, but always for reasons other than their denominational status (the criteria used were either strictly educational or concerned the oversupply of school places in the locality). In January 1998, however, the Minister of State for Education acceded to two applications from Muslim schools using the following form of words:

I am pleased to be able to approve sound proposals which demonstrate that these new schools will comply with the statutory provisions governing all maintained schools, such as delivering the national curriculum and offering equal access to the curriculum for boys and girls. (quoted in the *Independent*, 10 Jan. 1998: News sect., 4)

A week or so later, interestingly, a school run by Seventh Day Adventists achieved similar status, provoking, inevitably, a degree of public discussion about where such a policy will stop. The problem is a real one. The crucial point to grasp, however, is that each school must justify its educational credentials and its capacity to look after children—denominational status is insufficient in itself as a recommendation for aided status but should not constitute *per se* a bar to public funding.

## France

The French situation starts from the opposite end of the spectrum. Following the acrimonious debates in the early years of the Third Republic which culminated in (1) the creation of a state school system that was universal, free, and *laïque* and (2) the separation of church and state in 1906, the exclusion of religion from the public sphere in France has become the accepted way of doing things. Religion is strictly speaking a private matter. It follows that the role of the churches as either owners or managers of a section of the state school system was simply out of the question; nor was it possible to include the teaching of religion within the school curriculum (from the start a far more centralized affair than its equivalent across the Channel). The second point, and its consequences, will be dealt with in more detail in the following section. The first—the existence of private (almost always Catholic) schools in France—illustrates that practice within any given system leads at times to significant modifications in the policy intended at the outset.

Indeed one of the very first compromises effected by Jules Ferry and his advisers as they established the republican school system in France (in a series of Acts in the 1880s) was to permit the continuation of some private schools alongside the state school system and to allow sufficient space for Catholic (or other) catechesis outside school hours—hence the free day in the middle of the school week. The position and privileges of private or Catholic schools in France has continued as a source of friction (sometimes acute and sometimes less so) ever since. Only gradually did a *modus vivendi* emerge, driven once again by necessity (significant numbers of parents wanted such schools to continue).

There are several stages in this evolution. Before the war, for example, the argument concerned the right of private schools to exist at all. Since 1945 this right has been accepted as part of the freedom of choice given to French parents regarding their children's education. The debate continues, however, with respect to the degree of financial support such schools could expect from the state. A compromise was reached in the 1950s in which the schools concerned traded financial support for a certain degree of state control. The loi Debré (1959) codified the situation, offering three alternatives to private schools: integration into the state system, association by contract, or a simple contract—the latter two representing different combinations of freedom and financial support not all that dissimilar from the notion of 'controlled' and 'aided' schools in England and Wales (Allieu 1996). It is clear that financial support for private schools is accepted, but within limits; in 1994 the French public rejected the notion of additional state finance for these institutions over and above the 10 per cent agreed by the loi Debré.

What has emerged, in practice, is a system in which both sides in the original dispute have compromised to a certain extent, bearing in mind *both* the popularity of private or Catholic schools amongst French parents *and* their gradual secularization. They are, for example, no longer dominated by religious orders (most teachers, including the head teacher, are laypeople), their curricula are substantially similar to other schools, and they are obliged to offer an education which prepares young people for the world of work just like any other school. Conversely the advocates of *laïcité* have themselves shifted their position; or to follow the argument of Willaime (1996), *laïcité*—just like Catholicism—has experienced a form of secularization, adapting itself of necessity to a climate rather different from that which dominated the debates in the late nineteenth century. In other words, each side has come closer to the other, responding at least in part to the exigencies of a late-modern society in which parental choice plays a significant role.

In parenthesis, there is a further similarity between England and France in the marked underprovision of similar choices for Muslim parents. As in England and Wales, moreover, the Jewish minority—though considerably smaller than the Muslim community—has a significant number of schools in France, a privilege so far denied to Muslims.[8] Such a lack became a significant factor in the *affaire du foulard*, in that Muslim pupils denied access to the state system for wearing the *foulard* or *hijab* had nowhere else to go. Effectively these students were being denied access to the education system overall. The

---

[8] With one exception in La Réunion.

*affaire* itself will be discussed in detail in Chapter 7 for it raises wider issues of toleration and pluralism in European societies. Its significance as a catalyst of change in many aspects of the French education system, however, should not be overlooked.

It is possible, then, in bringing this section to a conclusion, to see more similarities than differences between the French and English systems. Starting from opposite ends of the spectrum, the two models begin to look increasingly alike. Effectively, the state is subsidizing if not funding a number of denominational schools which offer, relatively speaking, a high standard of education, for which reason they are sought after by significant numbers of parents with sufficient political influence to obtain (or maintain) what they want for their children. Other parents (particularly the parents of some religious minorities) are not, thus far, so lucky—though the situation in England and Wales is slowly beginning to change.

## Moral, Social, and Religious Education

A major area of confusion needs to be identified before this chapter can develop any further (Spinder 1992; Willaime 1993*a*). As a subject area religious education should be divided into two categories: confessional and non-confessional education. The former aims to foster a commitment to a world faith (or perhaps to a particular denomination); the latter aims to convey information about religion(s), to stimulate understanding about religion in general, and to enable the pupil to make an informed choice about his or her personal commitment. The distinction will be visible in all manner of ways: where and when religious education takes place, by whom it is taught, where it is placed in the curriculum, and what methods are used both in its teaching and its assessment. So far so good; this is an important distinction to bear in mind. But just like the case of denominational schools, what can be separated in theory is much more difficult to distinguish in practice. The legal framework may have one thing in mind, but practical application might convey quite another. Teachers and school managers may start out with one idea and parents and pupils absorb a different one, the point of view of parents very often reflecting what they themselves were taught a generation earlier. Further complexities arise, moreover, from the European situation itself, where the religious composition of the population is changing fast—changes which reflect both the global nature of the market in cultural ideas and the increasing mobility of labour. The classroom is not what it used to be. It becomes, in fact, a barometer of social change, reflecting the rapid evolution in both economic and cultural expectations.

It remains the case, none the less, that for very large numbers of young Europeans, any knowledge of religion—both of their own and that of the major world faiths—will come from the classroom rather than anywhere else. What, then, are they likely to learn, from whom, and in what circumstances? The following examples are by no means comprehensive, but represent a variety of European 'types',[9] from which a number of conclusions can be drawn. They include a Nordic example (Finland), a bi-confessional case (Germany), two virtual monopolies in Southern Europe (Italy and Greece), and two contrasting examples, one pluralist (the Netherlands) and one strictly secular (France).

## Some Examples

The first, the Finnish case, involves a system where religious instruction remains central to the school curriculum at both primary and secondary level. Whilst provision is made for the religious minorities in Finland (notably the Orthodox community), 97 per cent of pupils (1992 statistics) follow the courses relating to the Lutheran Church, reflecting once again the dominance of the state church in this part of Europe and its formative influence in the creation of national identity (indeed even the children of non-church members take part in these courses). On request from a parent or guardian, however, alternatives can be offered, including a philosophy of life course for children from families with no religious faith. The aims of religious instruction are broadly confessional, recognizing the role of the Lutheran Church in Finnish history, but include the need to acquaint children with religions other than their own and to foster ideals based on tolerance and respect of all individuals regardless of confessional identity. The teaching is done by specially trained teachers.

In examining the German case, it is necessary to bear in mind both the bi-confessional nature of the country and the relative independence of the *Länder* in establishing educational policy. What emerges in practice in most of the *Länder* is the provision of two types of religious education in almost all schools—one Lutheran and one Catholic, though clearly the proportions of children in each will vary depending on the make-up of the local population. The curriculum and textbooks are formally scrutinized by the state and by the churches and include a mix of confessional teaching alongside life themes, ethics, social issues, church history, and world religions (an alternative system based on ethics and philosophy is beginning to emerge in some places). German society is anxious to affirm its capacities for tolerance and respect for others whilst underlining the moral qualities that underpin its emergence as

---

[9] A country-by-country review of the situation across Europe which is more comprehensive than most and reasonably up to date can be found in Spinder (1992); this is a publication of the Inter-European Commission on Church and School. See also *Panorama*, the *International Journal of Comparative Religious Education and Values*, and the *International Journal of Practical Theology*. Robbers (1996) covers the law regarding religious education for the countries of the European Union. Copley (1997) gives detailed coverage of the British case.

one of Europe's leading democracies in the post-war period. It is clear, moreover, that religious education has been closely linked by policy-makers to peace issues and the moral nature of society, messages which are conveyed in the general clauses of the 1946 Constitution (MacNeill, forthcoming *a*). Pupils have, however, a right to withdraw from religious instruction—this requires written consent from their parent if the child is under 14.

The former East German *Länder* present an interesting and rather particular case as the dominance of communist ideology is removed from the classroom, as indeed from society as a whole. Several immediate and practical questions present themselves. It is clear, first of all, that a very large section of the former East German population no longer has contact with the Christian churches (the East German *Länder* form one of the most secularized parts of Europe). Is it, therefore, appropriate to impose on them the West German system, which assumes for most children nominal membership of one or the other of the two major denominations even if practice has dropped markedly in the post-war period? Hence in Brandenburg at least, there has been serious consideration of a system entitled 'Lebengestaltung, Ethik, Religion'—in other words non-denominational teaching which includes components on the major world religions (a move strongly resisted by the historic churches). A second point concerns the teaching of whatever curriculum is finally decided upon: where are the teachers to be found after forty years of communist domination and a dramatic reduction in religious knowledge as well as religious activity? The assumed desirability of the West German model remains, none the less, a dominant theme, despite the evident necessity for the latter to evolve given the changing nature of German society. The presence of a growing Turkish minority is a major feature of this evolution—not one accommodated very adequately within the German system. How, for example, can the issues of citizenship (never mind religious questions per se) be dealt with adequately in neighbourhoods where hardly anyone, by definition, is a citizen?

The Italian system is strongly confessional. The role of the school is to assist both family and church in introducing students to Catholic beliefs and practice, though provision is made for pupils to withdraw from the system if their parents so wish. In practice few do and the role of the Catholic Church continues to dominate, in, for example, the need for the Curia to approve support material for both teachers and pupils and to appoint the necessary staff (both clerical and lay). The Greek system is similar, though here the Orthodox Church is the dominant factor, whilst allowing some space for the Muslim minority which continues to exist in parts of Greece (the result of several centuries of Turkish occupation). Rather less allowance is made with respect to other Christian minorities. Despite some acknowledgement of change in the syllabus, there can be no doubt that the system remains permeated by the values and doctrines of Greek Orthodoxy—the nods to life themes and ethics are little more than nominal. Training for religious education teachers at secondary level is given in the theological faculties.

Two very contrasting situations can be found in the Netherlands and in France—the first retains a high degree of pluralism, the second has removed the teaching of religion from the school system altogether. In the Netherlands, there are, broadly speaking, three types of school: state schools, Catholic schools, and Protestant schools (there are in addition further private schools of a particular character, sometimes strongly confessional). The system embodies the pillarization, or vertical divisions, of Dutch society outlined in Chapter 1. At least at primary level, the provision of religious education reflects these differences, with the first group having no religious education provided by the school and the confessional schools offering whatever they feel to be appropriate and not permitting any student to contract out of religious education classes (a policy that causes difficulties when members of religious minorities choose confessional schools for their children). The situation at secondary level is more nuanced, with denominational schools torn between the realities of life, including an increasingly diverse school population, and the desire by some schools (and the parents that choose them) to retain a distinctive religious identity. A new subject has, in addition, been introduced for all children at primary level, one that is based on objective teachings about religious and secular world-views with the intention of preparing pupils for a multi-cultural society. This has been accompanied by a degree of innovation in forms of pedagogy; there is, however, no coercion regarding the implementation of such methods. Training for teachers varies across the system and the provision of textbooks operates according to the market.

The French system remains the great exception in Europe, bearing in mind that the former communist countries find themselves at different stages of development in their attempts to reintroduce religious education into their respective systems. Apart from the areas still controlled by the Napoleonic Concordat (i.e. Alsace and the *département* of the Moselle) there has been no provision for the teaching of religion within state schools in France for the best part of a century. It was systematically eliminated from the system in the reforms of Jules Ferry and his advisers in the early years of the Third Republic and replaced by a form of civic education, with its own array of symbols and illustrations. This is a well-documented story and a highly significant one in terms of French self-understanding (Baubérot 1990, 1998; Willaime 1996). In recent years, however, the situation has been changing. One reason for such reappraisal is a growing awareness that students growing up in the French educational system are inadequately prepared for modern living. Such inadequacies have resonance in a wide variety of fields: in the teaching of art and literature, in the comprehension of politico-religious conflicts in the modern world, and, not least, in the appreciation of the needs and aspirations of the sizeable Muslim community already living in modern France.

Those who demand change are variously placed in French society. Some, for example, can be found in the school system itself. The following citation reveals the anxieties of a head teacher responsible for the education of students for the twenty-first century:

The idea of setting up a series of lectures on religion at the Lycée Buffon grew out of an observation. In the course of conversations with students wishing to specialize in the plastic arts, I began to grasp their almost total ignorance of certain fundamentals of European culture. These students possessed some vague notions about Greek mythology, but had almost no knowledge of the Bible. How could they possibly appreciate either literary texts or works of art from the past without minimum reference either to scripture or to the Christian religion? . . .

. . . Or, from a more general point of view, how can young people today be expected to understand the events so widely reported by the media without a better knowledge of the various cultures, very frequently religious cultures, that divide the populations of the world? How can they possibly comprehend the sometimes violent manifestations of fundamentalism in some Muslim countries, the passions and actions observed in various European countries—passions and actions directed against Islam or against Islamic communities—or, finally, the displays of anti-Semitism that have occurred in both Western and Eastern Europe in recent years? (Ledanois 1990: 7–8; translation mine)

Other commentators have observed from outside the consequences of excluding religion from the school system, especially when this is accompanied by a dramatic fall in religious practice (Lebrun 1995; Monnot 1996). Whilst practice remained relatively high, the teaching of young people about the elements of Christian faith continued in classes for catechesis and in the home. As the figures for practice plummet (especially since the 1960s) what has emerged in France is a form of religious illiteracy, or in the phrase popularized by Henri Tincq—the religious correspondent of *Le Monde*—a pervasive 'analphabétisme religieux' (*Le Monde*, 10 Nov. 1988: 29). Tincq goes further than this in maintaining that such illiteracy is almost as true for teachers as it is for pupils (see below). Up to a point a similar situation is beginning to permeate the whole of Europe given the marked decline in religious practice. The combination of low practice and no religion in the school system is, however, particular to the French case. Clearly the effects are beginning to cause concern in some if not all sections of the French population.[10]

What is to be done? Despite the contentious nature of the topic and a considerable degree of prevarication, elements of religious education are currently being reintroduced into the French school system. Such a move has nothing to do with confessional teaching, but is an attempt to respond to the realization that the young adult who knows nothing about religion is not only poorly educated but is ill prepared to take an active role in modern societies, European ones included. The *affaire du foulard* was the catalyst that led to a

[10] A comparison with the American system is instructive at this point. Whilst religious education in the school system is forbidden by the American Constitution, religious practice remains high, relatively speaking, in most of the United States. The memory, for the time being, continues to be passed on to the new generation without the help of educational policies.

decision in this respect; indeed there are those who argue that the moment of truth brought about by the rejection of young women from the school system because of their religious convictions was of greater significance than the gradual erosion of Christian beliefs and values in French society as a whole (MacNeill 1998*b*). One of the most revealing, and for some distressing, aspects of the whole episode was the evident incapacity of many in the teaching profession—never mind the majority of pupils—to comprehend the aspirations of young people within the Muslim community.

## Cross-Cutting Themes

This examination of a representative range of national examples in terms of religious education in the school systems of Europe generates a number of cross-cutting themes. It is clear, first of all, that the teaching of religion as part of the school curriculum is at a turning point. In the cases outlined in the preceding paragraphs, the full spectrum can be seen—from almost undiluted confessional teaching (in Italy or Greece for example) to the conscious preparation of children for life in a world where a wide variety of religious ideas forms a significant part of cultural exchange (the Netherlands). Both, moreover, can be done well or badly. It remains the case, however, that religious education in Europe appears to be moving in one direction rather than another, in that those systems which confront the issues of religious pluralism more directly are, it seems, better adapted to the nurture of children in a modern, increasingly mobile world. Unsurprisingly, such systems are more likely to exist in those parts of Europe with immediate experience of religious diversity.

Such relationships are, however, far from straightforward and depend to a considerable extent not only on the political context from which they emerge, but also on the pressure groups that are active within this context. Such groups have markedly different agendas; some are looking for space to transmit the teachings of particular minorities, others are more concerned about the value system as a whole (Beckford 1998). The emphasis on complexity is the crucial one. It is reinforced by a consideration of pedagogical method. This can be almost as varied as syllabus content—as can the connections between them. It is perfectly possible, for example, to discover examples where innovative and creative teaching methods—including experiential rather than didactic learning—are used for confessional teaching, and with great effect. Indeed there is every reason to believe that a child well informed about his or her own faith (with a degree of personal commitment) may well be more, rather than less, capable of understanding the religious aspirations of someone else; the more so if that faith has been transmitted with an awareness that this is not the only possibility for spiritual satisfaction in the modern world. Exactly the reverse combination can also, regrettably, be true. A so-called multi-faith education can end up respecting the faith of no one and devaluing the concept of religion altogether. To be successful it requires both extensive knowledge and a developed capacity for empathy on the part of the teacher; it is no easy option.

Finally, a persistent set of confusions lies in the attempts to articulate the relationships between the teaching of religious education and the acknowledgement of (1) universal or human rights, (2) distinctly European values, and (3) national identities, confusions that lurk beneath the surface, but can be detected in, amongst other places, a close analysis of relevant texts. Such texts can be found at a variety of levels; they include, for example, the preambles to legal or constitutional documents, i.e. national constitutions and the Education Acts themselves (Lotz, forthcoming) but also the textbooks used for religious education in the classroom (MacNeill, forthcoming *b*). In both cases the assumption that Europe is Christian is consistently reaffirmed despite a growing awareness of universal rights and cultural change. At the same time, however, national differences are echoed and sometimes very strongly, notably with reference to the different arrangements of church and state across Europe and in attitudes to minorities. Indeed it becomes quite clear that pupils are receiving subtexts as well as texts in whatever form of religious education they are, or are not, entitled to. The careful use of discourse analysis as a means of discerning such processes marks a step forward in the sociological analysis of both the role of religious education and the task of nation building, and of the complex relationships that link these apparently separate activities.[11]

## *Evaluations of Religious Education in the School Systems of Modern Europe*

There is an in-built difficulty in assessing the 'success' of religious education in European societies, in that the aims and objectives surrounding the enterprise are at best unclear and more often than not contradictory. A parallel difficulty lies in the criteria to be used for assessment—both the assessment of the individual student and the appraisal of the system as a whole. As the system (or most of it anyway) moves away from the teaching of a particular faith to education about the nature of the spiritual or about world religions in general, the way in which success can or should be measured shifts accordingly. The concerns become increasingly 'academic' (testing the knowledge of religions alongside the knowledge of everything else) and less and less 'pastoral' (no longer associated with certain kinds of religious behaviour, notably regular religious practice). A system which aimed initially to reinforce the transmission of religious knowledge in the family or in the churches now criticizes a

---

[11] Two doctoral theses using discourse analysis are currently in progress in British universities: Dominique MacNeill (at the University of Exeter) is looking at classroom textbooks in Britain, France, and Germany; Stefanie Lotz (at the University of Lancaster) at the texts of Education Acts and other political documents in Britain and Germany. It is interesting that a similar methodology links these two pieces of comparative work.

whole range of religious ideas. It encourages the pupil to question as well as to accept, to empathize rather than to submit. Goals are likely to be long-term rather than short-term; their success (or otherwise) lies in the capacities of future generations to accommodate religious difference, rather than in the achievements of the generation currently in school.

A second difficulty concerns the practicalities of teaching. Even if the aims of each system are entirely clear-cut on paper (and that is seldom the case), they are unlikely to be so in practice, in that the teaching of religion as a school subject depends more than most areas of the curriculum on the teachers who take responsibility for it. For teacher and student alike, the lines between academic learning and personal involvement are fine. Empathizing with the religious or the spiritual requires almost inevitably a degree of emotional involvement; the more so if experiential methods are adopted. A further, often neglected, point should also be taken into consideration—namely the attitudes of senior management in the school. It is unlikely, for example, that religious education will flourish with even the most gifted of teachers if those teachers are denied adequate support from those in overall charge. There is bound to be a difference in effectiveness in those schools where religious education is well resourced and central to the school day compared with those where it effectively becomes a Cinderella subject, there simply to meet the requirements of the law, but considered by most people in the school to be a waste of curriculum time (an increasingly scarce commodity).[12]

## Religion and Young People: A Precarious Memory

How should this material be assessed within the theoretical framework of this book? It is essential, first of all, to keep in mind the wider role of young people in the evolution of the religious life of Europe. This requires looking back to the previous chapter, which outlined the shifting demography of modern Europe and in particular the prolongation of adolescence. This is the context in which the education systems play their part, both in terms of preparation for the world of work and in the transmission of values. In this respect they compete with an endless diversity of counter-currents in the colourful world of youth culture, itself a increasingly significant market-place. It is not one in which traditional forms of religion find an obvious outlet. Adolescence, the period between childhood and adult life, has always been a time of questioning moral codes and traditional values. It is precisely this period, moreover,

---

[12]  In many ways the point is similar to one that will arise in the following chapter on the role of the media. A religious correspondent, however gifted and well informed, is limited in his or her capacities to make an enduring contribution to the debate if the management of the paper does not permit sufficient space for articles. (I have discussed this point in some detail with Henri Tincq.)

that has lengthened disproportionately in late-modern societies. It follows that all those institutions concerned with preparation for adult life have had their task transformed; they are obliged to operate in the demanding circumstances outlined at the beginning of this chapter.

So much for the societal context. The teaching of religion within the education systems of Europe needs, in addition, to be set against the youth movements or programmes within the churches themselves; some of these will be considered in Chapter 8 and concern both traditional and innovative organizations. Central here is the appeal of emotional or experiential occasions rather than formats which emphasize the historical tradition or didactic learning (Hervieu-Léger 1994). An excellent example can be found once again in that country where religious education in the school system has been denied for so long. In August 1997, over a million mostly young people gathered in Paris for the Journées Mondiales de la Jeunesse (World Youth Days), a week of events which culminated in a Mass celebrated by the Pope on the race course at Longchamp. The numbers of people involved and the obvious success of the occasion defied all the pundits (see Chapter 6). Not only did this represent a considerable feat of organization, it demonstrated that certain forms of religious activity do still appeal to young people—even those with little experience of religious teaching in their schools.

It remains the case, however, that religious illiteracy is widespread in modern Europe amongst younger generations. With this in mind, it seems entirely possible that the religious memory of Europe—at least in its traditional form of a basic understanding of Christian teaching—might simply cease to exist, except as a branch of specialist knowledge; it is indeed precarious. The role of religious education in the school system is clearly a crucial factor in this possibility. The arguments are, however, complex. In some ways an obvious answer to the 'problem' (if such it is), religious education is itself changing as it responds to the demands of late-modern society and to the pressure groups that operate within it. Some of these groups may support the maintenance of a Christian, or mainstream, memory; others will favour education about (rather than in) a wider variety of faiths. It is a facet of modern European society that requires careful sociological analysis at every level: policy-making, political enactment, school administration, classroom teaching, and pupil reception. In many ways the task is only just beginning.

# SIX

# *Mediated Memory: Religion and the European Media*

THE relationship between the media and reality is inevitably complex, and nowhere more so than in questions of religion. Do the media reflect the realities of religious life or are these necessarily distorted if projected by the media—even to the point of becoming themselves an alternative source of symbols? (Arthur 1993; Stout and Buddenbaum 1996; Hoover 1998) This chapter will assume a symbiotic relationship. The media feed on the realities of life in order to exist at all; at the same time they inevitably create alternative images which not only dominate agendas, but may become, at least in part, a replacement for reality itself. The funeral of Princess Diana (already discussed in Chapter 4) illustrates all these tendencies: the funeral could not have been broadcast had it not taken place in Westminster Abbey; it attracted a truly global audience; it will, moreover, be the television images that are remembered in the years to come, rather than the reality itself—and within this, particular moments chosen for their mediatic appeal (Davie and Martin 1999).

What, though, do we mean by the term 'mass media'? There is an obvious distinction between the print media and those that deal with visual images—the position of radio broadcasting lies somewhere in between. Increasingly, however, it is necessary to take into account the exponential growth in electronic forms of communication, not least the Internet and the Web. It is still too soon to grasp the full implications of what is happening in this respect but the potential is, quite clearly, enormous—and with corresponding difficulties for control. All forms of the media are, moreover, used in two ways: both to spread information (including religious information) and as a medium of exchange in terms of comment. Newspapers, to give but one example, frequently contain a regular column of 'confessional' (though by no means always Christian) information; they also follow religious events as a form of

I must acknowledge my debt at several points in this chapter to Rosalind Fane, a student in History and Society at the University of Exeter (graduated in 1997), whose third-year BA dissertation on 'A Sociological Analysis of Religion on Television' became an inspiration for my own thinking in this field.

news. But the newspapers also take it upon themselves to offer comment not only on religious events, but on the faith that lies behind them, and the implications of both for society as a whole. The media become, in other words, both a source of memory itself and a form of commentary on this.

The distinction between the two is, however, complex, in that even the 'presentation' of news (as opposed to comment) is exposed to the immediacy of media deadlines and the need to produce soundbites. The longer-term agendas of religious individuals or the institutions for which they are responsible must inevitably be put on one side (Hoover 1998). Journalists, moreover—and especially those that specialize in religious affairs—are well aware of the different rhythms that dominate their own lives and those of their subjects; Longley (1991) and Bunting (1996), for example, have commented on this tension from a British point of view. A recent and more detailed discussion of similar themes can be found in Defois and Tincq (1997), a volume written jointly by the Archbishop of Reims and the religious correspondent of *Le Monde*. Both agree that relations between the churches and the press are a minefield of misunderstanding, yet religion as a topic intrudes repeatedly on to media agendas. One thing becomes crystal clear: religious institutions ignore the media (including the electronic media) at their peril. Contact with this increasingly powerful sector of late-modern societies requires professional expertise and careful management—it cannot be left to chance.

Within the sociological literature concerning religion and the media, one question dominates the agenda: that of televangelism, especially in its North American forms. The fact, however, that televangelism remains, essentially, a New World rather than European activity poses a central question for this chapter. Why is it that the attempts to transfer this form of broadcasting to the European context have had little success, relatively speaking? Yet why at the same time—in the course of continuing debates about the deregulation of the media—do so many Europeans fear the incursions of American-style broadcasting on to European soil? It is these questions that must detain us at the outset. Later sections of the chapter take a more positive form: they are concerned with the forms of broadcasting that do have some success in modern Europe, though sound sociological information in this respect is markedly more difficult to come by. Why this should be so is in itself part of the debate.

The final section has a different point of departure: the parallels between religion and other forms of leisure activity and their projection by the media. Two themes emerge from this discussion, both of which have been touched on in previous chapters. The first underlines that religion in modern European societies is essentially a form of leisure activity—it cannot be enforced; but second, its complex relationship with the media reflects the shifting nature of modern societies rather than changes in the religious sector *per se*. The latter will have important adjustments to make; so too, however, will those responsible for the management of sport—to give but one example. One question cannot be avoided in conclusion: is it indeed the case that the media have, themselves, become the message (or perhaps the memory)? Or to put the same point even more sharply: in dominating the agendas of so much of modern society, are they (the media) a form of religion in themselves?

## The Televangelism Debate: Contrasts between Europe and the New World

The phenomenon of televangelism in its American context has generated a lively sociological debate. Much of this has centred on the discrepancy between the media's self-portrayal of what is going on and the rather more measured assessments of the academic community—namely that televangelists are primarily preaching to the converted, themselves a relatively restricted sector of modern American society (Hadden 1987; Hoover 1988; Bruce 1990; Peck 1993). Two points, however, are essential in understanding this much-discussed phenomenon. The first concerns the presence of the 'converted'—who these people are and where they are located within the profile of American religion; the second relates to the structures of the media themselves. Both, and indeed the combinations between them, account for much of the difference between the religious life of the United States and that of modern Europe.

The electronic ministries of American televangelists such as Robert Schuller, Jerry Falwell, Pat Robertson, and Jimmy Swaggart are part and parcel of an evident revival in conservative Protestant theology in the 1960s and 1970s; such evangelists propagate a strongly evangelical message. It is crucial to remember, however, that this revival—unforeseen by most contemporary sociologists—had a considerable effect on the realities of religious life in America, just as much as their projection by the media. Both, moreover, are intimately related. The most accurate predictor in terms of attraction to tele-vangelistic broadcasts is denominational allegiance. For conservative Protestants there is a persuasive congruence between the theological messages of the churches they attend, their own beliefs, and their electronic endorse-ment via the media. For those whose theological predilections lie elsewhere, televangelism holds limited attraction (Hoover 1988; Peck 1993). Peck goes further than this in drawing to our attention the considerable diversity within televangelism, but still maintains the necessary fit between the viewer's own religion and the electronic message. There is, in other words, convincing evidence to indicate that televangelists do indeed preach to the converted.

Why, though, should conservative and Protestant forms of theology come to such prominence in the mid-postwar decades and, apparently, so much more so in America than in Europe? They are part of the 'restructuring' of modern American religion, researched in considerable detail by Wuthnow (1988) and Roof, Carroll, and Roozen (1995). Such restructuring takes the form of a movement away from the centralized denominational organizations of mainstream America, in favour of new (or more accurately *re*-newed) religious identities—among them the Protestant movements already described, attractive to a particular generation of Americans born for the most part between 1946 and 1965 (Roof, Carroll, and Roozen 1995). Peck (1993) describes this constituency in some detail. Up to a point a similar trend can be seen in Europe in the *relative* prosperity of conservative theology both inside and outside the mainstream churches (see Chapter 8 for a more developed discussion of this point), but—comparatively speaking—such movements involve very limited numbers of people. It is the size of the American constituency that draws attention, not least its capacities to produce a viable television audience. Crucial in this respect is the propensity of this audience to contribute financially to the programmes they enjoy. Their numbers reflect the vibrancy of American religion taken as a whole.

A second point follows on: the relative accessibility of the American media to a diversity of religious groups. The American broadcasting system has always been more open than its European equivalents; moderately small organizations (both religious and secular) have been able to purchase airtime, first on the radio, but later on television (Wallis and Bruce 1986). The rapidly shifting nature of the technology (notably the emergence of satellite and cable), coupled with the necessary computer resources to deal with the correspondence involved, simply increases the possibilities. Conservative Protestant groups, moreover, proved themselves not only willing but able to react to these possibilities, paradoxically so in view of their profound mistrust of secular television. Here is a classic example of groups which are ideologically opposed to modernity using the technologies of modernity itself to promote an alternative vision of society (Linderman 1993: 13–14).

The question of ability (as opposed to willingness) in the reactions of such groups to the opportunities offered refers, of course, to questions of finance. It is the existence of sufficient numbers of conservative Protestant groups—as an empirical as well as electronic phenomenon—that permits the televangelists to prosper:

In order to succeed in reasserting the evangelical cause, televangelists have to have a compatible, and already extant, religious sensibility in society with which to resonate. Their distinct 'religious media cultures' have to match the distinct 'religious real cultures' of their audiences. This match is essential for the survival of television ministries, given that they are funded by donations from television viewers. (Fane 1997: 20)

There is, however, another side to this question. The existence of the fit between conservative Protestantism on the ground and its electronic endorsement may be the principal reason for the existence of televangelism in modern America. It is, however, a self-limiting factor. Preaching to the converted may well result in financial underpinning; it does not imply extension beyond the matching sphere.

Attempts to introduce televangelism into Europe have had little success so far (see below). Despite this, there is visible unease in Britain to give an easily illustrated example. There is a firmly held conviction that if deregulation of the media is permitted, there will be an immediate influx of 'un-British'—with the strong implication of distasteful—televangelistic broadcasting (quite apart from the scandals associated with American televangelists). Such unease can be discovered in a variety of places: in, for instance, the research monograph written by the Independent Television Commission on religion and television in the 1990s, whose findings illustrate that all the faith groups represented in the enquiry expressed reservations about televangelism. So, too, do wider publics, of no particular religious persuasion, who feel that televangelists should be denied access to mainstream channels (*ITC Summary Report* 1994: 4). A more developed argument can be found in the case study of the supposed 'hidden agenda' of the then Independent Broadcasting Authority relating to the passage of the 1990 Broadcasting Act (Quicke and Quicke 1992). Once again the argument turns on the supposed threat to British society and to the balance of public service religious broadcasting.

Are such apprehensions justified? Or to put the question in a different way, why does it appear to be more rather than less difficult for televangelists to gain a foothold in Europe, even in Britain where the language barrier is more easily surmountable? The first and most obvious barrier lies in the prevalence of public service broadcasting, which remains pervasive throughout Europe, but with an inevitable and growing degree of deregulation—driven partly by the increasing influence of the market but, even more so, by the rapid evolution in media technology. Given the exponential growth in outlets it is impossible to control them all, even if mainline channels remain within a public framework. Hence, precisely, the unease of many Europeans.

Two case studies—of Germany and Sweden—are interesting in this respect, in that they demonstrate the difficulties for televangelistic enterprise on this side of the Atlantic, even after access is secured. Schmied (1996) follows a series of experiments in televangelism in Germany, a story that lasted approximately ten years. A point of departure was provided with the introduction of a pilot cable system in the early part of 1984. From these beginnings, a German Pentecostal group called 'Media-Vision'—to give but one example—set up a programme in association with Jimmy Swaggart, on the Eureka-TV outlet. The venture was, however, short-lived in view of the problems that arose when Eureka-TV was sold, as the only way that Media-Vision could continue in business was to pay on the basis of rates charged for advertising. As Schmied (1996: 96) demonstrates, this simply was not possible and the Pentecostal group lost their airtime. A similar fate met Robert Schuller's *Hour of Power*. The financial question remains central in these affairs, though it may be posed in different ways. Either the programme concerned must be sufficiently successful (in terms of viewers) to attract commercial advertising; or time must be paid for by a willing constituency (that is, effectively, sufficient numbers of conservative Protestants). At present, neither situation appears to obtain in modern Europe.

The Swedish case (Linderman 1993) is different in that it involves rather more indigenous attempts at a form of televangelism, thus refuting to a certain extent the argument that this kind of programming is necessarily 'foreign' in its culture. Once again the technological factor has to be taken into account with the presence of satellite and cable, through which at least some of the American evangelists (including Robert Schuller and Kenneth Copeland) have attempted to find an outlet in Sweden. The Pentecostal 'TV Inter' has operated as broker in these enterprises (both in radio and television), but has also produced its own programmes. It has, moreover, advertised for subscriptions to cover expenses for such activity (Linderman 1993: 43–4). Here is an excellent example of the changing climate in religious broadcasting in Sweden in which local churches (for example Livets Ord—a huge American-style evangelical church in Uppsala) have also been implicated. Linderman, in fact, goes further than this, arguing that there is a gradual but increasing discrepancy between the patterns of church life on the ground and a more independent, media type of religion. There is at least a hint that the latter may not only prosper but offer more time to evangelistic broadcasting. Whether or not such innovations will be able to succeed remains an open question (as yet few of these new phenomena have been subject to scholarly analysis).[1]

They raise, however, the central question of this section (and indeed of the chapter as a whole): will America-style televangelism become an integral part of religious broadcasting on this side of the Atlantic or will this not be possible in view of the incapacity of European churchgoers to constitute an adequate base (1) as an audience and (2) crucially (if indirectly) as a source of finance? Has there, in other words, to be a resonance between the realities of religion and their uptake by the media? The media—despite the immensity of its technological potential—can be surprisingly limited in its attempts to *create* a religious agenda. If Europeans simply turn off their television sets when confronted by America's (or indeed their own) evangelists, there is little that the latter are able to do. That is one point of view. Elvy (1986, 1990), however, offers a slightly more nuanced response,[2] arguing that the televangelists may indeed make inroads into Europe as public broadcasting systems crumble. This is more likely to be true of radio than television (radio is very much cheaper) and more likely to happen in Northern Europe than in the Catholic countries

---

[1] What is clear is the overall drop in the size of the Swedish audience for religious broadcasting taken as a whole (Linderman 1993: 50). There is, moreover, a strong match between the audience for Livets Ord in general and the audience for TV Livets Ord in particular—a situation that mirrors the American situation very precisely. It also suggests limited penetration into the wider society. A case study of Livets Ord itself can be found in Coleman (2001).

[2] Additional information was gained in conversation with Peter Elvy (Sept. 1998). Elvy's published work also provides an admirable introduction to the myriad religious broadcasting associations operating in modern Europe.

further south, where cultural resistance is higher (Gutwirth 1998). The most successful case so far in television is the evangelical channel (Evangelische Omroep) in the Netherlands, a nice example of re-pillarization within Dutch society. It is ironic that a noticeable proportion of this constituency decline on principle to watch television, including the programmes produced in their name.

## Religious Broadcasting in the European Context

If American styles of broadcasting meet with a certain hostility in Europe, are there others which are able to do better? It is at this point that the lack of appropriate material becomes apparent, reflecting at least in part the incompatible agendas of sociologists of religion and those who study the media.[3] A subtext lies behind this incompatibility: namely that disproportionate numbers of those who have little or no interest in religion (in both a personal and professional sense) are present in the circles which dominate the media. Such dominance may, moreover, be one (possibly the principal) reason for the persistence of dismissive attitudes to religion in modern Europe. Such attitudes are particularly prevalent at management level in media circles, a fact which can colour the life of the journalist interested in the subject. Despite considerable knowledge about the complex evolutions of religion in modern societies, some professionals in the field feel that they have insufficient space or time to develop these views in the necessary detail (Hoover 1998).[4]

The dearth of systematic information on religion and the media presents a real problem. In contrast, for example, with the availability of excellent comparative material on the teaching of religion in the education systems of Europe, there is no equivalent concerning the opportunities for and the regulation of religious broadcasting in the media systems of either the European Union as a whole, or its constituent nations (or indeed further afield). Messner (1998) has attempted to establish a framework in this respect but not without difficulty. In terms of the European Union itself, the least that can be said is that religious groups normally find themselves in the same position as other voluntary or intermediate organizations; in other words they are covered by

---

[3] Arthur (1993) and Stout and Buddenbaum (1996) offer interesting collections of articles on religion and the media, but with almost no reference to Europe. Conversely the publications of the Euromedia Research Group (e.g. Østergaard 1992) make no reference to either religion *per se* or the European churches. The best single source of information is Elvy (1990)—although a subject index would have helped to systematize the material. The case studies on Denmark and Norway are particularly useful (ibid. 106–17).

[4] A comparison between The *Guardian* and The *Times* would be interesting in this respect; clearly the managements of the two papers have made very different decisions with respect to religious coverage. The point parallels that made about school management and the teaching of religion in the previous chapter.

the law in terms of the right to propagate information about themselves.[5] Conversely there is a certain protection for religious groups from attacks or bias on the part of the media, but—once again—such protection is couched in terms of human rights rather than anything specifically religious. The situation in the emergent democracies of Central Europe—still beyond the frameworks of the European Union—is even more difficult to research systematically. The very lack of 'orderliness' in the former communist countries of Europe offers, however, opportunities that are denied further west; religious groups (some internal and some external) have been quick to take advantage of this situation (Elvy 1990: 45).

## Public Network Broadcasting

Whatever the complexities of the legal arrangements, public broadcasting networks—systems which undoubtedly privilege the mainstream denominations—remain the norm in most of Europe. Access to the media depends on the proportion of members (often assessed in nominal terms) thought to be present in that country.[6] Different European countries find different solutions to the problem of media access (Elvy 1990: 71–6). In France, for example, the public service channel (Chaîne 2) devotes most of Sunday morning to mainstream religion, though it allows certain religious minorities proportional access. Jewish, Muslim, and Protestant minorities have been present for some time. The relative newcomers in this case are the Buddhists, who gained access to Chaîne 2 in January 1997 (Kone-el-Adji 1998). The question of 'scope' in the context of an increasingly pluralist continent is raised once again (as it is elsewhere in Europe). If access to the media is publicly—as opposed to financially—controlled, there has to be some mechanism to decide which groups are and which are not allowed access to this sought-after commodity.

The case study of French Buddhism is interesting for an additional reason. In a small way it illustrates, once again, the essential theme of this chapter—i.e. the complex interactions between diverse forms of religious reality and their projection by the media. The exigencies of the latter have produced a particular image of Buddhism in France—as indeed they did in Germany (Kone-el-Adji 1998: 10)—which in its turn has altered the way that Buddhist centres operate on the ground. Not all of the latter, for a start, were equally enthusiastic about a television outlet, raising inevitable questions about the

---

[5] The crucial clauses in this respect come from the European Convention on the Rights of Man (Arts. 9 and 10). Austria and Germany are partial exceptions to the general rule—offering a particular status to the churches, in the sense that they are public institutions (Messner 1998).

[6] In fact the minorities do better than might be expected from this type of arrangement; if a strict proportionality was enforced, they would have almost no media time at all in most modern European societies—which is clearly not the case. There is an even stronger argument for the media participation of other-faith populations at local level, especially in places where their numbers are disproportionately high.

typicality of what is seen. Linked to this has been the need to attract a viable television audience, an aspiration which has clashed at times with the desire to promote something authentically Buddhist. A third illustration of necessary modification can be found in the pressure to follow Christian practice and to produce an identifiable Buddhist 'creed'. And given the response generated by exposure through the media, something approximating an organization or bureaucracy is beginning to emerge—again a feature which jars to an extent with the spirit of Buddhism.

This, in microcosm, is a tension that all religions experience when they project themselves on the media, and notably on to television. Images emerge which are in tension with structures (or conversely the absence of these) built up over centuries and the theologies that underpin these. In the case of Christianity, the requirement of attendance, Sunday by Sunday, in a particular place and in the presence of specified professionals, is clearly overridden by broadcasts of the liturgy, provoking an inevitable set of questions concerning the theological validity of what is going on (notably in the case of the Mass or a Eucharist). But the churches—of whatever denomination—know only too well that their capacities to reach those who are unwilling to attend churches, whether regularly or less so, are enormously enhanced by both radio and television and with a quality of presentation that cannot be guaranteed by each and every parish.

An inevitable question follows from this: who exactly watches these broadcasts? Is it the case that those responsible for European religious broadcasts are, like their American counterparts, simply preaching to the converted (albeit a rather different constituency from those attracted by the televangelists), or it is possible to create an additional set of viewers? In this respect, the British case appears to be a partial exception to the rule. Those programmes which are based on hymn singing and the culture that goes with this, whether on television (*Songs of Praise*) or on the radio (*Sunday Half Hour*), are able to attract an appreciable audience—larger, for example, than their equivalents in sport (Davie 1994: 112). The existence of disproportionate numbers of older people within this audience is hardly surprising. These are representatives of a generation which grew up knowing these hymns—if not directly from the churches, then at least from a wide variety of parachurch organizations in the years before the Second World War (Gunter and Viney 1994). It is a moot point how far these audiences will continue once this generation no longer exists and is replaced by groups of people who never knew the hymns in the first place, and have little interest in their electronic endorsement. This is a form of religious memory that could well cease to exist; at present it is maintained to a considerable extent through the media. Some parallels to this wider audience exist in the Nordic countries (Linderman 1993: 51–2);[7] elsewhere in Europe it seems

---

[7] A more detailed discussion of the significance of hymn singing in Scandinavia can be found in Ch. 9.

that it is those who regularly attend church that are most likely to watch both broadcast versions of the liturgy and other religious programmes.

The relationship between religion and broadcasting, however, goes much deeper than this. One area of research which needs further (and comparative) exploration concerns the image of religion that is projected in secular rather than religious programmes *per se* (Knott 1984). Knott concludes in this detailed but largely exploratory study that the media present to us what religion 'is thought to be' rather than 'what it is'; stereotypes emerge in line with popular culture but with a dubious connection to reality (1984: 33).[8] The relationship with reality is, however, complex: the media can at times be wrong and be forced to change their tack. An excellent illustration of this can be found in the Journées Mondiales de la Jeunesse in Paris in August 1997 (an event already noted in relation to the religiousness of young people). Gloomy prognostications predicted an embarrassingly low turn-out and general lack of interest in this rally of young Catholics from all over Europe. A day or so later, exactly the same pundits were endorsing a remarkable success.

## *Media Portrayals of Religion: Personalities and Celebrations*

The example at the end of the previous section is interesting in a different way: the Journées Mondiales de la Jeunesse are indicative of a type of religion which not only appears to flourish at the turn of the millennium, but which is more readily accessible to media presentation than week-by-week devotions. Central to these presentations are the media personalities of modern religion, and by no means least among them the present Pope (Dayan 1990; Willaime 1991). The capacity of John Paul II to make full use of this form of communication has, once again, created images which influence reactions. There were many young people in Britain, for example, who were so accustomed to an image of a travelling pontiff that the visit of a pope to Britain in 1982—for the first time for several centuries—was seen as commonplace rather than extraordinary (in its literal sense). If the Pope travelled to every other country, there was no reason to suppose that coming to Britain was all that unusual.

The capacity of John Paul II to sustain an image in the media for more than twenty years is worthy of note in itself. Here, an actor by profession has learnt the techniques of media projection and has used them to the full. The case is all the more interesting for its political repercussions in the years leading up to 1989. Indeed they began a full ten years earlier in the celebrated journey of John Paul II to a firmly communist Poland in 1979. Watched by the entire world, the Pope addressed the assembled crowd at Jasna-Góra (the symbolic heart of Polish Catholicism). Poland was transformed (and at least in part by

---

[8] The series of chapters concerning soap operas in Arthur (1993) to some extent undertakes the same task, but with a slightly different focus. In the main these are trying to identify an alternative set of values in the 'soaps' rather than noting references to popular religion as such.

the media) from a Soviet satellite to a centre for Catholicism—initially an out-post, but increasingly a centre or hub of the entity known as Europe. The communist authorities were powerless to prevent this. The visit in 1979 unleashed a whole series of subsequent events, many of which included further visits to Poland by the Pope. Each of these drew a world-wide television audience, undoubtedly instrumental in taking the Polish people step by step to political emancipation.

Other papal visits have been rather more contentious, especially in those parts of Europe where the conservative nature of Vatican politics is viewed with some dismay. The visit to the Netherlands in 1985 was one such, in a country where the collapse in churchgoing is very marked indeed in the later post-war period and where the churches are subject to internal pressures, as yet less developed in other parts of Europe. The visit to Austria in 1998 (the third since 1979) was another; here a church racked by internal scandal and potential schism illustrated the difficulties of Catholicism in coming to terms with a rapidly changing social climate.[9] Visits to France have been contentious for a different reason—the developed *laïcité* of the French state. In France there will be difficulties if the visit from the Pope involves public or political gestures which may be wrongly interpreted. The commemoration in 1996 of the fifteen-hundredth anniversary of the baptism of Clovis, King of France, looked as though it might fall into this category; it became a disputatious affair, not least in terms of finance. Who exactly was paying for this visit? A notable feature of the subsequent débâcle however, was the incapacity of the *laïques* to muster an effective counter-protest and in the end the visit, carefully managed by the French Catholic Church, passed off peacefully enough (Davie 1999*a*).

There is, however, a negative side to papal exposure. In the early years of John Paul II's papacy, his portrayal as an energetic, multi-lingual, pastoral, and charismatic figure was systematically relayed throughout the world. Such images are associated with the notion of the Pope as a powerful and effective critic of communism—a striking and positive combination (fleetingly re-created in 1998 during the visit to Cuba). Equally ubiquitous, however, are the later images of a frail and increasingly sick individual, this time accompanying a rather less popular message of intractable conservatism in matters of sexual morality. Which of these contrasting images will dominate in the decades that follow this remarkable papacy may well reside largely in the hands of the media. Physical frailty is not, however, synonymous with a negative media image. Mother Theresa, l'Abbé Pierre, and Sœur Emanuelle are evidence to the contrary, all of whom are known (partly through the media) for their humanitarian convictions and personal restraint; all three provide positive—and charismatic—role models for the younger generation in particular.

Media amplification of a different sort of celebration can be found in a whole series of national events—whether these be joyful, such as coronations

---

[9] It is interesting that the nature of the Austrian scandal concerned sexual abuse—it was very much an affair of the late 1990s (see *The Tablet*, 27 June 1998: 831).

or royal weddings, or less so, in the case of national disasters or a royal death. (Somewhere in between, and infinitely ambiguous, can be found the royal divorces.[10]) The power of television to transform the armchair viewer into a participant personally present at these national or even international celebrations has been analysed in some detail by Dayan (1990, 1998). The viewer becomes, in fact, a witness or pilgrim, not only watching but appropriating the event accordingly, then taking the event forward with the media experience taken into account. This process is particularly profound if the specialness of the episode requires that the home itself become a place of sociability and viewing take place in groups rather than alone. The fact that so many of the events have *ipso facto* a religious dimension is simply part and parcel of what is going on; like everything else, however, it is differently experienced by those who are physically present compared with those who watch at home.

Two exceptional funerals were analysed at the end of Chapter 4, primarily in terms of the necessity of religious markers at the time of death in two moderately secular European countries. The ambivalence of both events was the principal point to grasp, together with the representativeness of both individuals in terms of the religious cultures of France and Britain. Exactly the same events can, however, be looked at in terms of their projections by the media. In the case of President Mitterrand, the French public were permitted to see— on a divided screen—the two funerals that took place simultaneously on the morning of Friday 7 January 1996. One displayed an international gathering in Notre-Dame, whose start was delayed until the plane carrying the President's body had arrived in Jarnac for the private ceremony; the other represented provincial France (*la France profonde*), not with images of the funeral (closed to all but the family) but with careful use of the camera during the subsequent journey of the cortège through the village of Jarnac itself. A juxtaposition of two images of France—cosmopolitan and deeply rural (both dear to the President)—were achieved through media technology (Hervieu-Léger 1996, 1999*b*).

In the case of Princess Diana, a remarkably similar moment was achieved almost by chance. During the singing of the psalm (*De profundis*) in a short memorial service at St Paul's Cathedral on the day that the Princess died— broadcast in place of the scheduled *Songs of Praise*—the camera incorporated shots of the plane that carried Diana's body from France preparing to land at RAF Northolt (Davie and Martin 1999). The moment was clearly anticipated by the BBC but provided for the television viewer—though not for the

[10] Royal divorces are ambiguous in so far as royal individuals (or couples) who behave like everyone else inevitably lose their royal/sacred status. 'Royals' are supposed to be different or 'set apart' (to use the Durkheimian phrase) and to embody values that the rest of us appear to have discarded. In this respect these public figures find themselves in a very similar position to the professionals of the state churches; they embody a memory of traditional family life on behalf of the population as a whole (see Ch. 3).

participants at either event—one of the most potent images of the whole extraordinary week. The evocations were all the more powerful in view of the fact that the marriage of Prince Charles to Diana Spencer had taken place in St Paul's Cathedral in 1982. The fleeting character of the image is the essential point to grasp. The role of the media more generally in the week as a whole remains more difficult to quantify. Was it the case that enormous numbers of individuals went spontaneously to London (or elsewhere) in order to lay their flowers or to sign a book of condolence; or was such activity the result of media exposure and associated exhortation? The symbiotic relationship of reality and the media is clearly illustrated: initial reactions by some individuals were turned—at least in part by the media—into a flood of human sentiment by the middle of the week.

## Positive and Negative Images

Undoubtedly negative, though entirely in tune with the images of popular culture, are the media presentations of new religious movements. Interesting in this respect is the well-documented case study of the Solar Temple movement (Campiche 1995). The Solar Temple was a small, hitherto little-known and somewhat esoteric new religious movement based primarily in Switzerland and Quebec. The episode which brought the movement to public attention was far from typical of new religious movements as a whole, in that it ended abruptly and disastrously in October 1994 with the discovery of numerous bodies in both Switzerland and Canada. It was entirely predictable, however, that the press—throughout the Western world—should give the tragedy maximum exposure. Equally easy to anticipate, though rather more regrettable, were the inevitable condemnations of all new religious movements (indeed of all religious non-conformism)—strongly endorsed, indeed articulated, by the media as a whole. In reactions such as these, there is clearly a mutually reinforcing interaction between public opinion in most European countries and the messages conveyed by the media; there is, conversely, very little connection between the *realities* of these unconventional but normally peaceful religious movements and their portrayal in newspaper, radio, or television.[11]

Campiche (1997*b*) scrutinizes such tensions in terms of the responses of the media to different types of religious activity. In relation to sects or new religious movements, the impact of a strongly negative press portrayal is both considerable and persuasive; the more so in that relatively few members of the general public have first-hand experience of how such movements operate.

---

[11] There is a huge sociological literature on new religious movements. Almost all those who study such groups are agreed on the following point—i.e. that most religious movements are entirely harmless, and many provide frameworks within which certain individuals are able to flourish and to lead socially effective lives. The portrayal in the press remains, however, almost universally negative.

Such a lack is not the result of secrecy on the part of the movements themselves, but simply an indicator that—despite their prominence in the media—they remain a very small part of European religious activity. The effect of repeated negativity in the media influences legislative decisions as well as popular points of view: in short, new religious movements are seen as pernicious (see Chapter 7). Media portrayals of mainstream religion are less persuasive, since most Europeans have at least some idea of what happens in these churches; they have, moreover, been part of the European environment for centuries. There is no harm in these religious institutions; they are, simply (in terms of media discourse), marginal to the functioning of late-modern societies and so easily dismissed as irrelevant.

A different, but again decidedly negative, case study comes from Poland and concerns the programme known as Radio Maria (Radio Maryja). This has achieved a certain notoriety not only in Poland but outside it in terms of the extreme, and at times distasteful (to say the least), nature of its content. Radio Maria was the creation in 1990 of a Catholic priest, Father Rydzyk; in terms of its position on the airwaves, it is extremely difficult to avoid and has, undoubtedly, a loyal following amongst a certain kind of Polish Catholic. Father Rydzyk himself uses the programme to propagate ultra-conservative views on moral and political issues which lead from time to time to suggestions that those who do not share these attitudes, or indeed those who are not Catholics, are not welcome within Polish society. It is the tone of the broadcast which is offensive, just as much as its content. A relatively recent episode for example concerned the debate in Poland's lower house of parliament (the Sejm) relating to changes in the abortion law in 1997. Father Rydzyk suggested that those who had voted in favour of a relaxation in the existing law should have their heads shaved 'so that they would look like women who had consorted with members of the German occupying forces during the Second World War' (*The Tablet*, 28 Feb. 1998: 292). Outrage leading to questioning by the prosecutor's office of Torun provoked, in turn, a storm of protest from Rydzyk's supporters; despite initial backing by the Polish bishops the case was eventually dropped.

In terms of religious memory an interesting postscript to this section on positive and negative images can be found in the use of religious symbols in advertising. Understandably enough the discussion of such images is usually formulated in terms of taste and suitability; certain references are considered offensive to particular religious communities and advertisements which fail to take account of this run the risk of prosecution. There is, however, an additional point to make. The use of religious images in advertising—whether distasteful or not—depends on sufficient numbers of the general public being able to pick up the resonance. The widely displayed Benetton advertisement of a young priest kissing a nun (which had nothing to do with the promotion of certain kinds of clothing) was a case in point. A young priest in a shovel hat and a young woman in full habit are unusual sights in modern Europe; the resonance remains sufficient, however, to provoke a second glance (the aim of all advertising). Biblical and artistic references are similarly used (Cottin and Walbaum 1997; Freysinnet-Dominjon 1998), offering an index—albeit indirect—of which parts of the tradition or memory are not only chosen, but sufficiently intact to have a positive reference in terms of the market. Apples are clearly seductive (even to computer buffs), serpents rather less so. Whether or not the average Apple Mac user grasps the relationship between the pivotal 'apple' key and the biblical reference to the tree of the knowledge of good and evil is harder to say. The notion of paradise, finally, is attractive—not only to the advertiser (notably the travel agent) but to the public at large; how the idea of paradise is portrayed in an advertisement becomes in itself an indicator of how the notion is perceived by Western Europeans at the turn of the millennium.[12]

# Mediated Memory

This chapter has assumed a symbiotic relationship between religion and the media. It is now important to put this into a wider context and to recognize that if the media both amplify but at the same time distort (or even replace) the patterns of religious life established over centuries in Europe, this ambivalent relationship is also true of other activities. The partial parallels between religion and sport provide the most obvious illustration. Both, for a start, are leisure activities and depend for their existence on attracting sufficient numbers of enthusiasts to maintain viability. The world of sport, moreover—just like the world of religion—has been subject to a marked degree of individualization. It is the sporting activities that can be pursued alone or informal groups which prosper in the final decades of the twentieth century, rather than the team games encouraged in earlier generations.[13] This does not mean, of course, that team games have entirely disappeared—indeed they flourish at a professional level; they have, simply, become less widespread within the population taken as a whole. Exactly the same is true of religion: it is clear from the evidence presented so far that European individuals increasingly discover their own religious agendas independently of the institutional churches, while the latter continue to offer significant points of reference. Convincing parallels can be seen in other ways as well. The fall in attendance at professional football matches in Britain, for example, more or less mirrors the decline in religious practice; both graphs fall at the same time and for similar reasons (the population no longer 'gathers' for its entertainment in the way that it used to). In both activities, moreover, what might be called the 'top'

---

[12] Several ideas come together in the notion of marketing perfume (Lolita Lempicka for example) in apple-shaped bottles!

[13] *Social Trends* regularly provides ample evidence for this statement within a British context.

divisions continue to flourish; the lower divisions (or average parish church) very much less so.

In terms of this chapter, there is in addition a certain similarity in both cases between 'reality' and its projection on the media. If fewer people than previously are paying to watch football matches (i.e. to attend the more modest as well as the exclusive games) it is equally evident that relatively large audiences watch football on television, not least the World Cup. The interest is still there, though expressed in a different way and with a different register of experience. Up to a point this is also true of religion: regular attendance drops but larger numbers of people access a form of religion on the media (notably the great ceremonial occasions), but again with a different subjective experience. (There are, of course, rather fewer great ceremonial occasions than there are top-class football matches.) And in many ways those who take responsibility for the organization of amateur sport and those who make decisions about parish activities have to take the same factors into account when scheduling local events. If these clash with popular programmes (of whatever kind) there are inevitable and negative repercussions; it cannot be otherwise in a media-dominated society.[14]

Bearing these similarities in mind, it seems increasingly clear that it is society as a whole which is changing rather than simply the religious sector within this. The economic and technological evolutions of society have, however, immense and immediate *consequences* for religion in all its manifestations, and not least with respect to its ambivalent relationships with the media. On the positive side, the media quite clearly amplify the religious message (just as they do in the case of politics). In one radio or television broadcast, for example, it is possible for one preacher (or one politician) to reach more people than in a whole lifetime of preaching (or speech-making). The crucial question to ask at this point, however, is whether the nature of the message alters with the manner of transmission. This is particularly true of an activity which hitherto has depended almost exclusively on the regular attendance of individuals in a specified place and has developed a theology to go with this. It seems increasingly clear, moreover, that even if the broadcast sermon is exactly the same as the one heard in the church or cathedral, it is experienced differently by those who are listening or watching at home. At one and the same time, therefore, the memory is both endorsed and subject to mutation.

But the sermon is seldom exactly the same, for *by its very nature* broadcasting creates pressures which are likely to alter the substance of what is being said. The sermon is manipulated and refined to produce material appropriate for a very different medium—even if those responsible for the broadcast are basically in sympathy with what is going on. Soundbites are demanded which

---

[14] Indeed even prestigious first-division football clubs fear competition from simultaneous broadcasts; the timing of matches is carefully negotiated with this in mind. Matches are seldom broadcast live on Saturday afternoon in view of the effect on gate receipts.

are rarely compatible with the subtleties of theological argument or elements of the liturgy are arbitrarily discarded in view of time constraints. A sympathetic broadcaster, however, cannot always be assumed. It is quite possible, for example, for the message to be deliberately 'mediated' in order to question or distort its meaning (or simply to produce a good story), with the result that the media have a negative rather than positive effect on religious memory.[15] This can happen in a variety of ways, some of which have been illustrated in the previous sections, notably with reference to new religious movements. Larger memories are also if less immediately vulnerable, particularly in the hands of those who have little understanding of religion—but in this case, following Campiche (1997b), some knowledge of mainstream religion on the part of viewers may serve to correct the worst distortions.

A final question cannot be avoided in conclusion. In their dominance of late-modern societies, increasing all the time by means of new technologies, and with their propensity to 'order' society according to their own terms, have the media become *de facto* a form of religion in themselves? Even the word 'media' implies that this is so, in the sense that the world and what goes on within it are interpreted on our behalf—an assertion that can be supported by a wide range of empirical material. Despite the immensity of their resources, the media are, however, limited in what they can achieve in that they depend on connections with reality in order to begin at all. Televangelism, for example, has not so far made significant inroads into Western Europe. And whatever the media said about young Catholics coming to Paris in the middle of August, the reality proved to be different (and independent of the mediated message). The question returns once more to the starting point of this chapter; without some resonance with reality, the media simply cannot function. It is true that the religious memories of Europe can be subject to considerable distortion, manipulation, and censure by the media, but *within limits* (Elvy 1990: 69).

In terms of functional equivalents, moreover, both the sporting illustration and the possibility of usurpation of the place of religion itself by the ever-increasing presence of the media come up against the same unavoidable question (just like the French Republic in the case of François Mitterrand). Neither have an answer to the existential questions of human living, and notably those that surround the finite nature of human existence. In the last analysis, the media coverage of Princess Diana's funeral could only amplify what took place in the established church of a Northern European country. It was the church, not the media, that has been (and still is) the guardian of liturgies which both individuals and societies require to mark the turning points of human existence.

---

[15] Postman (1986: 114–24), drawing mostly on American material, goes further than this and argues that the authentic religious experience is impossible on or through television. Television is primarily entertainment, with a strong bias towards secularism; if religion becomes the content of television shows, the risk is always there that television shows may become the content of religion.

# SEVEN

# *Alternative Memories 1: Pluralism and the Law*

THE idea of increasing religious diversity in modern Europe has already been introduced in previous chapters—in the initial overview of the religious situation in Europe in Chapter 1 and in the brief discussion of demographic change at the beginning of Chapter 4. These were paragraphs which stressed that the presence of religious minorities in post-war Europe is largely, though not wholly, explicable in terms of economic change, and more particularly by the demand for additional supplies of labour in the expanding economies of the 1950s and 1960s. Outline facts and figures were presented; so, too, some information about the provenance and social composition of the other-faith groups present in different European societies.

The notion of 'scope' has also appeared in a number of places—in, for example, the discussion of financial arrangements and in matters of marriage, education, and the media. In each instance, essentially the same question has presented itself: who does or does not have access to whatever rights or privileges are involved for entities known as 'religious organizations' in modern European society? In the last analysis the question becomes, therefore, one of definition (what counts as religion and what does not)—hence, amongst other things, the legal dimension of the debate. The fact that a set of obligations or responsibilities might accompany such rights and privileges is seldom articulated in quite the same way, though it is undoubtedly an important part of these complex and delicate arrangements. Both sides of the equation need to be borne in mind in the pages that follow.

Underlying the whole question are the concepts of tolerance and pluralism. Neither is self-evident and both need careful scrutiny in light of the circumstances with which this book is dealing: i.e. the later post-war decades in a part of the world which has been inseparable from a primarily Christian tradition for two millennia (and all the institutional arrangements that go with this), but which is now faced with the need to accommodate a diversity of faith communities—some of which embody aspirations that do not fit easily into the historical frame. From a sociological point of view, questions of tolerance and pluralism were initially posed through a widespread engagement with new religious movements; hence the first section of the chapter. More recently the debate has shifted to the other-faith communities in modern Europe, and notably to Judaism and Islam. Each raises very different substantive issues which must be considered in turn. A thematic approach re-emerges, however, in two case studies of Islam: that is, the Rushdie controversy in Britain and the *affaire du foulard* in France, in that the principal points at stake in both cases concern not only the Islamic community in itself but its interaction with the host society in question. In both cases the deposits of law and law-making were a crucial element in the discussion.

Pluralism and the law asserts itself, finally, in an entirely different way. In all societies it is necessary to have some way of determining outcomes to the complex ethical and moral issues that emerge as an integral part of human living, but in an accelerated form in late-modern societies in view of the speed of discovery in modern science. Unsurprisingly the frame in which such issues have been decided in Europe has traditionally been Judaeo-Christian thinking, and more especially the branch of knowledge known as moral theology. Two evolutions challenge this predominance at the turn of the millennium, only one of which is the arrival of communities with alternative ethical frameworks. The other is the growing proportion of Europeans who would deem themselves secular as opposed to religious, in any sense of the word. Still a minority, this group has an important part to play in the establishment of new ways of deciding policy in these difficult areas, including, for example, research on the embryo or the decisions relating to the ending of lives whose 'quality' is no longer thought to be acceptable. The fact that many of these issues concern the beginnings and endings of human lives simply heightens their proximity to traditional understandings of the sacred.

# New Religious Movements

The sociological literature on new religious movements[1] is huge and, unlike equivalent studies of the media, includes a literature on Europe. A recent annotated bibliography on new religious movements in Western Europe (dealing with the period from 1960 to the present day only) has, for example, almost 2,000 entries covering well over 300 pages (Arweck and Clarke 1997). Other useful collections, including a number of detailed case studies, can be found in Towler (1995), Champion and Cohen (1996), Meldgaard and Aagaard (1997), and Barker and Warburg (1998). A proportion of these publi-

---

[1] The distinction between new religious movements and the movement known as the New Age is blurred. Some new religious movements display tendencies associated with the New Age, others are quite different; conversely some aspects of the New Age are moderately well organized in the form of movements or organizations, others very much less so. In the main this section deals with new religious movements; the New Age will be discussed more fully in Ch. 8.

cations began their life as conferences, meetings which frequently attract public as well as sociological attention.[2] Accounting for such disproportionate
attention to groups which are numerically very small is part of the sociological task; clearly new religious movements disturb the European mind—
whether this mind be secular, religious, or sociological. For secular Europeans,
new religious movements challenge assumptions of rationality; for the
traditionally religious, they throw up disconcerting alternatives to Christian
teaching; and for the sociologically inclined, they offer not only ample material for case studies, but more importantly, insights into the nature of
European society itself—notably its capacities to tolerate difference.

## New Religious Movements and the Law in Modern Europe

Arweck and Clarke (1997) provide a useful overview of the presence of new
religious movements in most countries of Western Europe—both in terms of
a country-by-country summary (albeit a brief one) and in noting a number of
overall themes. Similarities and differences between European societies are
explained by a combination of the movements themselves and by geographic,
historical, and cultural differences in the European nations—not least their
religious and political structures. Unsurprisingly,

> the more culturally uniform and homogeneous societies with little direct cultural
> contact or involvement over time with the wider world, from which many of the
> new movements derive their inspiration, tend to be less receptive to certain types
> of new movements, in particular those non-Christian movements that demand
> total commitment and set themselves up as alternatives to the existing order.
> (Arweck and Clarke 1997: p. xxv)

And as an example of the extreme case, Arweck and Clarke cite the Irish
Republic, where (until recently) high levels of both practice and belief have
tended to act as a 'dam against the inflow of new religious movements' (ibid.
p. xxvi). The opposing extreme is not, however, in Europe at all, but in the
United States, where religious pluralism is built in, both historically and constitutionally, in a way that no European society can emulate. Compared with
the US, no European society can be considered pluralist, in that its history has
always been weighted towards a state church of some sort, even if the legal
arrangements have been modified over time to permit the existence of various
alternatives. New religious movements have, however, adapted to the
European scene; they exist in profusion. They also evolve as the decades pass,
as do their alter egos, the anti-cult groups (also varied in terms of both their
stances and their tactics). The picture, therefore, is complex, as different movements at different moments provoke controversy for different reasons in different European countries.

[2] A good example of such public attention can be found in the 1996 meeting of the
Association Française de Sociologie Religieuse on 'Nouveaux Mouvements Religieux et
logiques sectaires' (Champion and Cohen 1996).

How can a sociologist get a handle on what is happening? The answer lies in careful empirical analysis, which includes a comparative element. Particularly useful in this respect is the work of scholars who are able to bridge the gap between sociological and legal knowledge. A excellent example can be found in the work of Richardson (1995), who has scrutinized the workings of the emergent pan-European institutions with respect to minority religions and basic human rights in the European Union. Essentially this is a study of social change which should be understood in two ways: first in terms of institutions as a pan-European socio-legal framework begins to emerge (thus permitting, theoretically at least, appeals over and above the national courts); and, secondly, in terms of a growing pluralism as 'European religion' gives way to an increasing diversity of religions in Europe—new religious movements are one element in this diversity. Richardson is not, on the whole, optimistic in his conclusions concerning either the realities or the futures of tolerance and pluralism. *De facto*, the European Courts have shown a strong pattern of deference towards the nation state, rarely overturning judgements that relate to freedom of religion.[3]

A second socio-legal contribution can be found in the work of the European Consortium for Church–State Research and notably their 1997 Conference on 'New Religious Movements and the Law in the European Union'.[4] The principal approach of the conference was a country-by-country analysis of the legal cases provoked by the presence of new religious movements and the implications of their respective resolutions (satisfactory or otherwise). Such an approach permits a close study of the courts involved and the way that these are used in the different European nations: who, for example, brings the case, how it is argued, and by whom—all of which are essential elements in a comparative analysis. The Conference papers also include a contribution on the place of new religious movements in international law (Duffar 1999), a study which complements the work of Richardson. New religious movements are clearly relevant to the application of the Rights of Man, and more immediately to the directives emanating from the European Convention (especially Article 9 on the Right to the Freedom of Thought, Conscience and Religion and Article 2 from the Additional Protocol on the Right to Instruction and Education). Following Duffar, the law will deal more easily with those groups whose existence derives, even indirectly, from one of the traditional religions, than with new religious movements, where the connections with the entity recognized as 'religion' by the Articles in question are rather more difficult to discern. How inclusive, in other words, is the understanding of the term 'religion'?

[3] This is not always so. The CESNUR website in October 1998 (see n. 5) provided details of four religious liberty cases concerning the situation in Greece, which were brought to the European Court of Human Rights between 1993 and 1998. Greece lost all four of these cases. (There have been others since.)

[4] See European Consortium for Church–State Research (1999).

A third lawyer to take an active interest in the evolution of new religious movements in Europe is Massimo Introvigne, the director of CESNUR—an Italian centre for the study of new religions and strongly supportive of their right to exist.[5] Particularly useful from the point of view of this chapter are Introvigne's summaries of the various official (or semi-official) reports that have emerged in a number of European countries with respect to new religious movements in the late 1990s (Introvigne 1998*a*). The French, for example, published *Les Sectes en France* in 1996, an event which both responded to and invigorated a major national debate; this led in turn to the establishment of an Observatoire interministériel français sur les sectes, which itself published a report in 1997.[6] The tone of both these documents is strongly anti-cultist. The Swiss and the Belgians have followed suit—the Swiss in February 1997 (in the wake of the Solar Temple affair described in Chapter 6), the Belgians in April of the same year. All three (French, Belgian, and Swiss), following Introvigne, are Type I reports casting new religious movements in a strongly negative light. The German and Italian equivalents (1997 and 1998) are rather more moderate (Type II) reports, but the attitude of the German authorities towards Scientology remains—in Introvigne's opinion—repressive, regarding this as a politically subversive group rather than a religious organization (see below). The Italian report is primarily a police document, a fact that can be discerned in its format, style, and aims. Substantially, however, it is comparatively restrained in its approach; in this case (and indeed in so many others) the problem lay in its instant translation by the media into negative and judgemental headlines (see Chapter 6).[7]

If questions of 'scope' are difficult both to determine and to apply in the context of the relatively stable political systems of Western Europe, how much more is this the case in the emergent democracies of Central and Eastern Europe, where constitutions are still evolving and where notions of inclusion and exclusion raise immediate political as well as juridical questions. This is a part of the world where the mainstream religions have suffered severe discrimination. In re-establishing their own rights, they are not always among the most generous in extending such privileges to a whole range of hitherto little-known movements (see Chapter 1).[8] An excellent collection of papers in

[5] The work of CESNUR is most easily accessed through its multilingual website—www.cesnur.org. The site lists a wide range of documents, press releases, and legal cases; it is regularly updated.

[6] One year later (October 1998) this Observatoire was itself replaced by a stronger and more aggressive Mission interministérielle de lutte contre les sectes, led by prominent anti-cultists. The earlier organization was felt to be insufficiently effective.

[7] Even more recent and continuing the more moderate trend are the reports of the Swedish government (1998) and the Canton of Ticino in Switzerland (1998). A report to the European Parliament (presented in July 1998) remains as yet unofficial; it has not yet been passed by a plenary session of the Parliament.

[8] In the West, the French Protestant community is interesting in this respect. Mindful of their own history of persecution in previous centuries they are unusually sensitive to issues of religious tolerance. The smaller evangelical groups, however—paradoxically

this respect can be found in Borowik and Babiński (1997), which contains amongst other things a further overview by Richardson, this time on the Central and East European situation (Richardson 1997). In this Richardson explores the tension between the need for historical continuity (often expressed through the historic churches) and the demands of diversity (reflecting genuine religious liberty). There are no easy answers to these questions. Among the case studies covered in the book are the Unification Church and ISKCON in Poland and the Hare Krishna movement in Hungary. All three relate the evolution of the movement in question to the extremely rapid economic and social transformations of the societies of which they are part.

## *Is Scientology a Religion? The Response of the Italian Supreme Court*

Definitional questions pervade this difficult area, nowhere more so than in the case of Scientology. The following quotations concern the decision of the Italian Supreme Court as to whether Scientology is or is not a religion (8 October 1997). They are taken from the CESNUR summary in English of the court case (Introvigne 1998*b*). The quotations are largely self-explanatory and put into perspective the persistent debates within the sociology of religion about what should or should not be included in this area of study. The lawyers, it seems, have as much difficulty as the sociologists. Equally significant for the argument of this chapter, however, are the remarks of CESNUR in the final paragraph concerning the implications of definition for both the understanding and practice of religious liberty in modern European societies. They form a bridge to the sections on other-faith communities:

While some Italian courts (including Rome and Turin) have considered Scientology as a religion, a different conclusion was reached by the Court of Appeal of Milan. Reforming a first degree decision favourable to Scientology, on November 5, 1993 the Milan appeal judges found a number of Scientologists guilty of a variety of crimes, all allegedly committed before 1981, ignoring the question whether Scientology was a religion. The Italian Supreme Court, on February 9, 1995, annulled the Milan 1993 decision with remand, asking the Court of Appeal to reconsider whether Scientology was indeed a religion. On December 2, 1996 the Court of Appeal of Milan complied, but maintained that Scientology was not a religion. Not unlike their Turin homologues, the Milan appeal judges noted that 'there is no legislative definition of religion' and 'nowhere in [Italian] law there is any useful element in order to distinguish a religious organization from other social groups'. However, among a number of possible definitions, the Milan judges selected one defining religion as 'a system of doctrines centered on the presupposition of the existence of a Supreme Being, who has a relation with humans, the latter having towards him a duty of obedience and reverence'. Additional criteria based on the case law of the Italian Constitutional Court are considered, but these

those that look most like new religious movements from a sociological point of view— resist the teaching of so-called 'cults' on theological grounds.

are clearly ancillary to the main definition. Theoretically, the reference to a 'Supreme Being' may be interpreted in a non-theistic sense. This was the interpretation in the case law of the U.S. Supreme Court interpreting the Universal Military Training and Service Act of 1948, also including in its definition of religion a reference to 'a relation to a Supreme Being'. The Milan judges, however, interpreted 'Supreme Being' in a theistic sense. As a consequence, they could easily exclude the non-theistic worldview of Scientology from the sphere of religion. . . .

The Italian Supreme Court 1997 decision on Scientology includes one of the most important discussions—so far and at an international scale—of how courts may apply existing laws apparently requiring them to decide whether a specific group is or is not a religion. It argues that the non-existence of a legal definition of religion in Italy (and elsewhere) 'is not coincidental'. Any definition would rapidly become obsolete and, in fact, limit religious liberty. It is much better, according the Italian Supreme Court, 'not to limit with a definition, always by its very nature restrictive, the broader field of religious liberty'. 'Religion' is an ever-evolving concept, and courts may only interpret it within the frame of a specific historical and geographical context . . . (Introvigne 1998*b*: paras. 2, 10)

## Other-Faith Communities

So much for the discussion of new religious movements. How far can the analysis be extended to the other-faith communities of Europe? Two of these will be discussed in detail; the two, possibly, that present the greatest contrast in terms of their historical connections with Europe.

### European Jewry

The presence of Judaism within Europe is hardly new.[9] Jewish communities have played a crucial if at times tragic role in Europe's history, not least in the twentieth century. No one who has visited the major cities of Central and East Europe can come away without sensing the loss of a rich and vibrant culture which contributed in multiple ways to what it means to be European—in terms of the economy, the arts, and intellectual life. Vilnius, once known as the Jerusalem of the North, is an admirable illustration of this point—if less well known than its larger equivalents in Poland, Czechoslovakia, or Hungary. Its newly established Museum of Judaism tells the story of the Jewish community in Lithuania, both before and during the Nazi occupation.

The establishment of the museum is interesting in itself. In the communist period, those Jews who lost their lives in the war were simply Soviet victims of German hostilities; they had no identity beyond this. Only since Lithuanian independence from the Soviet Union has it been possible to establish a specifically Jewish memory in the Baltic states. Most of the material is photographic,

---

[9] See Ch. 1, n. 8.

much of it taken from the communist archives; its visual impact is considerable. As you enter the museum, for example, a large inter-generational family photograph taken before the war hangs on the wall—only two or three of the family (poignantly ringed) were still alive six years later. Even more revealing, however, were the reactions of my young Lithuanian guide and interpreter. At my request we sought out the museum and made our way round the collection, reading the various inscriptions. By the end of the visit, she was visibly shocked, having discovered an aspect of Lithuanian history that quite clearly she knew nothing about.

Nor are such tragedies confined to Central and East Europe. Anywhere in fact where the Nazi occupation took hold, the Jewish communities of Europe suffered appallingly. This is as true for Amsterdam[10] or for Vienna as it was for the capitals further east; only British Jewry (and the small communities in Sweden and Switzerland) escaped the devastating impact of Nazi policies.[11] The statistics alone demonstrate the success of the 'final solution' (see Table 7.1), quite apart from the accumulation of individual or family histories; a frighteningly large proportion of European Jews lost their lives in the course of World War II—a reminder that religious communities can indeed be destroyed by persecution, together with the memories that they sustain.

What, then, has happened to European Jewry in the post-war period? In many ways the story becomes even more poignant. It is wonderfully told by Wasserstein (1996), whose theme of a 'vanishing diaspora' fits easily into the overall argument of a book centred on the concept of memory. Wasserstein's portrait should, however, be read against the collection of essays brought together in Webber (1994a); the latter provide an equally informative but rather more nuanced account of the complexities of Jewish identity in the new (post-1989) Europe. At the heart of this discussion lies the question of what it means to be Jewish: is this an imposed, given, or created identity in late modernity (Webber 1994b: 74–85)? Different people will give you different answers.

Both accounts cover all parts of Europe plus the former Soviet Union, together with a range of thematic issues; in addition, that is, to documenting the evolution of the major Jewish communities in different European societies. The thematic issues include the emergence of the state of Israel, the memory of the Holocaust, and a developed discussion of the relationship of Jews and Christians (more especially the Catholic Church) in Europe. In terms of the national communities, particular attention is given to the two largest— i.e. the British and the French—together with what Wasserstein calls the three Germanies (the West, the East, and Austria). The contrast between France and Britain is instructive in that it demonstrates once again the continuing import-

[10] The plight of Dutch Jewry has been epitomized in the story of Anne Franck. The presentation of her story to subsequent generations will be referred to again in Ch. 9.
[11] Nazi policy was patchy, however (or more effectively countered), permitting some communities to survive for longer, or in marginally better circumstances, than others.

TABLE 7.1. *Jewish populations in Europe, 1937–1994*

| | 1937 | 1946 | 1967 | 1994 |
|---|---|---|---|---|
| Austria | 191,000 | 31,000[a] | 12,500 | 7,000 |
| Belgium | 65,000 | 45,000 | 40,500 | 31,800 |
| Bulgaria | 49,000 | 44,200 | 5,000 | 1,900 |
| Czechoslovakia | 357,000 | 55,000 | 15,000 | 7,600[b] |
| Denmark | 8,500 | 5,500 | 6,000 | 6,400 |
| Estonia[c] | 4,600 | — | — | 3,500 |
| Finland | 2,000 | 2,000 | 1,750 | 1,300 |
| France | 300,000 | 225,000 | 535,000 | 530,000 |
| Germany | 500,000 | 153,000[a] | 30,000 | 55,000 |
| Great Britain | 330,000 | 370,000 | 400,000 | 295,000 |
| Greece | 77,000 | 10,000 | 6,500 | 4,800 |
| Hungary | 400,000 | 145,000 | 80,000 | 56,000 |
| Ireland (Republic) | 5,000 | 3,900 | 2,900 | 1,200 |
| Italy | 48,000 | 53,000[a] | 35,000 | 31,000 |
| Latvia[c] | 95,000 | — | — | 18,000 |
| Lithuania[c] | 155,000 | — | — | 6,500 |
| Luxembourg | 3,500 | 500 | 500 | 600 |
| Netherlands | 140,000 | 28,000 | 30,000 | 25,000 |
| Norway | 2,000 | 750 | 1,000 | 1,000 |
| Poland | 3,250,000 | 215,000 | 21,000 | 6,000 |
| Portugal | n/a | 4,000 | 1,000 | 300 |
| Romania | 850,000 | 420,000 | 100,000 | 10,000 |
| Spain | n/a | 6,000 | 6,000 | 12,000 |
| Sweden | 7,500 | 15,500 | 13,000 | 16,500 |
| Switzerland | 18,000 | 35,000 | 20,000 | 19,000 |
| Turkey[d] | 50,000 | 48,000 | 35,000 | 18,000 |
| USSR/CIS[d] | 2,669,000 | 1,971,000 | 1,715,000 | 812,000 |
| Yugoslavia | 71,000 | 12,000 | 7,000 | 3,500[e] |
| Total | 9,648,100 | 3,898,350 | 3,119,650 | 1,980,900 |

*Note*: These figures, collated from many sources, are of varying reliability and in some cases are subject to a wide margin of error and interpretation. This warning applies particularly to the figures for 1946, a year in which there was considerable Jewish population movement. It must also be borne in mind that the boundaries of many European countries changed between 1937 and 1946.

n/a = not available.

[a] Includes 'Displaced Persons'.  [b] Total for Czech Republic and Slovakia.  [c] Baltic States included in USSR between 1941 and 1991.  [d] Excludes Asiatic regions.  [e] Total for former Yugoslavia.

*Source*: Wasserstein (1996: p. viii).

ance of immigration for the changing profiles of the other-faith populations of Europe. French Judaism is the only Jewish community to demonstrate appreciable growth in the post-war period, in view of the arrival of substantial numbers of Sephardim from North Africa following the withdrawal of France from the Maghreb. Not only has this brought new life to the French Jewish community, it has also changed its nature (Wasserstein 1996: 67–8). In Britain there has been no equivalent; here—as in most of Europe—out-migration is a far more significant factor, notably to Israel.

Indeed it is the unrelenting tilt in the demographic balance of European Jewry that forms the principal theme of Wasserstein's work (see also DellaPergola's essay in Webber 1994*a*). This is presented in various ways. With respect, for example, to the improving dialogue between Christians and Jews, Wasserstein remarks in conclusion that both Christians and Jews in Europe are in many respects ill prepared to confront the challenges of secular society. It is undeniable that Christians face a certain degree of decline and an evident loss of influence, but for the Jews the threat is altogether of a different order: 'They faced the prospect of dissolution and eventual extinction' (Wasserstein 1996: 158). The number of deaths begins systematically to outweigh the number of births and marrying out becomes an increasingly natural occurrence in an assimilated community. These facts, alongside appreciable out-migration, point to a steady reduction in the number of Jews in Europe, despite the significant counter-tendencies found in the small, if vociferous, orthodox enclaves (where large families remain the norm).

Paradoxically, it is precisely the tolerance of an open and welcoming society—rather than ethnic or religious hostility—that poses the main threat to the future of Judaism. The ambiguities associated with assimilation become the key to understanding this process. For decades the aspiration of large numbers of Jews in Europe, 'assimilation' has become in recent decades almost a word of abuse. Clearly it is a two-sided affair: welcome in some respects, it has negative and inevitable consequences for community life.

In multicultural, pluralist Western Europe, the Jew is no longer obliged to efface his Jewishness. This very fact has a *disintegrative* effect on Jews no longer bound by religious, cultural or political ties to their Jewishness. (ibid. 281; emphasis in original

In achieving their goal, the Jews have put the life of their community at risk. Wasserstein ends his epilogue with a brief reference to a small Jewish settlement in China (established in the twelfth century on the Silk Road). For eight centuries the group survived intact before it finally lost its sense of identity and became indistinguishable from the surrounding culture. Will the same thing happen to European Jewry? Or will this remarkable people find some way of re-establishing themselves as a viable unit in the Europe of the twenty-first century?[12] Only time will tell, but the real vulnerability of Judaism in Europe puts the as yet rather far-fetched claims about the end of institutional Christianity into a proper perspective.

## *Muslims in Modern Europe*

[12] The regenerative capacities of Judaism should not be underestimated. They are emphasized in the interpretation offered by Jonathan Sacks in Berger (1999). Following Sacks, the demographic account as it is traditionally presented is inadequate. Non-marriage, late marriage, and low birthrates are as much to blame as out-marriage; the latter, moreover, has relatively little influence on the 'engaged' community compared with the less engaged. The problem, therefore, is one of disaffiliation rather than out-marriage *per se* (Sacks 1999).

A whole clutch of books on Islam in Europe have appeared in the 1990s, reflecting the preoccupation of Europeans with this subject. Among the most important—quite apart from any number of journals which have published special issues on this theme—are Lewis and Schapper (1994), Shahid and van Koenigsveld (1995), Nielsen (1995), Nonneman, Niblock, and Szajkowski (1996), and Vertovec and Peach (1997a). Most of these combine a country-by-country approach with a variety of horizontal themes, with the exception of Shahid and van Koenigsveld. Theirs is a book with a rather more legal approach, including a very extensive bibliography. In many ways the material presented in this more analytical publication fits well into the approach adopted in my own, notably the emphasis on church and state, on religious organizations, on faith and ceremonies (including those relating to the life-cycle), and on education.[13] Each of these topics is, however, presented from the point of view of the Muslim minority rather than the dominant tradition, providing a useful counterpoint to this text.

For the most part, recent publications on Islam in Europe are (quite rightly) concerned with the post-war period and with recent and sizeable immigrations into the larger nations of the continent. It is, however, necessary to point out—as indeed most of them do—that there were earlier deposits of Islam in this part of the world (mostly at the peripheries). Some of these early initiatives were forcibly removed in the course of Europe's history, not least both the Muslim and Jewish communities that had provided such a notable example of fruitful co-existence between the Abrahamic faiths in medieval Spain.[14] A second set of settlements remained on the South-eastern edge of Europe, unknown to most modern Europeans until the eruption of violence in the Balkans in the 1990s. Such settlements, however, provide a helpful reminder that at times in European history, the Muslim presence came considerably further west with the periodic advance of Turkey across the Austro-Hungarian Empire as far as Vienna itself. A visit to the Museum of the City of Vienna will provide striking visual evidence of the significance of 1683 (the last siege of Vienna) and of the manner in which Europeans depicted the 'infidel'. In the form of both models and paintings, the museum contains an 'iconography of difference' in its repeated manifestations of the defence of Christendom against the Turk. The siege of Vienna was a defining moment (in terms both of boundary and stereotype) in the history of Europe.

These, moreover, are memories which persist in the European mind, albeit latently. They provide the background against which more recent debates take their place, prompted not only by the post-war arrivals into Europe, but by the continuing reappraisals of Islam in the modern world. This is an area in which the globalization of both religion and politics plays a major part. One way of

[13] In addition to these examples, a useful pair of studies on Muslims and the media can be found in Vertovec and Peach (1997a).

[14] The ambivalence of 1492 as an anniversary has already been pointed out (Ch. 1, n. 11).

quantifying this lies in listing some of the major shifts in global politics in the later post-war decades: these would include the oil crisis, the Iranian revolution, war in the Lebanon, the Arab–Israeli conflict, the Gulf War, and continued unrest in Algeria, not to mention civil conflicts within the Sudan and Nigeria. Indeed the end of the Cold War itself has had a major influence on the balance of power in the Middle East and on the manner in which Islam is perceived. The list could be continued indefinitely, but the point remains unchanged: domestic affairs, and notably the accommodation of Islam, cannot be isolated from the wider world, dominated for the most part by forces beyond the control of European governments.

The size, provenance, and nature of the major Muslim communities in Europe have already been outlined in Chapter 1. This outline can now be expanded in the following representations, both taken from Vertovec and Peach (1997a). Table 7.2 indicates the most accurate figures available in the mid-1990s, bearing in mind the difficulties involved in collecting them; Figure 7.1 shows the same material in a more visual form, emphasizing the scale and provenance of Muslim immigration into Europe. Both should be filled out with reference to the country-by-country analyses in the publications listed above. One point, however, needs firm underlining right from the start. In contrast to the Jewish population, most European Muslims are recent arrivals in Europe and demonstrate the economic and social vulnerablities of communities that suffer disproportionately from a downturn in the economy or a shortage of money available for effective supporting services. Nor do the Muslims, in contrast to the Jews, have wealthy sponsors in the United States; their situation in European society is altogether different and must be analysed accordingly.

What, then, are the principal interests at stake for these communities and how do European populations respond to these? One way of approaching this question is to compare the two episodes in the 1990s in which the Muslim communities of Britain and France were caught up. Both reveal the intractability of the central issues at stake in each case, many of which derive as much from the host society as from the minority community in question. The principal events will be outlined for each episode, followed by a discussion of the points they have in common (at least from a sociological perspective).

### The Rushdie Controversy

The polemic surrounding the Rushdie controversy has been such that the sequence of events are sometimes forgotten. The following offers an outline of the principal stages in the controversy.

September 1988: *The Satanic Verses* is published in the UK by Viking Penguin.

November 1988: the novel wins the Whitbread Best Novel Award.

January 1989: book burnings begin in Bradford; Muslims demonstrate in Hyde Park and petition Penguin Books.

TABLE 7.2. *Estimates of the composition of the Muslim population of selected West European countries, by country of origin, 1990 (thousands)*

| Country of origin | Belgium[a] | France[b] | Germany[c] | Destination Netherlands[d] | Switzerland[e] | United Kingdom[f] | Total |
|---|---|---|---|---|---|---|---|
| Turkey | 84.9 | 201.5 | 1,657.1 | 203.5 | 64.9 | 12.0 | 2,241.90 |
| Algeria | 10.7 | 619.9 | 6.7 | 0.7 | 2.5 | 3.6 | 644.10 |
| Morocco | 141.6 | 584.7 | 67.5 | 156.9 | 3.2 | 9.0 | 962.90 |
| Tunisia | 6.3 | 207.5 | 25.9 | 2.6 | 2.5 | 2.4 | 247.20 |
| Yugoslavia[g] | 0.6 | 5.2 | 65.3 | 1.4 | 11.7 | 1.4 | 98.00 |
| Iran | | 50.0 | 89.7 | | | 3.2 | 172.00 |
| Afghanistan | | | 30.0 | | | | 30.00 |
| Pakistan | | | 17.0 | | | 475.8 | 492.80 |
| Bangladesh | | | 23.0 | | | 160.3 | 183.30 |
| India[h] | | | 12.0 | | 3.8 | 168.2 | 184.00 |
| Indonesia | | | | 9.5 | | | 9.50 |
| Other | | 1,000 | | 67.2 | | 139.2 | 1,206.40 |
| Total | 244.1 | 2,668.8 | 2,012.2 | 441.8 | 88.6 | 975.40 | 6,430.90 |

[a] Based on SOPEMI (1992).

[b] Based on SOPEMI (1992). The 'Other' category refers to 100,000 West Africans, 300,000 Harkis, and 600,000 Beurs.

[c] SOPEMI (1992). The German census of 1987 gives a figure of 1,650,952 Muslims.

[d] SOPEMI (1992). The *Statistical Yearbook of the Netherlands* (1990) gives a figure of 405,900 Muslims. The Indonesian figure comes from this source. The 'Other' figure is a balancing term to arrive at the *Yearbook* total.

[e] These figures are taken from the *Statistisches Jahrbuch der Schweiz* (1992: table 1.30, p. 39).

[f] Based on an update of Peach (1990) and special tabulations from the 1991 census.

[h] The Yugoslav figures represent the 10% of the population which is thought to be Muslim.

[h] The Indian figures represent the 20% of the population which is thought to be Muslim.

*Source:* Vertovec and Peach (1997a: 16).

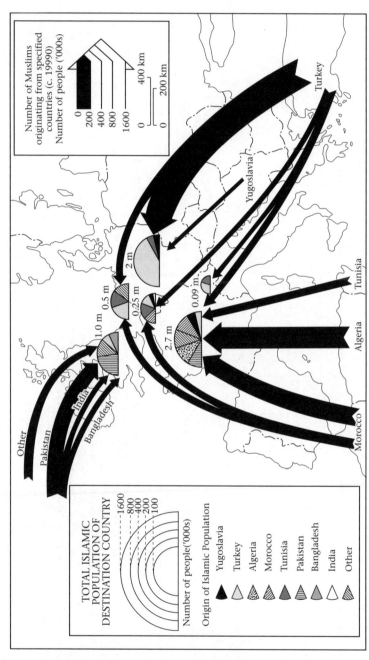

FIG. 7.1. Number of European Muslims originating from specified countries and total Islamic population of European destination countries, c. 1990

*Source*: Vertovec and Peach (1997a: 17).

February 1989: Ayatollah Khomeini, the religious leader of Iran, proclaims a *fatwa* declaring Rushdie guilty of blasphemy; a price is placed on his head, forcing him into hiding.

March 1989: Iran breaks off diplomatic relations with Britain.

February 1990: Rushdie breaks his silence and publishes 'In Good Faith' in the *Independent on Sunday*, reopening the debate about *The Satanic Verses*.

September 1990: Iran and Britain resume diplomatic links.

December 1990: Rushdie claims to 'embrace' Islam, indicating that he will not publish the paperback edition or permit more translations while further risk of offence remains.

February 1991: Iranian religious authorities reaffirm the *fatwa*, rejecting any idea of a compromise.

July 1992: Professor Hitoshi Igarashi, a Japanese translator of the novel, is stabbed to death.

October 1993: William Nygaard, the Norwegian publisher of *The Satanic Verses*, is injured in a gun attack in Oslo.

May 1994: *The Satanic Verses* is published in paperback in the UK.

June 1995: the Iranian government gradually distances itself from the *fatwa*.

September 1995: Rushdie speaks at the pre-publicized 'Writers against the State' event at Westminster Central Hall; he is seen in public more and more.

September 1998: the Iranian government formally dissociates itself from the *fatwa*; diplomatic negotiations bring Rushdie's ordeal to an end, though the *fatwa* remains in force.

How, then, should this sequence of events be understood? Why was *The Satanic Verses* so deeply offensive to Muslims? Why was it so important to the Muslim community to ban the publication of a 'blasphemous' book which no one had to read unless they wanted to? It is these questions that the average Briton (indeed European) finds almost impossible to answer. In order to grasp the issues at stake, a huge imaginative leap is required by the European mind— not only to master a different set of assumptions but to empathize with the emotional impact that *The Satanic Verses* made on an already vulnerable community.

The point derives from Europe's past. Whether they realize this or not, Europeans have absorbed the legacies of the Enlightenment; they think in ways that separate subject from object, or observer from observed, and have difficulty with a worldview that cannot make the same distinction. This is as true for Christians as it is for non-believers. Christians nurtured in a post-Enlightenment climate may not like works of art that mock or make light of Christianity, but they none the less have the capacity to distance not only themselves but their beliefs from such onslaughts. For Christian believers, such episodes may lack both taste and discretion; they do not, however, damage faith itself. For the believing Muslim, this distinction is altogether more difficult—hence a rather different understanding of blasphemy. For many Europeans this concept is barely relevant at the turn of the millennium; for Muslims it is central to daily living.

Indeed the most crucial point in the whole affair came two years or so after its inception when Rushdie claimed to have 'embraced' Islam. With every appearance of sincerity, he declared himself a Muslim (see, for example, the *Guardian*, 17 Jan. 1991: 21–2), apologizing to his co-religionists for the problems caused by the book and acknowledging that some passages were offensive to believers (an admission of blasphemy). Financial contributions from the book's royalties would be made to those who had suffered injury as a result of protests (in other words reparations would be made). The attempt to build bridges seemed genuine enough and brought some comfort to the Muslim community. In so doing, however, the gesture provoked an equally potent reaction from the opposing camp, an interesting counterpoint to the whole affair. The outrage of the secular liberals at this point could hardly be contained, revealing an alarming illogicality at the heart of their campaign: Muslims should be tolerant of offensive books, but liberals cannot tolerate the writer who becomes a Muslim. Tolerance was clearly a social construct, to be applied arbitrarily.

Rushdie's 'embrace' of Islam turned out to be a temporary phenomenon; before the end of 1991 he was once again displaying a critical view of Islam (in for example an attack on the Archbishop of Canterbury's plea for greater understanding of the Muslim position).[15] The flirtation with religion was clearly a mistake, openly acknowledged as such as the controversy came to an end: 'There were times when I attempted to compromise, when I said things that weren't true. I'm not a religious person and I shouldn't have rediscovered religion' (*Guardian*, 26 Sept. 1998: 9). Mistake or not, the second about-turn was bound to wound the Muslim community almost as deeply as the original insult. They were now twice betrayed. Whilst few Muslims in Britain had any interest in the *fatwa* they were understandably mistrustful of a writer who had humiliated both them and their religion for a second time. Salman Rushdie's attitudes epitomize the European who has difficulty in 'taking religion seriously'.

## *The* Affaire du Foulard

Liederman (1996) provides a helpful summary of the series of events that became known as the *affaire du foulard*; the sequence of dates is markedly similar to the Rushdie controversy.

October 1989: three Muslim schoolgirls wearing the Islamic headscarf are sent

---

[15] See the Morrell Address on religious toleration given by the Archbishop at the University of York, 22 Nov. 1991.

home from the Collège Gabriel Havez in Creil (north of Paris).

November 1989: the first Conseil d'État ruling, which affirms that, in principle, the wearing of the Islamic headscarf as a symbol of religious expression in public school, though not encouraged, is not incompatible with the French school system and the principle of *laïcité*.

December 1989: publication of the first ministerial circular (*circulaire Jospin*) stating that teachers must decide on a case-by-case basis whether or not to ban the wearing of the Islamic headscarf.

January 1990: three girls are asked to leave the Collège Pasteur in Noyon (north of Paris).

April 1990: parents of one schoolgirl file a defamation claim against the head teacher of the Collège Gabriel-Havez in Creil.

October 1993: teachers at a *collège* in Nantua (eastern France) strike in protest against the wearing of the Islamic headscarf in school; publication of the second ministerial circular on the need to respect the principle of *laïcité* in state schools.

September 1994: publication of the third ministerial circular (*circulaire Bayrou*), which attempts to distinguish between 'discreet' religious symbols which should be tolerated and 'ostentatious' symbols, including the *foulard*, which are to be banned from public schools.

October 1994: student demonstrations at the Lycée Saint-Exupéry in Mantes-la-Jolie (north-west of Paris) in support of the freedom to wear the *foulard* in school.

November 1994: approximately 24 veiled schoolgirls are expelled from the Lycée Saint-Exupéry in Maintes-la-Jolie and from the Lycée Faidherbe in the city of Lille.

March 1995: a Conseil d'État ruling upholds the expulsion of two veiled schoolgirls from the Collège Xavier-Bichat in Nantua.

July 1995: a further Conseil d'État ruling indicating that the wearing of the *foulard* is not by nature 'ostentatious'—and so not in itself grounds for expulsion—unless it is accompanied by some other disruptive behaviour.

Even a cursory reading of this chronology reveals the degree of indecision and ambivalence which pervades the whole affair. Not only were there several attempts at buck-passing between the schools and central government, but the *circulaire Bayrou* requires a consistent definition of 'ostentatious', a far from simple concept. Each case has to be considered on its merits.

The issue generated an enormous public controversy in France in both the written and the broadcasting media. Baubérot (1998) discusses this in terms of the tensions between freedom of conscience (claimed by the Islamic families) and freedom of thought (claimed by the teaching establishment); if pushed to the extreme, the two are incompatible. The affair was further complicated by a significant number of middle-class intellectuals who interpreted the wearing of the *foulard*, not only as a challenge to the *laïcité* of the French school system, but as a restriction on the rights of women. There were, in consequence, two reasons to oppose its acceptance in state schools.

The *affaire du foulard* cannot, however, be properly understood without reference once again to the notion of *laïcité* itself (see Chapter 4) and the two tendencies that have always existed within this: first, the universalist claim based on reason and excluding all religions from the public space, and second, a more pragmatic emphasis which attempts to come to terms with the specificities of the contemporary situation in each generation (Baubérot 1990, 1997, 1998). Both have existed from the outset, sharply contested in the heated debates of the Third Republic. A similar tension can be seen in the *affaire du foulard*, in which each understanding of *laïcité* points in a different direction. The first, fearful of the destructive forces of Islam in Europe, adopts a primarily defensive attitude. In so doing it is effectively—if not intentionally—discriminatory, for it implies that some religions are more acceptable than others. Christians and Jews get a better deal than Muslims. The second approach is more pragmatic and continues to look for new definitions of *laïcité* and new accommodations as France becomes an increasingly plural society. Questions, however, are easier to come by than answers. The irresolution of the *affaire du foulard* is indicative of the difficulties involved in the second position. Realistic in its intentions, it has yet to produce an enduring solution to this problem.

Why, then, have two such very different episodes caught the attention of the public on both sides of the Channel? One significant factor has been the mutual incomprehension in each of these countries of the other's difficulties. The French, for example, cannot understand the British preoccupation with a blasphemy law—a concept that the French consider totally outmoded in a modern democracy (as indeed do many on this side of the Channel). In this respect the contribution of Webster (1990) is particularly pertinent. Here a self-confessed atheist argues strongly that in the interests of social harmony the law on blasphemy should not be abolished but reformulated in order to protect all religious groups and not only the historically privileged. Webster's disturbing analysis of blasphemy in the European context, however, goes much deeper than this; in *A Brief History of Blasphemy*, he demonstrates that this unpleasant trait is in fact embedded in the European mind, so much so that it is hardly noticed until it is turned against those things that Europeans hold dear. For centuries, the Jews have been the particular target of European blasphemy (a fact that can be amply demonstrated in the visual as well as the literary arts). Massive guilt since 1945 has brought Europeans up short; not so much, regrettably, as to kick the habit altogether, but to find alternative victims—one such is clearly Islam, the more so given its increasingly high profile both in Europe and elsewhere.

So much for French observations of Britain. The British in their turn have equal difficulty coming to terms with French understandings of *laïcité* and the fact that a young woman wearing a *foulard* could not attend a state school in France as she was wearing a religious symbol. It is important to realize that the British escaped this particular problem more by luck than good judgement. It threatened to present itself as a school uniform issue (a subject close to the hearts of the British), but was defused in the form of a compromise: Muslim scarves could indeed be worn but only if they were the appropriate school colour (grey, navy blue, etc.).[16] For the French, no such compromise was possible, a point incomprehensible to most British people, whose schools are full of religious symbols, some of which—for example the holding of a daily assembly—are required by law. What, then, was all the fuss about? This was a point even more difficult to grasp once the British were made aware that the more modest symbols of Christianity and Judaism (the cross and the skullcap) were in fact tolerated in French schools. The difference between the latter and a Muslim *foulard*, deemed an 'ostentatious' religious symbol, was not easy to define even for French lawyers, let alone for their neighbours across the Channel.

In many respects the British and French seem as far apart as ever in their attitudes to religion in public life, but looked at from the Muslim point of view, such mutual incomprehension is simply a sideshow: neither British communalism nor French *laïcité* has provided a satisfactory answer to the question and in both situations the newly arrived minority community continues to find itself at a disadvantage. A further reason for the intractability of these episodes lies in the ever-present tensions of the international situation, particularly in North Africa as far as the French are concerned and in the delicate power balances in the Middle East for the British. The point to grasp in this respect is that the necessarily difficult negotiations between newly arrived religious minorities and the host society—hard enough to deal with within the stable democracies of Western Europe—are almost impossible to separate from the very much more tense situations in other parts of the world, some of them not so very far away. Algeria, for example, is uncomfortably close to France, a fact which is felt implicitly if not explicitly in every debate about Islam within the Republic. It is also clear that the shifting political climate in the Middle East coloured the Foreign Office agenda with respect to Salman Rushdie. The Middle East, moreover, is a part of the world where political differences can very quickly turn into dangerous and armed confrontations; they cannot be taken lightly.

For the British, moreover, the continued attempts at translation of Rushdie's novel have periodically revived the controversy; so, too, the presentation of literary prizes to Rushdie himself. Both have provoked reactions, sometimes fatal ones (see above) and in unexpected places. One of the last of these (in November 1996) took place in Denmark, a European nation noted

---

[16] Very real problems remain for the Muslim community in the British educational system, however—in terms, for example, of acceptable clothing for PE lessons and mixed classes for swimming.

for its open government and freedom of speech (Denmark was an early champion of Rushdie against the Iranian *fatwa*). The offering of the European Union's Aristeion Prize for Literature to Salman Rushdie during Copenhagen's turn as European City of Culture was, therefore, to be expected. Much less anticipated was the refusal to allow Mr Rushdie the chance to collect the prize in person, on the grounds that the Danish authorities could not guarantee his safety. The reason given was the preoccupation of the Danish police with Nordic biker gangs at the time of the ceremony.

## Ethical Issues and the Law: A Secular View

Alternatives to the Christian memory can take a whole variety of forms. So far this chapter has concentrated on a range of 'religious' alternatives, with more of these to come in Chapter 8 (albeit with a slightly different focus). But the statistics presented in Chapter 1 indicated that a sizeable proportion of the European population declare either that they do not believe in a God of any kind, or that they have no affiliation with any religious organization whatsoever. These figures need to be treated with a degree of caution in that at least some of those who so declare do in fact have a religious service at the end of their lives; indeed both belief and practice may evolve in the course of the life-cycle. The proportion of Europeans in the 'unbelieving' category is none the less considerable. As a group they merit considerably more attention than they have received so far.

It is probably safe to say that around 30 per cent of Europeans not only live their lives without reference to the institutional churches or to credal statements of any kind, but with a more or less conscious awareness that Western societies need to establish an alternative source of values—not only for everyday living but also for the making of law relating to difficult moral or ethical questions. It is here, however, that the difficulties begin, for we know very little indeed both about the kind of people represented in this category and about the views they uphold. We *do* know that the size of the constituency varies from country to country; this much can be seen from the European Values Study. France and the Netherlands, for example, are in a very different position in this respect from Poland and Ireland. It is also clear from the same source material that the social composition of the non-believing group is far from random: amongst others it will include significant numbers of intellectuals who have systematically thought through their position and whose actions (in this case lack of churchgoing) are reflected in their philosophical position. These people are disproportionately present in certain areas of European societies, not least the media (see Chapter 6) and the university systems. Younger men are more likely to be found in this category than older women.

Rejection of religious values is however one thing, finding an adequate alternative quite another. It is unlikely to be the case, for example, that the whole 30 per cent will agree on their answers even if they acknowledge the urgency of the question. Unbelief is at least as multiform as belief and probably more so—but there is very little evidence on this point. The *possibility* of disagreement can, however, be seen in the numbers wavering between agnosticism and atheism in different sociological enquiries, depending on the precise nature of the questions asked;[17] these are by no means hard and fast categories. A second indication can be found in the shifting positions of church and state in England. Here there are periodic calls for the disestablishment of the state church, but almost no discussion about what to put in its place, or how to handle the voids in society that the debate begins to reveal. Indeed a close scrutiny of the disestablishment issue uncovers a marked lack of consensus (in other words a whole range of subtexts) about what each 'faction' hopes to achieve in dislodging the Church of England from its privileged position (Modood 1997).[18]

Two facts, none the less, are clear in the European context. The first is that unbelief just as much as belief in Europe is coloured by historical tradition. In other words the God that some Europeans do not believe in is more likely to be a Judaeo-Christian God than any other formulation. Indeed in some parts of Europe it is only half-facetious to use the terms 'Catholic atheist' or 'Protestant atheist', a statement that implies not only the specificity of the rejection but the enduring influence of cultural patterns whatever the state of belief. The French case illustrates this well. Both in terms of culture and in institutional forms, the anticlerical response in France is inseparable from the Catholic tradition. Each depends so much on the other than it is difficult to determine the future of anticlericalism in a country where the Catholic Church is no longer the force it used to be. Anticlericalism, following Willaime (1993*b*), is subject to secularization just as much as its alter ego. This oppositional stance is markedly different from the pillarized societies of Belgium and the Netherlands, which have produced considerably more nuanced and tolerant (live-and-let-live) forms of unbelief (Wachtelaer 1998).

The second fact is rather different. It is crucial to remember, in assessing these possibilities, that a large part of Europe in the twentieth century had imposed upon it both the values and institutions of an alternative, aggressively secular, belief system, and did not on the whole enjoy the experience. Dominant for some seventy years in the Soviet Union and its satellites, com-

---

[17] In general, the greater the space allowed for doubt in the questionnaire, the fewer the number of convinced atheists.

[18] There are, broadly speaking, three alternatives: a radical break with the past, often related to calls for the abolition of the Monarchy and the Peerage; a kind of creeping disestablishment which unpicks the system a bit at a time; and an altogether different view which extends the advantages of establishment to a wider range of religious communities. It is interesting that the other-faith constituency is not, on the whole, in favour of the first two—fearing the secular state considerably more than the presence of an established church (Davie 2000).

munism as both a creed and a way of life collapsed dramatically in 1989. And despite a certain nostalgia for the privileges that it brought to some people and an understandable rejection of the hardships of the transition period that has followed, there are few Europeans who would readily re-embrace this option.

Are there any others? Here the lack of a single, clear-cut alternative to Judaeo-Christian teaching needs careful underlining. Europe is in a state of transition; in the process of losing one system, it has not yet found an adequate replacement (Barker, Halman, and Vloet 1992: 7). What seems, however, to be emerging in practice is a mixed economy. Since there is a degree of urgency in making decisions—not least concerning the criteria by which to judge what is or is not allowable in the making or taking of human life—commissions are established to create frameworks for decision-making in these difficult areas. It is quite clear that these organizations are no longer the sole preserve of the religious sector of society and their appropriately trained specialists (the moral theologians). But the opinion of such specialists is still sought—alongside that of others—either as members of the commissions in question or as respected and independent authorities on the matter in hand. Other 'experts' (moral philosophers, lawyers, scientists, and doctors, to name but the most obvious) are also consulted, with the final decisions subject to the democratic process. And if it is clear that the churches, and more especially the Catholic Church, have effectively lost the debate in terms of abortion or divorce and remarriage (all three are widespread in Europe and accepted by the greater part of the population), the situation is very much less clear-cut with respect to research on the embryo or euthanasia. In terms of the deliberate ending of life, the emergence of AIDS in the 1980s and 1990s is a crucially important factor; it has re-opened questions to which Europeans (especially younger ones) thought they already had the answers.

## Memory and the Middle Ground

If no clear-cut alternative to the historically dominant tradition has emerged up to now, is there likely to be one in the near future? It is almost impossible to say. One way of approaching the question is, however, to consider the notion of the middle ground in these complex evolutions. Roughly speaking 30 per cent of Europeans remain relatively committed to their churches and another 30 per cent are living their lives almost entirely beyond their boundaries. What of the group in the middle? Sociological opinion varies: Bruce (1995) for example would argue that this section of the population is drifting steadily away from the churches and that the influence of religious organizations is diminising all the time. Other are not so sure—partly in view of the capacity of the churches to act vicariously (see Chapters 3 and 4) but also in view of the *lack* of conviction on the part of many in the population about any of the alternatives on offer. These are no longer held in the esteem than they used to be, and if science was once thought of as the solver of humanity's problems, it is more and more envisaged as the creator just as much as the solver of difficult issues (Davie 1994; Sjødin 1995).

A second, rather more historical point, should also be taken into account. The turn of the third millennium is not the first time that the value consensus of Europe has been brought into question. Studies of *fin de siècle* Vienna make this abundantly clear—*Die Fledermaus*, for example, is hardly an embodiment of traditional family values. Nor is Schnitzler's play *Der Reigen*, which reveals all too clearly the hypocrisy of both public and private life at the turn of the century (and in each social class). Marital infidelity was commonplace though rarely acknowledged in public. A more discursive analysis of the period is provided in Hermann Broch's intellectual biography of Hofmannsthal, a contemporary of Schnitzler, which takes as its central theme the disintegration of values in the Western world (Broch 1984). Two phrases stand out in Broch's study: 'value vacuum' and 'gay apocalypse'. Apart from the slippage of meaning in the term 'gay', the terms are equally applicable to the mood of Europe almost a century later. That is one side of the question. A second can be found in the *contrasting* attitudes towards the theatre. Schnitzler's *Reigen* remained unperformed until the 1920s, when it became (first in Berlin and then in Vienna) a *cause célèbre*. Condemned by many for undermining the moral fibre of the nation, the play attracted additional attention in view of its Jewish authorship. After the furore in Vienna, Schnitzler himself placed a moratorium on performance for fifty years. Seventy years later—well after the fifty-year ban expired—a partially rewritten and far more sexually explicit version (*The Blue Room*) has been overwhelmingly endorsed by both critics and audience in London and New York.[19]

The nature of these shifts is central to the analysis of values and value consensus in the ongoing life of Europe. It also raises crucial implications for pluralism and tolerance. Is it possible to escape both the hypocrisy and anti-Semitism of the interwar period without offending—under the guise of toleration—the deeply held convictions of significant sections in the population (the issue at the heart of the Rushdie controversy)? Or to put the question slightly differently, is indifference a necessary consequence of tolerance—be this religious or political (Bell 1976)? In coming to a conclusion it is necessary, once again, to take into account not only those who are firmly for or firmly against a particular book, play, film, or painting, but the middle ground between them. Assent (or resistance) to change can be passive as well as active: simply by failing to respond in the way that they might have done in previous generations, the majority may reveal a marked change in public opinion.

---

[19] Sexual intercourse is indicated in the original text by a row of dots; on stage the room was darkened, a curtain lowered and lifted again after a few seconds.

# EIGHT

# *Alternative Memories 2: Religious Innovations*

THIS chapter, like the last, deals with alternative memories, but begins from a different position. It is concerned with the nature and forms of religious innovation that have emerged within the mainstream tradition, rather than documenting the existence of alternatives outside this. The *process* of innovation forms an important part of the discussion. New forms of religious life seldom present themselves spontaneously; they emerge out of older ones and in dialogue with them. Nor do they occur in a vacuum, but are related to wider processes of economic and social change. Indeed an obvious inspiration for innovation lies in shifting perceptions about the modern world and the place of religion within this, a point that will be discussed in some detail. The forms of innovation which occur are, moreover, infinitely varied. Sometimes they emerge as clearly identified movements such as Communione e Liberazione or Opus Dei (the two developed case studies in this chapter), but new ways of thinking may also appear in less organized ways—in liturgical style, for example, or in ecclesiological evolutions, in which the real significance of what has happened is only perceived in retrospect. One repeating theme can be found across a number of examples cited in this chapter—namely a change in emphasis away from more regular forms of gathering towards the special occasion, often containing a stress on spontaneity and emotion. Old and new, finally, can come together in forms of religion which reinvent the past within a modern context.

The emphasis on process alongside the substance of innovation leads at the end of the chapter to a discussion of mutating rather than alternative memories, taking care to articulate the tension between the two. From time to time mutations become alternatives, challenging rather than supporting the tradition from which they emerged in the first place. 'How far can you go?' becomes a constant refrain in the study of mutation; it will be introduced in this chapter but developed more fully in the conclusion to the book as a whole.

Before embarking on the chapter as a whole, however, there will be some discussion of the phenomenon known as the New Age. Here the overlap with the previous chapter is at its most evident, given the blurred nature of the distinction between new religious movements and the New Age. Clearly these are overlapping categories, but the emphasis in each is rather different. The sections on new religious movements included an important legal element, provoked at least in part by the organizational claims of the movements themselves. The New Age is much less likely to become embroiled in such issues, in that it is less a collection of movements than a coming together of tendencies. An examination of these tendencies and their complex relationships with both the modern world and more traditional forms of religion (an ambivalent affair in both cases) will provide the focus for the first section of this chapter; it leads naturally into the discussion of religious innovation *per se*.

## A 'New Age'

Heelas (1996) has provided an admirably well-organized book on the New Age movement. The word 'well-organized' is carefully chosen in that charting a path through the multiplicity of activities associated with the term 'New Age' is a challenge in itself. Heelas himself is primarily concerned with British and (to a lesser extent) American material, but gives occasional references both to what is happening in continental Europe and to sociological studies of this (1996: 120–1). In terms of the French literature on the subject, Champion (1989, 1992, 1993) provides a way in, coining the evocative phrase 'une nébuleuse mystique-ésotérique' (1993: 751) to characterize the elusive world she is trying to describe.[1] In addition, however, to academic introductions to the field, the New Age movement itself produces a *mountain* of published material, a fact that can be ascertained across Europe in any general bookshop with a section on religion. A large proportion of this section is likely to be taken up with books on or about various manifestations of the New Age; very much more, in fact, than material on mainstream religion or the historic churches. Why this should be so is part of the puzzle; or to ask the same question more directly, who are the people who buy these publications—some of which are expensively produced? A clear-cut answer would reveal a great deal about the constituency involved in New Age activities.[2]

Heelas's book is divided into three parts: the first develops a portrait of the New Age in all its diversity, the second places this material into a theoretical perspective, the third assesses the effectiveness of New Age teaching and

---

[1] In many ways, Champion's approach is similar to that of Heelas, notably the stress on the self and on holism (Champion 1993: 752–3).

[2] Some evidence exists in the literature with respect to the socio-economic background of New Agers; it is clear that middle-class professionals (a book-buying public) are prominent among them.

practices. The following paragraphs select two themes in particular for further amplification—the underlying unity of New Age phenomena and their complex relationship with the modern world. A third element concerns the continuing tensions between the New Age and mainstream religion, an area covered in rather less detail by Heelas.

Trying to get a handle on the sheer diversity of the subject turns out to be easier than expected—what might be termed an organizing principle can be found in the notion of self-spirituality:

Beneath much of the heterogeneity, there is remarkable constancy. Again and again, turning from practice to practice, from publication to publication, indeed, from country to country, one encounters the same (or very similar) *lingua franca* to do with the human (and planetary) condition and how it can be transformed.

This is the language of what shall henceforth be called 'Self-spirituality'. New Agers make the monistic assumption that the Self is sacred. . . . There is thus general agreement that it is essential to shift from our contaminated mode of being— what we are by virtue of socialization—to that realm which constitutes our authentic nature. (Heelas 1996: 2)

Herein lies the *fil conducteur* that allows an observer to make a consistent assessment of what should or should not be included, whether these manifestations occur in the medical world (in the form of alternative therapies), in the ecological sphere (as green movements or alternative life-styles), or in the much more hard-headed environments of management training or commercial publishing. A second common theme can also be discerned: that of holism. New Agers bring back together what in the Western tradition has been separated. Individuals are to be whole and whole implies body, mind, and spirit; they are, in addition, related not only to each other in a multiplicity of ways (not all of them immediately discernible) but also to the universe in all its created forms. In other words they 'connect' (ibid. 33–4). This is equally true internationally, in that the New Age is very much part of the globalization of modern religion; it draws together elements from both the Western and Eastern traditions and repeatedly illustrates the facility of cultural as well as economic interchange in the modern world. Heelas's discussion of India is interesting in this respect. If some aspects of New Age thinking were initially imported into Europe or North America from the East, these are now travelling back again: a 'westernized East' interacts in new ways with the traditional East (ibid. 123) to create particularly Indian versions of the New Age.

The globalization of modern religion, and more specifically of the New Age, is one indicator of its relationship with a rapidly changing world. A more detailed discussion of this relationship reveals profound ambivalence. At one and the same time the New Age is both a continuation or extension of key aspects of modernity (global communication being an obvious illustration), and a rejection of these (preferring, for example, an altogether simpler and more human scale of living). In some ways it affirms the cultural trends of modernity, appealing more often than not to the successful or professional classes; in other ways it retains a counter-cultural element, a more or less explicit rejection of the societal aspirations epitomized in the middle-class life-style. Heelas (1996: pt. 2) deals with this ambivalence by looking at the New Age from two angles: the modern and the post-modern (see also Davie 1994). The latter implies that the New Age is at its core a counter-cultural movement, rejecting or calling into question the capacities of modern society to solve the problems of human living. It favours very different perspectives, with, for example, a strong preference for the natural healing processes of the human body over the impersonal technicalities of modern medicine. It is equally pos-sible to argue, however, that the New Age is a natural extension of modernity rather than a reaction to this. In other words, the emphasis on 'self-realization' is entirely compatible with modern living and indeed depends upon it. From this point of view, the New Age becomes a form of religion ideally suited to the modern world, far more so in fact than traditional forms of religious teach-ing, at least in their Western forms.

It is at this point that the ambivalent relationship with Christian teaching needs further exploration, for at one and the same time the New Age both affirms and contradicts the message of the historic churches (Champion 1993: 753–5; Davie 1994: 41–2). The affirmation can be found in the emphasis on the spiritual—that human beings are indeed body, mind, and spirit and that there is more to life than the accumulation of wealth or knowledge (or as one commentator has put this, 'we are more than the sum of our shopping'). The New Age is essentially non-materialistic and looks elsewhere for human satis-faction and fulfilment; it is in this sense an ally of the traditional churches. But the form that New Age spirituality takes—in other words the absence of obligation to an external authority and the stress on the self and on self-realization—is, clearly, profoundly antithetical to Christian teaching, so much so that a number of more conservative Christians envisage the New Age not only as an antagonist, but as the principal source of evil in the modern world.[3] Not all Christians, however, react in quite such a negative way. Others, for example, have been willing to reconsider at least some elements of traditional teaching in light of New Age insights. Attitudes towards creation and the cre-ation story illustrate this point well. The 'revised' versions or interpretations look at the traditional text in a new light and allow rather more space than previously for the view that humanity is part of creation rather than its undis-puted master (the gendered term is significant)—a view which echoes among other things widespread unease about the future of the created order and humanity's responsibility for it.[4]

[3] An interesting study could be made of the evolution of the 'other' as perceived by evangelicals. In the early post-war period, rationalism was the principal enemy. Communism gradually replaced this through the 1960s and 1970s. Since 1989 New Age ideas are beginning to fill the vacuum left by the fall of communism; it is worth noting that this is a spiritual other rather than a secular ideology (Newport 1998).

[4] Changing attitudes to the environment have already been mentioned in Ch. 3. The Christian response to these changes can be found in the threefold formula 'Justice, peace

A final point concerns the significance of the term 'New Age' itself. Is this indeed something new or is it simply a millennial form of an ongoing feature of European religion—in other words the persistence of informal and from a Christian point of view dubious patterns of religion alongside formal beliefs and practices, in a part of the world where the institutional churches have never been able fully to control every aspect of religious life? The historical existence of popular forms of religion in Europe is an enormous subject which can only be touched on briefly;[5] there can be no doubt, however, that this—like all forms of religion—is something that evolves over time, depending partly on the relative authority of the Christian churches but also on the alternatives available to European populations. The post-war period has seen a decisive shift in both respects: a marked weakening in the influence of Christianity and a rapidly increasing range of alternative possibilities. The idea of a new millennium or a New Age is simply one more factor in these complex evolutions, whose direction is extremely difficult to predict as the twenty-first century gets under way.

Whatever the case the New Age is clearly an important feature of modern European life, sufficient to worry the representatives of the institutional churches and to offer to a significant—if not huge—section of the population new ways of religious thinking and activity. Some of these innovations embrace an acceptance of modern life-styles, others reject them, an ambivalence that will be repeated in the sections that follow. In the mean time and at the very least, the New Age offers further, if not conclusive, evidence that Europeans are only very partially secular populations if by secular is meant 'an increasing approximation of average thinking to the norms of natural and social science' (Martin 1969: 107). This is simply not the case for a large proportion of the European population at the end of the twentieth century.

## Two Case Studies of Catholic Innovation

The two case studies which follow are totally different in that they describe tightly organized confessional movements, in some ways the complete antithesis of the New Age. Each, however, portrays an organization faced with the continuing tension of Christian teaching: how to be in but not of the world (an ambivalence implicit, if not always explicit, in New Age dealings with modernity). Being in but not of the world is, moreover, a tension that becomes ever more complicated depending on how 'the world' is perceived. Is this something essentially benign, from which both Christian churches and Christian people can learn and whose insights (of whatever kind) bring posi-

and a sustainable society'—the idea of a sustainable society joined the former two in the course of the 1990s.

[5] Thomas (1971) and Obelkevich (1976) are classics in this field.

tive advantages for human living? Or is the world something far more sinister, necessarily harmful to the essence of Christianity and about which Christians should be very careful indeed, at all times keeping a safe, not to say distrustful, distance?

Which of these views predominates depends on a multiplicity of factors: quite clearly they change over time and relate to the dominant cultural mood; they will also vary between different sections of the religious constituency, who perceive the possible advantages and disadvantages of worldly activity in contrasting ways.[6] A full discussion of these shifts and balances goes well beyond the scope of this chapter (it would involve a history of social and cultural change in a global perspective). It is, however, crucial to grasp the scale of the shift in the international—never mind European—'state of mind' that took place between the optimism of the 1960s and the far more cautious assessment of possibilities that gradually became the norm a decade or so later.

Whichever way you look at it, the 1960s posed an enormous challenge to the churches; this was a decade in which all institutional forms of authority were radically questioned and in which secular optimism was at an all-time high—it offered a very attractive alternative. This, after all, was the decade in which man (*sic*) landed on the moon. Ten years later, global recession (usually associated with the oil crisis of the early 1970s) was taking hold, public expenditure was under pressure and unemployment rising. Life for many Europeans was considerably less certain than many had anticipated and the secular alternatives looked far less secure than they had done when economies were expanding in a manner that appeared to be limitless.

These are the shifting parameters of post-war Europe. Within Catholicism (and indeed its significance spreads well beyond the Catholic community itself) a further, almost unimaginable change took place in the 1960s in the form of the Second Vatican Council. Undoubtedly this is a form of innovation in itself, so radical and so widespread that Hastings describes it as the most important ecclesiastical event of the century, never mind of the 1960s (Hastings 1986: 525). It is clear, moreover, that in terms of the rather more limited argument of this chapter, the Council represents a movement towards the world, itself perceived more positively than had previously been the case; it represented, in its own phrase, an *aggiornamento* or bringing up to date of the Catholic Church in line with modern, or at least more modern, ways of doing things. Saying Mass in the vernacular is one of the most visible examples of this process; so, too, is the recognition of non-Catholic Christian churches as entities with whom dialogue could take place.

Other Catholic movements fit the same sort of model; some of these predate the Council by several decades whilst others more or less coincide with it. Catholic Action illustrates the former, emerging in a variety of European countries in the interwar period. It was the voluminous writings of Pope Pius XI

[6] See Davie (1994: ch. 3) for a discussion of such changes in the British context.

(1922–39) that gave to Catholic Action 'a charter, a spirit, and an apocalyptic vision' (Geaney 1967: 262). Moreover, a strong emphasis lay on praxis: in an encounter with the needs of the world, which, though real, should be addressed according to the principles of social justice and Christian charity. There was, in other words, an optimism about the world; a sense that—given the right conditions—the values of the world are in keeping with the gospel. The discerning member of Catholic Action should be alert to these signs not only of commonality, but of the common good and be trained to build them up (De Antonelis 1987). Liberation theology is a more extreme statement of the same approach, bringing together the notion of eternal salvation (redemption) and the struggle for social justice (liberation). Essentially a Latin American movement, it found public affirmation at the Second General Conference of the Latin American Bishops at Medellín in 1968. Articulating an 'option for the poor', base communities became the units in which such thinking was put into practice. Discussions of everyday life in difficult conditions led to calls for action. Biblical themes of love and justice translated themselves into social activism, often of a radical nature.

This, briefly, is the background, both secular and religious, against which to see the rather different forms of innovation described below. Both movements—Opus Dei and Communione e Liberazione—are Catholic in inspiration but have evolved in ways rather different from those so far discussed. They are far more suspicious of the world, but find innovative ways of coming to terms with it. Both, moreover, are highly controversial. Their respective histories and organizations will be outlined before considering a number of cross-cutting themes.

## *Opus Dei*

Opus Dei has been described as 'the doyen of the neo-conservative movements in the Catholic Church' (Walsh 1992: 176). The phrase 'neo-conservative' provides the key to understanding this complex, influential, and much-discussed movement. At one and the same time, Opus Dei *both* challenges the traditional—in terms, for example, of the economic and financial institutions of Franco's Spain (initiating reforms that were long overdue), *and* maintains the status quo in relation to the political sphere. (The latter is hardly surprising given that improvements in the Spanish economy in the 1950s and 1960s significantly advantaged the middle class, bolstering, almost inevitably, their support for the existing political order.) The moral conservatism of the movement is even more marked.

What then were the origins of Opus Dei and why has it become so controversial?[7] It is associated with one man in particular: José Maria Escrivà de

---

[7] One index of the degree of the controversy can be found in the number of entries on Opus Dei to be found on the Internet—both the site sponsored by the movement itself (www.opusdei.org) and those which use the Web to reveal what they feel are the more sinister aspects of the organization.

Balaguer, who not only founded Opus Dei (in 1928), but became and remained its leader and inspiration until his death in 1975. Amid considerable controversy Escrivà was beatified in 1992—an event interpreted by many as further evidence of Opus' extensive influence within the Church. Organizationally Opus went through several stages in its early years. What eventually emerged was a primarily lay movement with separate organizations for men and for women. An article in the *New Catholic Encyclopaedia* (1967) describes the movement as follows:

an association of the faithful, whose members dedicate themselves entirely to the apostolate and to the practice of an intense spiritual life in the world without abandoning their own social environment or the exercise of their profession or secular occupation. The purpose of *Opus Dei* is to spread the life of sanctity among people of all walks of life, especially among those of intellectual pursuits. (Gramunt 1967: 709–10)

Opus Dei is divided into different membership categories: numeraries, who pledge to remain celibate and live in Opus Dei houses; associates, who take vows of poverty, chastity, and obedience but for family reasons do not live in designated houses; supernumeraries (the majority of Opus Dei members), who are married and continue living in the secular world; priests, who belong to the Society of the Holy Cross; and co-operators, who offer various kinds of support but are not considered to be members. Nearly 80,000 people belong to the movement world-wide; 30,000 of these are Spanish.

Walsh (1992) considers a number of perspectives from which Opus Dei can be understood in sociological terms: as a religious order, as a new religious movement, or simply as a movement (one among many) within the Catholic Church. Each of these suggestions has advantages and disadvantages. Clearly Opus displays some of the characteristics of a religious order but is essentially a grouping of lay people very much in the world, rather than an order set apart. Most members are married, remain in secular employment, and perceive their calling in these terms. Perspectives from the literature on new religious movements—attractive to those who note the difficulties that some members have had in leaving Opus and the authoritarian nature of its structures—fit only very partially with an organization whose emphasis on and loyalty to traditional Catholic teaching is paramount. Finally, Opus is indeed one movement amongst others within the Catholic Church, but has at the same time a particular status—that of a personal prelature achieved in 1982 (the date of its most recent constitution). A personal prelature is a relatively new idea within Catholicism; it amounts in effect to a world-wide diocese with a certain independence from local bishops. Opus Dei is the only organization to merit such a status within the Catholic Church at the present time.

A defining moment came with the Second Vatican Council. In some ways Opus anticipated the Council in its developed emphasis on the lay Christian and his or her role in the life of the church. In this respect it also anticipated the dramatic decline in vocations to the priesthood in the European context

(Pérez Vilariño 1997). In other ways, however, Escrivà was profoundly out of sympathy with the Council and distressed by its recommendations. *Aggiornamento* (accommodation with the world) was not what he or Opus Dei stood for and should be rigorously resisted. Changes in liturgy, for example, were seen as disruptive rather than liberating and firmly controlled within Opus Dei houses; priests continued to celebrate in Latin and with their backs to the congregation.

A rejection of *aggiornamento* is, however, only half the story for in terms of the economy, there is a markedly different emphasis: one that affirms economic success, almost to the point of indulgence (an attitude epitomized in the 'dinner table apostolate'). The legitimacy of personal gain and professional advancement is entirely in keeping with Opus values, a position which inevitably endorses a middle-class life-style. The 'apostolate of non-giving' is the logical conclusion of this stance—the complete antithesis of 'an option for the poor' (Walsh 1992: 108). At one and the same time then (rather like the New Age, from which it could hardly be more different) Opus both affirms and rejects the values of modernity. It sits easily alongside capitalist enterprise, not least in terms of its own organizational wealth, but uses such assets to resist the advance of modernity in other ways—notably in the political and the moral spheres.

## *Communione e Liberazione*

Communione e Liberazione grew out of an Italian student organization which began life in the 1950s. The original movement was known as Gioventù Studentesca; it was the inspiration of Mgr. Luigi Giussani, who gathered together students from a high school in Milan, a part of Italy where the movement continues to flourish. The name Communione e Liberazione came later (1969), chosen to express the conviction that the Christian event lived out in communion is the foundation of an authentic liberation. Numbers in Italy are estimated at 100,000; international representation is growing, with groups in most parts of the world.[8]

From a sociological point of view, the most useful source of information is the book-length case study of Communione e Liberazione published in French in 1989 (Abbruzzese 1989), the more so given the developed discussion in this text of the relationship between the movement and contemporary social change. Abbruzzese sets the affirmation and development of *Communione et Liberazione* in Italian society of the 1970s—that is, in the midst of an economic, political, and cultural crisis. This decade of uncertainty was felt especially sharply in Italy, where economic difficulties and high levels of unemployment were compounded by political prevarication and acts of terrorism of a particularly brutal kind (Abbruzzese 1989: 136, 155). Side by side

---

[8] Information from the Communione e Liberazione website, www. communioneliberazione.org.

with such manifest economic and social unease came the realization that the Catholic Church could no longer command the allegiance of substantial numbers of Italians. The results of the referenda on divorce in 1974 and on abortion in 1981 are often cited as evidence for this assertion. The reality is, however, rather more complex in that it becomes increasingly clear that significant elements within the Catholic Church (not least sections of the Catholic Action movement) were beginning to wonder how far the Catholic Church *should* participate in the political process with respect to moral decision-making, a shift in perspective which indicates a step back from the world rather than renewed commitment to it.

Within this confusing situation, Abbruzzese places Communione e Liberazione firmly on the side of the conservative forces in terms of moral order (Abbruzzese 1989: 154). Here was a movement that affirmed both the distinctiveness of Catholic teaching and the right (indeed the duty) to articulate this view within the political process. The contrast with Catholic Action could hardly be more marked. Indeed Abbruzzese uses this contrast to illustrate the innovative nature of Communione e Liberazione. The discussion fits squarely within the argument of this chapter in that it asks how particular sections of the modern church come to terms with the values of the world, in a society which has lost any illusions it might have had with respect both to modernity itself and to the cultural climate it engenders (Abbruzzese 1989: 157).

Two possibilities emerge: the first (already described) is epitomized by Catholic Action, the second by Communione e Liberazione—the latter a movement as complex as it is distinctive. On one hand the thrust is reactive: Communione e Liberazione becomes the representative of a particular form of Catholicism, separated from the world and hostile to the facile optimisms of earlier decades. On the other, it is pro-active: not turning its back on the world but looking instead for new modes of insertion—offering a solid base for a generation of young people disillusioned by the failures of the society of which they are part. The originality of Communione e Liberazione lies in the manner in which this is done. It is a movement that confronts modernity on the basis of its own distinctive structure. Moral authority comes from the charismatic nature of its leadership, not the rational-legal representations of modern bureaucracies. Hence the emphasis on a developed spirituality which empowers the membership both to confront and to negotiate the pressures of modern living. The notion of community must be constantly reaffirmed to permit effective engagement with economic and social realities. The mode of engagement is, moreover, highly modern—whether in terms of education (the university world), political life, the economy (engagement with the market and the organization of labour), or the mass media and the publishing world, Communione e Liberazione has made its mark in Italian society.

How, then, does the material relating to these two movements fit into the underlying theme of innovation? Both, it seems, are representative of a wider category within the religious life of the modern world—groups, that is, that use the means of modernity to oppose its message. In North America, a similar combination can be found in the world of televangelism, a form of religious communication that has made relatively little impact in post-war Europe (see Chapter 6). Pairing conservative Catholic movements with American televangelists may seem an unlikely combination but the essential paradox is the same in each case. Both perceive the world negatively; both, however, are quick to appreciate the economic and technological potential of modernity—a proper use of these facilities permits possibilities unknown in previous generations.

In drawing such elements together, it is difficult to avoid altogether the concept of fundamentalism, so frequently misunderstood in sociological thinking.[9] It is significant that a recent discussion of this term by Italian sociologists (Pace and Guolo 1998) involves its possible extension to certain kinds of Catholic organizations, notably Communione e Liberazione (1998: 73–84). The movement is seen as a 'fondamentalismo ben temperato'; it is, in other words, a partial illustration of fundamentalism, displaying some of the 'family resemblances' (see note 9) but lacking any sustained reference to a sacred text. The profoundly ambiguous relationship with the modern world (using the means of modernity to subvert its ends) is, however, the crucial point. In this respect the Catholic movements described in this section fit the model; in so doing they illustrate an important set of innovations within the religious life of modern Europe.

## Sociological Approaches to Religious Innovation

There are, however, other possibilities for change in religious life and at this point it is important to pick up illustrations from previous chapters. One obvious example can be found in the gradual acceptance of women in the professional ministries of most Protestant churches in Europe, the real significance of which has yet to be seen. Parallel to this (indeed in some respects part of the same reassessment) is the far greater role given to laypeople than in previous decades in the churches as a whole. This is equally true in both Catholic and Protestant circles and leads to very different divisions of labour in ecclesiastical organizations. A third shift might be seen in the relative attractiveness to

---

[9] An excellent source of information on the nature and forms of fundamentalism can be found in the publications of the Fundamentalism Project, based at the University of Chicago through most of the 1990s. These volumes are edited by Martin Marty and Scott Appleby. The last of these includes a definition of fundamentalism, pointing out the 'family resemblances' between different movements—in other words an 'ideal type' in the Weberian sense (Marty and Appleby 1995). It is interesting that Communione e Liberazione is one of the very few European case studies covered in the Project as a whole (Zadra 1994; Marty and Appleby 1995).

young people of one-off or special occasions rather than regular week-by-week attendance at Mass. The Journées mondiales de la Jeunesse in August 1997 is simply an international version of a wider tendency.[10] The annual Greenbelt Festival in England is a Protestant version of the same sort of thing, albeit with a sharper doctrinal edge in view of its evangelical inspiration.

Such events are not necessarily the preserve of young people; the attractiveness of an experiential or emotional element in such gatherings—more important, perhaps, than the historical or cultural dimensions—can be seen in the charismatic movement as a whole, both in its Catholic and Protestant forms. Almost all European churches have been subject to such tendencies in the later post-war decades, tendencies which are welcomed up to a point by those with institutional responsibilities (they can after all be life-giving), but which are regarded, inevitably, with a certain degree of suspicion. Tensions between the charismatic group and the host institution are almost unavoidable as conventional forms of authority are challenged in the name of something both more immediate and more personal.[11] Sometimes the differences of opinion or of worship style can be contained within the church in question; at other times they lead (painfully) to schism and the formation of new communities.

A rather different and in many ways very impressive embodiment of charismatic Christianity can, however, be found in the forms of worship characteristic of the Afro-Caribbean churches of modern Britain. Albeit a special case, these churches are some of the most vibrant Christian communities in Europe at the turn of the millennium. It is their dual nature that makes them special: in some ways they are part of the Christian mainstream, but in others they exemplify the features of immigrant churches—notably the relative activity of their members and a distinctive style of worship. They form a natural and highly effective focus for the Afro-Caribbean communities in post-war Britain.[12]

The last part of this chapter will consider three further examples of religious innovation. Two of these pick up the theme of the special occasion: the first comes from Germany, the second from Scandinavia. The final illustration is a blend of old and new in the form of local religious festivals in Spain—here it is the innovative nature of the combination that counts rather

---

[10] The Paris meeting itself was but the latest in a whole series of encounters between the Pope and young people. Earlier meetings were held in Santiago de Compostela and Denver.

[11] The débâcle of what became known as 'The Nine O'Clock Service' in Sheffield (culminating in May 1996) illustrates the negative side of these tendencies; this was a case in which charisma was seriously misused. The Service began as an evening meeting for young people under Anglican auspices; its leader was an ordained priest. Gradually, he began to abuse his position, demanding sexual as well as other favours from the female faithful, some of whom were very young.

[12] A partial parallel might be discovered in the Hungarian Catholics living in Slovakia. They are indeed Catholics, but at the same time distinct from the Hungarian majority.

than newness in itself (the festivals themselves are very ancient). All three examples quite clearly edge towards the notion of pilgrimage, an increasingly popular form of religious life in modern Europe. In this respect they form a bridge between this chapter and the next, in which there will be a greater emphasis on a particular place or building as a positive element or goal in the religious experience in question. In this chapter, the stress lies on the act of gathering or coming together rather than on the place in which this occurs. The line between the two is, however, a fine one and should not be applied too rigorously.

## The German Kirchentag

The Protestant Church in Germany initiated the idea of the 'Kirchentag' in 1949 with the intention of gathering, encouraging, and instructing the laity (Lukatis 1989). The immediate post-war period was a time of reconstruction for both churches and society in Germany, a process that put an inevitable stress on matters internal to the organization rather than the prophetic voice. The Kirchentag attempted to counteract this tendency and to offer a wider perspective on the world. Regular meetings established themselves soon after, settling to a pattern of every two years (similar events for the Catholic Church are held in intervening years). The 1997 meeting was held in Leipzig, the first to take place in the former East since 1989. Kirchentag meetings last for four days and draw around 100,000 participants for the full duration of the meeting (and several tens of thousands more in terms of casual visitors). One obvious function in this respect is to offer to German Protestants the experience of fellowship in a large gathering at a time when regular attendance is diminishing in most German parishes. The stress on an independent lay movement is crucial—manifested amongst other things in the choice of speakers (the preserve of the Kirchentag committee, not the church authorities).

Lukatis (1989) has analysed both the participants themselves and their expectations at three meetings of the Kirchentag in the 1980s. Young people and young adults constitute by far the largest category of visitors and come mostly from well-educated sections of German society. They come with the expectation of relating their faith to socio-political problems but with a parallel stress on self-discovery. Simply being there is important, especially the opportunity to be with large numbers of like-minded young people. The stress on youth ensures a constantly renewed constituency, though significant numbers return for a second time. The relationship with parish life and regular churchgoing is ambivalent; in some ways the meetings reinforce the message of the local church, in other ways it is challenged. Unsurprisingly the Kirchentag offers to those disillusioned by parish life an opportunity to re-establish the connections between faith and life. For others, however, the Kirchentag is the positive culmination of preparation in the parishes and forms a natural expansion of what goes on week by week.

The stress on gathering for a special occasion is none the less important—the Kirchentag takes people away from the immediate locality or community. A temporary 'utopia' is created in which new and different forms of worship and fellowship are experienced and in which the elements of a better society are imagined and discussed. Generation gaps diminish as common experiences (including somewhat primitive conditions) forge common bonds. Following Lukatis (who draws in particular on the German literature in this field), such experiences are equally associated with pilgrimage, described by Brückner (1984) as a form of 'sanctioned opting-out of everyday events'. The difference lies in the location. Kirchentag meetings do not take place in specially denoted sacred places; indeed in many ways they concern a metaphorical journey to the profane (not the sacred) in a sustained attempt to relate aspects of Christian teaching to the realities of the modern world.

## The Thomas Mass in Finland

The Thomas Mass is both similar and different. Its origins lie in the attempts by the Finnish Lutheran Church to attract more people to the worshipping life of the church. The Thomas Mass has become the most successful of these attempts; moreover, it has been carefully documented from a sociological point of view by the Research Institute of the Lutheran Church in Finland (Kauppinen 1992). The first Thomas Mass was celebrated in the Agricola Church in Helsinki in 1988, a practice which has subsequently spread to all the major towns of Finland and indeed beyond—achieving a certain institutional status. Kauppinen's 1991 study relates to the situation in Tampere, a city to the north of Helsinki, which has hosted the Mass since 1989—interestingly the first of these events coincided with the Kirchentag held in that city.

The most striking fact about the Thomas Mass is its capacity to fill the church in which it takes place, attracting attendances that are five times those on an average Sunday.[13] The Mass itself combines both old and new elements. The structure is given by the traditional liturgy; this, however, is used flexibly, allowing considerable room for manœuvre (notably in the style of prayer and music). The result is a service significantly longer than most, normally lasting for two hours or more. The reference to Thomas in its title is deliberate—the Mass is constructed with the intention of attracting doubters or half-believers, those in other words on the edge of the church rather than at its centre. In terms of those it does attract, the statistics are noteworthy, especially in terms of age and social class. The Thomas Mass draws people of all age-groups and from a diversity of social backgrounds. Attempts to be equally inclusive in terms of gender have been less successful in a country where the contrast

---

[13] It is important to remember, however, that the total figures for the whole series of Thomas Masses in Tampere remains a small fraction of the churchgoing population as a whole. An occasional large event does not compensate for the loss of attenders on a regular basis (Kauppinen 1992: 7).

between men and women in religious life is particularly marked; the women continue to dominate. It is also clear that the Thomas Mass in Tampere draws people from all over the city and not only from the immediate neighbourhood (in this respect it is at least as successful as the major sporting or musical events in the area). The turnover of participants is high—a quarter of those attending in 1991 were first-timers.

A further point is also significant: the media image of the Thomas Mass (including presentations in the secular press) is extremely positive. The Mass is commended for its openness, the lay participation, the presence of young people, and the large number of people present. Why do they come? They come first for a eucharistic celebration, although only two-thirds of the con- gregation take communion. The music—distinctive, yet familiar—is a further attraction together with an evident sense of unity (in the sense of participat- ing in an act of worship with a great variety of people). The sharing of the peace becomes a significant factor in this respect.[14] Prayer is central and reflects the emphasis of the Mass on silence and contemplation rather than the spoken word, a considerable shift given the traditional patterns of worship in the Lutheran churches of Northern Europe. The relative freedom of the liturgy is symbolized by the movement of people within the church in the course of worship. Part of their movement, however, is prompted by requests for intercessory prayer; some two hundred are deposited at each service, reflecting a mass of spiritual questions in the midst of modern living. Human needs (both individual and collective) are brought to the Mass in the know- ledge that prayer will continue on behalf of those that have asked—the notion of vicariousness appears once again. How this should be managed in the cir- cumstance of European living at the turn of the millennium preoccupies Kauppinen in the second part of his monograph. He concludes with the sug- gestions that the Thomas Mass should become a specialized form of urban ministry, alongside rather than replacing more traditional liturgies, and that diversity should be seen as a resource, as potential richness, not—as is often the case in the Finnish Church—as evidence of 'a fall from grace' (Kauppinen 1992: 60).

## Local Festivals in Spain

The last example is quite different and returns once again to Spain. The mate- rial is taken from an anthropological account of local religious festivals, which remain extraordinarily popular in a part of Europe where the fall in religious practice in the later post-war decades has been particularly marked (Albert- Llorca 1996). In assessing the significance of these events, it is important to remember that they take place in a multiplicity of locations, only some of which (the Holy Week celebrations in Seville, for example) are known outside

---

[14] In an event of this size it is possible to share the peace without jeopardizing anonymity (a much more difficult combination in the local parish).

the country. At a regional level (not least in terms of the local media), the festival is given sustained attention; it is a major event for the population, growing rather than diminishing in significance.[15] How, though, should these manifestations be understood? Are they 'religious' in any conventional understanding of the term or are they simply spectacles based on local folklore encouraged by the growth in the tourist industry? This is the central question addressed by Albert-Llorca on the basis of her close observation of a series of festivals in Valencia—both those associated with the celebration of 'Moors and Christians' and those associated with the *fallas* (funeral pyres), where huge, ornate, and costly statues are ceremonially burnt.

A central theme in her presentation lies in the evolving meaning of 'local' and its significance in a late-modern society. The attachment to locality (to a *pueblo*) has always been strong in Spanish society, cemented historically by devotion to a local virgin or a local saint (Christian 1972, 1989). As the nature of modern living enforces both greater centralization and economies of scale, the sense of locality might well diminish accordingly. This, it seems, has not occurred in Spain in the way it has in other parts of Europe. It follows that the means for expressing such loyalties within the Spanish context become more rather than less significant at the close of the twentieth century.

Devotion to the local virgin and to the place associated with her presence are, moreover, part and parcel of this process. Indeed Albert-Llorca offers convincing evidence for elaboration, rather than diminution, in the religious dimension of local festivities. In Valencia itself, for example, the presentation of flowers to the Virgin des Desemparats has become ever more central in the festival of the *fallas*, symbolizing the unity of the city—the coming together of different sections of the community, each of which burn their *falla*, but create symbolically an immense garment of flowers for the Virgin (1996: 245–6). Such gestures are described in some detail and assessed sociologically. In terms of the latter Albert-Llorca argues convincingly that such behaviour is genuinely religious (to say otherwise is to misunderstand it). She does not, however, claim that it represents an expression of Catholicism in its more conventional forms. Indeed there are numerous examples in Albert-Llorca's text of local dignitaries who do not 'believe' in any credal sense, but who see no incompatibility between their participation in the local festivities (including the religious aspects of this) and their formal stance vis-à-vis the church. This is not a question of religion versus non-religion, but of different manifestations of the sacred. Obligations, moreover, can be equally developed in both cases: non-participation on the part of local dignitaries in the religious aspects of these festivities would not be tolerated.

---

[15] Rather as an aside Albert-Llorca remarks that the change in attitudes to women is one reason for the growth in the numbers of participants in some places: women are now welcomed on an equal footing with men into the fraternities responsible for the enactments of past events (1996: 236).

Albert-Llorca appreciates the complexities of the situation. Local festivals in this part of Spain (and indeed other parts) are not simply hangovers from the past. They perform an important function in a rapidly modernizing society. Up to a point they illustrate the distinctiveness of the Spanish case in modern Europe, not least its attachment to locality. More than that, however, they reveal the inherent tension in the meeting of tradition and modernity, a tension that can lead to immense creativity—in, for example, the detail of each and every one of these festivals and the seriousness with which participants assume their roles. This is a more positive view than one which regards tradition and modernity as mutually exclusive categories, an attitude which will necessarily fail to appreciate not only the essentially modern nature of the local festival, but also the significance of the religious factor within it.

# Mutating Memory

Mutation in a scientific sense implies a change in genetic form in order that the species in question will be more suitably adapted to its environment. In many ways this is exactly the process that this chapter has tried to describe (using a variety of case studies), bearing in mind that different religious organizations have different ideas about what 'more suitably adapted to its environment' might mean. The emphasis lies, however, on the process just as much as on the substance of the mutation; how it occurs and why is as important as what happens.

One means of illustrating this point in a different way might be to link the material in this chapter with the alternatives presented in the last, for an obvious example of 'mutation' can be found in diaspora communities. Religious minorities are never able to behave in the ways that majorities do, a fact that has already been emphasized. They have instead to find new ways of surviving, always asking themselves whether this or that course of action will be appropriate and how far they should go in adapting to the mainstream culture. Many of the points of conflict which arise occur when the mainstream culture asks for one thing and the minority community cannot deliver. The lack of mutual comprehension is the problem: what appears reasonable on one side of the dispute is seen in an entirely different light on the other. According to the majority of the British populations, Muslims were 'unreasonable' in their demands that Salman Rushdie's book should be banned. For Muslims, on the other hand, the book was blasphemous and banning but the logical conclusion, once this was understood. In France, the educational authorities thought that the wearing of a *foulard* in the school system was a step too far; those, however, who considered this not only a normal but a necessary item of Muslim dress for young women thought it 'unreasonable' to have the *foulard* forbidden in the establishments of education to which their daughters or sisters were entitled.

A second stage in the argument follows from this: are Christians in modern Europe now themselves in a diaspora situation, at least *de facto* if not *de jure*, in which case some of the same arguments would begin to apply? A fuller answer to this question will form one theme in the concluding chapter, where an attempt will be made to assess how much of the Christian memory is still intact. At this point, it is sufficient to stress once again that the weight of tradition and culture remain firmly on the side of the Christian churches and that innovation within the Christian tradition is as much a feature of European life as alternatives outside this. But this in turn provokes a subsequent question: are such innovations truly Christian? How malleable, in other words, is the Christian tradition in terms of innovation and who is going to decide where the limits lie? Or to put the question in a different way, when does a mutation become a distinct, different, and possibly competing species? A sociologist can indicate the nature of the tension; setting the limits, however, must be the task of a different discipline.[16] Both debates, however, are necessarily ongoing in that the tension of being in the world but not of it can never be fully resolved. The world is constantly changing, inviting in every generation new ways of responding or reacting to this. Yesterday's answers are, almost by definition, inadequate.

---

[16] Lodge (1980) provides a fictional account of precisely this process. How far can the church go in adapting to the world before it loses its entire *raison d'être*?

# NINE

# *Aesthetic or Symbolic Memory: The Cultural Sphere*

A FULL discussion of pilgrimage has been held over until this chapter, which introduces a different set of elements into the understanding of memory. These include the significance of a particular place or building which in itself embodies something special; simply being there is important, quite apart from what you do or who you are. Pilgrimage, however, is only the starting point: from here the discussion moves outwards to a variety of aesthetic or cultural fields in which religious memory can find expression. In order to do this, the argument works at two levels. The initial step is institutional and focuses in particular on the connections between cathedrals and museums. Examining the links between these evidently overlapping institutions and the motives of the people who enter each or both of them is a fascinating area of enquiry. The second level is cultural and concerns the equally intricate relationship between the religious and the aesthetic. Both, for example, find inspiration (amongst other things) in understanding better the meaning of life and the place of the individual person in the cosmos but do this in different, if closely connected, ways.

'Telling the story' becomes a key phrase in this chapter: stories that are told in stone, in art, in music, and in literature. The examples offered as illustrations are, however, highly selective; they are chosen to exemplify a particular point or theme, not to provide anything that might be considered a complete or coherent account of the European artistic heritage in so far as this relates to religion. The point in fact lies elsewhere, in the capacities of Europeans to 'read' or 'hear' the story that is being told. It is in this idea that the chapter joins up with those that have preceded it, notably the passages that refer to the changing capacities of European generations to understand what the artist or architect is attempting to portray. It is, in other words, the interaction between art and its audience that becomes the key to what can, or can no longer, be considered a memory in Europe at the turn of the millennium.

# Pilgrimage and Place

The popularity of pilgrimage in the late twentieth century is undeniable. It can be documented in the increasing number of pilgrims year on year in almost all the major pilgrimage sites of Europe (Giuriati and Lanzi Arzenton 1992)[1] and in the literature produced to facilitate such journeyings (evident in bookshops all over the continent).[2] A similar tendency is reflected at a more mundane level in the increasing flow of visitors to religious buildings in general, whether these be designated pilgrimage sites or not (English cathedrals are an excellent example of this tendency). What, though, is the sociological significance of these rising figures? Are these modern visitors simply spiritual dilettantes, flitting from one site to another as part of their holiday experience, or are their visits symptomatic of something more profound in the religious life of Europe? In answering this question, it is important to grasp from the outset that the line between pilgrimage and tourism (even religious tourism) is extremely difficult to draw. Pilgrims and tourists must be recognized as overlapping categories and one reason, surely, for the apparent growth in the number of pilgrims is, simply, the relative ease of travel in late modernity; it is very much easier than it used to be to get to the sites in question (Urry 1990; Lash and Urry 1994). But—following exactly the same logic—it is equally easy to get everywhere else; the heritage industry is booming (Walsh 1992). So why do increasing numbers of people seek out the spiritual in their choice of destinations? Some of the answers may emerge in the paragraphs that follow.

The chosen destinations are both old and new: they range from the medieval routes west to the shrine of St James at Santiago de Compostela in northern Spain, through the Marian shrines that have established themselves at various points in European history (including Częstochowa in Poland, Lourdes in the Pyrenees, Fatima in Portugal, and Medjugorje in Croatia), to

---

[1] Hard facts and figures are not easy to obtain, partly because of the difficulty of classifying visitors—which ones are pilgrims and which are not. Giuriati and Lanzi Arzenton (1992) is none the less a useful source, documenting a noticeable rise in numbers across the various Marian shrines between the late 1970s and mid 1980s, a rise sustained thereafter. At the time of their investigation Lourdes welcomed 4–5 million per annum and Fatima over 2 million; the numbers at Medjugorje had not yet stabilized. Iona—a tiny and almost inaccessible island on the west coast of Scotland—welcomed 200,000 people in 1997; Taizé expects between 3,000 and 6,000 young people each week throughout the summer period. Statistical indicators are complemented by a different source of information—the growing number of accounts by journalists/pilgrims who visit the major shrines of Europe and then write them up as journeys of spiritual discovery (see e.g. Seward 1993; Tóibín 1994).

[2] Such literature is eclectic and covers a wide range of activities. At one end are the major pilgrimage sites of Europe; at the other are carefully compiled lists of convents, monasteries, and retreat houses ready to welcome all types of people. Many of the latter are anxious to escape the atmosphere of conventional tourist sites, opting instead for the simplicity of a religious house (often, it must be said, a very much cheaper option). It is as necessary to book ahead for these as it is for accommodation in a ski resort.

more recent points of reference such as Iona in western Scotland or Taizé in eastern France. The fact that all of them display the same tendencies towards growth is significant in itself, tendencies which can be explained in terms of both commonality and difference. Santiago, for instance, has clearly benefited not only from renewed attention to the spiritual, but also from an impressive injection of European money into the pilgrim route across northern Spain—effectively turning this into an international commodity, particularly, though by no means exclusively, in Years of the Saint (i.e. when the feast of St James falls on a Sunday). It is equally clear that the Spanish tourist board has played a major part in this undertaking. The emergence of Częstochowa is rather different. The Jasna Góra Monastery has been a place of pilgrimage for centuries, and particularly so since the time of the Swedish invasion of Poland in the seventeenth century. The monastery, however, took on a new significance under the communist domination of Central Europe in the post-war period and became a gathering point for Polish (and indeed European) Catholicism; it was visited by the Pope at critical moments in the years preceding 1989. The painting of the Virgin it houses became, moreover, an icon of Polish resistance.[3] Lourdes, Fatima, and Medjugorje, in contrast, are places associated with appearances of the Virgin (Lourdes in 1858, Fatima in 1917, and Medjugorje from 1981). All report increasing numbers of visitors in recent decades (Giuriati and Lanzi Arzenton 1992: 20–1), despite, in the case of Medjugorje, the vicissitudes of war. The Catholic Church keeps a watchful eye on the healing ministries associated with these places, taking great pains to authenticate any claims to miraculous cures. The shrine at Medjugorje is particularly problematic; despite growing popular appeal the appearances of the Virgin have never been fully legitimated by the Catholic authorities.[4] Iona and Taizé, finally, have a different sort of history. Iona is an ancient religious site on the west coast of Scotland from which St Columba brought Christianity to northern Britain; the present community, however, dates from the late 1930s and grew initially as a place of retreat for those working in inner-city Glasgow. Taizé goes back to the war years but 'took off' as a place of pilgrimage in the middle decades of the post-war period. Neither Iona nor Taizé are Catholic in origin and both welcome visitors of all denominations; each, moreover, has developed its own style of spirituality which has become associated with the place in question. Taizé music, for example, is an industry in its own right.

Who, then, are the pilgrims? Giuriati and Lanzi Arzenton (1992: 25–35) produce a profile of the typical pilgrim visiting the major Marian shrines of Europe in the late 1980s (their study includes Lourdes, Fatima, and

---

[3] In addition to the people coming to the icon, the icon was also taken to the people in the communist period. When even this was disallowed by the communist authorities, simply the frame was taken in procession—a powerful illustration of symbolic representation (Micewski 1982: 274). (Information from Irena Borowik, Feb. 1998.)

[4] Bax (1996) explains this ambivalence in terms of the shifting power balance between the diocesan regime in Mostar and the Franciscan presence in this part of Croatia.

Medjugorje). Large numbers are relatively young (i.e. under 30), there are more women than men (except at Medjugorje), and about half are making the visit for the first time. Most are regular Mass attenders. Relatively few are simply tourists, in that the great majority indicate that they come with a religious motive of some kind. The precise nature of these motives varies, however; they also evolve through the course of the visit as the pilgrim reflects on what he or she is doing. Watching the patient queue of pilgrims (at the grotto in Lourdes for example) is indeed a moving experience; it is hard to doubt the sincerity of what is going on, bearing in mind the evident ill-health of a substantial proportion of participants. Equally impressive are the large numbers of young people who spend some weeks at the shrine in the summer in order to help those who are ill or unable to walk the considerable distances involved. Indeed the whole enterprise offers a striking combination: explicitly spiritual aims run alongside the rational organization of modern tourism, with its rapid turnovers, practical requirements, and commercial acumen (some of it of a very tawdry nature). Pilgrimage, in this sense, builds on to rather than contradicts the infrastructure of modern life, just as the possibility of miraculous healing complements rather than replaces modern medicine (some patients are pushed to the grotto attached to complex medical apparatus).

The process, moreover, is ongoing. The beatification of Padre Pio in Rome in May 1999 illustrates the continuing power of the 'miraculous' in the lives of many very ordinary Europeans. Despite—or perhaps because of—huge popularity during his lifetime, Padre Pio suffered periodically at the hands of the ecclesiastical authorities. In this sense miracles are often contentious in that they challenge conventional religious authority.[5] They do not, however, appear incompatible with (1) daily European living even at the turn of the millennium (images of Padre Pio are part of the everyday lives of many Italians—in their homes, cafes, and local shops) or (2) modern forms of communication (Padre Pio, like most of the major pilgrimage sites in this chapter, has his own dedicated website—in his case sustained primarily by devotees in the United States).

Taizé offers a further variation on the theme. Between 3,000–6,000 young people (including a number of disabled) from all over Europe and beyond gather at the Taizé community for most weeks of the summer with a minimum of infrastructure and resources. The emphasis here is firmly on the 18–35 age group and reflects a community that sits lightly to worldly possessions. Once again, it is difficult to observe this phenomenon with complete detachment. These are young people looking for something more satisfying

---

[5] The contentious nature of the miraculous is a central theme in a recent account of Lourdes published in English (Harris 1999). The dispute took place on two fronts: on the one hand with the ecclesiastical authorities and on the other with the secular nature of nineteenth-century France (or at least its dominant elites). The significance of gender in this process is firmly underlined. If Lourdes has survived to become one of the world's leading Catholic shrines, this is largely due to the faith of women.

than a world of commerce and consumption; they exist on surprisingly little. Such values leak out of the community itself. No one passes the last turning to the village without offering a lift to the young people waiting by the roadside and the notice board asking for lifts all over Europe is one of the most optimistic that I have ever seen.

The great majority of the pilgrimage sites have as their focus a particular building or basilica. Such a building (with the partial exceptions of Taizé and Iona) has been lavishly constructed in order to mark or honour the sacredness of a particular locality: where a miracle or vision has quite literally 'taken place' (as in the case of the Marian shrines), or where a particular relic (the remains of St James) or a revered icon (the painting of the Virgin at Częstochowa) is housed. The cathedral at Santiago offers an excellent illustration. Here a glorious building (added to over many centuries) welcomes the pilgrim, who is invited on arrival to place his or her hand into the central column of the Tree of Jesse just inside the main door, giving thanks for a safe journey. The depth of the fingermarks on the stone column connects the pilgrim to the countless number who have come before. The second stage of the pilgrim's 'arrival' is to embrace the silver statue of St James himself behind the high altar (the figure of St James is dressed as a pilgrim).[6] A mass for pilgrims is said at noon each day in which a number of pilgrim groups are greeted by name. Those, moreover, who have walked or cycled a specified distance are entitled to collect their *compostela* (or certificate) from the pilgrims' office not far from the cathedral; here is the proof both of participation and completion.[7]

Giving thanks for a safe arrival is understandable enough, but cannot, surely, mean the same for the modern visitor (complete with travel insurance and support vehicle) as it did for the medieval pilgrim, whose journey took many months, if not years. Travelling to and from the site remains, none the less, part and parcel of the pilgrimage experience—one which reveals, once again, an ambivalent relationship with modernity. On the one hand, it is clear that pilgrimage sites have developed alongside modern forms of communication, permitting larger and larger numbers of people (including the sick or disabled) to make the trip in person, rather than by proxy. Lourdes, for example, has unusually good rail and air connections for a small town in the Pyrenees. On the other, appreciable numbers of people at the end of the twentieth century quite deliberately choose *not* to travel by modern forms of transport, putting themselves instead through a degree of physical hardship in order to achieve their goal. Many walk to Częstochowa from the major Polish cities, for example, as they do to Santiago from various points along the pilgrim route, or to Chartres from Paris. It is the element of choice which places the debate squarely in its late-modern context: these are chosen rather than necessary

---

[6] The associated image of St James the Moor-slayer is rather more difficult to accommodate for the modern pilgrim.

[7] Such proof was particularly important in earlier centuries, when significant numbers of pilgrimages were undertaken by proxy.

hardships, offering opportunities for spiritual refreshment denied by the speed of modern living, not least the speed of modern transport. The need for such refreshment becomes, in fact, a recurring theme in the study of pilgrimage. Modern Europeans are, it seems, looking for opportunities to step back from the world and to find time for reflection; one way of doing this is to seek out a designated place and to take time in getting there. This is particularly true for the busy (and possibly self-indulgent) middle class with sufficient resources to 'buy time', and for the young—and more impecunious—visitors at Taizé searching for some meaning to life. It is unlikely to have quite so much resonance for the terminally ill and their carers.

With the significance of travelling in mind, it is relatively easy to widen the definition of pilgrimage to include its symbolic as well as physical applications. Quite apart from the growing popularity of pilgrimage sites, the idea of life as a journey becomes a metaphor for modern living—a way of understanding the world that applies not only to religion but to life itself, especially in its late-modern forms. The idea, in fact, is hardly new: life was just as much a journey in the ancient world as it is now. The metaphor has, however, picked up particular resonances in late modernity as we become less and less sure about the point of arrival in modern societies and reflect interminably on the process of getting there. Life becomes a form of perpetual seeking, a virtual reality in which the boundaries always recede: following Hervieu-Léger (1986), the closer we get to our goals, the more we realize that the ultimate prize or certainty eludes us. This, she argues, is the symbolic space in modern living that only religion can fill, though not necessarily in its conventional forms. It is interesting that Hervieu-Léger's current writing looks at the religious life of modern societies in terms of two ideal types: the pilgrim (*le pélérin*) and the convert (*le converti*) (Hervieu-Léger 1999a). In adopting these essentially mobile models, Hervieu-Léger is rejecting the historical emphasis on regular practice (*le pratiquant*), which has dominated sociological thinking in the past. It is clear that it is becoming less and less useful for a proper understanding of modern European religion; the decline in regular practice is but one part of an increasingly complex picture.

The contrast between static and mobile models, moreover, helps us to understand the tensions between parochial structures and the pilgrimage experience. The latter, traditionally, enhances the former and allows the regular worshipper an experience over and above week-by-week attendance at the local church—to which they return with renewed enthusiasm and commitment. It can, however, become an alternative, rather than a supplementary, model, rivalling rather than enhancing more static forms of religion, which look increasingly out of date. As we have seen, the latter tendency may be particularly true for young people, who enjoy the company and the emotional high of the pilgrimage experience, but for whom dogmatic teaching and regular practice have less and less appeal. If this is truly the case, the consequences for religious memory are likely to be considerable.

### *The Memorialization of War: An Alternative Form of Pilgrimage*

A rather different form of pilgrimage must be mentioned in conclusion, one that has pervaded a great deal of European experience. War is part of Europe's common memory (Davies and Wollaston 1993; Winter 1995). War memorials and war cemeteries, moreover, can be found throughout the continent and continue to draw people from all over the world (given the nature of the last two wars) for both personal and public anniversaries. These are powerful places which evoke the tragedies of Europe's past; they are central to the understanding of what it means to be a European. They are equally crucial for a proper grasp of European religion in that they bring together a sense of national identity and some sort of religious (usually, but not exclusively, Christian) teaching. In the vast majority of cases, for example, the inscription implies that the individual died for God as well as their country; war graves are marked with religious symbols and the cemeteries themselves are sacred ground. In the associated museums, visitors are expected to dress correctly, *as if* they were entering a church (see below).

Despite the shared experience, however, sharp national differences remain, nicely illustrated by the different placing of the tomb of the unknown warrior in Britain and in France. In France, this symbol of national pride is located on secular soil; the tomb is placed beneath the Arc de Triomphe in the heart of the capital city and reflects the *laïcité* of public life (unusually—in European terms—there is no religious inscription on this tomb). In Britain, on the other hand, the same symbol lies just inside the main door of Westminster Abbey, where institutional Christianity (embodied in Anglican form) meets the secular world or indeed the world of popular belief. The 'burial' of the unknown warrior in Britain in 1920 took the form of a representative funeral under the auspices of the state church, at which the King was the chief mourner, a pattern reflected in the annual celebrations of remembrance held at the Cenotaph each November. In France there is no king, no state church, and a strictly secular ceremony.

## From Cathedral to Museum

The significance of a cathedral or basilica at a pilgrimage site has already been mentioned. Europe's cathedrals, however, have a far greater resonance than this in that they embody in architectural form the religious heritage of Europe. It is no exaggeration to say that Europe's religious past can be 'read' from these buildings, as indeed it can be in microcosm from the countless churches, chapels, and synagogues all over the continent. Over-familiarity is in many ways the problem; Europeans simply take these buildings for granted and cease to recognize either the structures themselves or the history they contain.

Only when a building is threatened with demolition does the local community react, frequently with vehemence, appreciating (sometimes too late) how much of their common memory resides, both directly and indirectly, in what they are about to lose.[8]

Not only do the buildings themselves embody the past, they have become in addition one place where significant collections of artefacts have accumulated. The motives for such accumulation are many and varied—by no means all of them are religious. Local pride and the existence of patronage have been equally influential, leading in some parts of Europe not only to rampant and competitive building but also to conspicuous consumption on a lavish scale. The result, however, is an immense richness of art and architecture, posing difficult questions of oversight, maintenance, and access. Only a fraction of this debate can be engaged in this chapter, but a fruitful pivot for the argument can be found in the vexed question of payment for access. The intricate connections between cathedral and museum form an integral part of the same discussion.

An interesting set of examples in this respect can be found in Tuscany in north Italy, a part of Europe in which the artistic heritage is at its richest. The cathedrals in Florence, Pisa, and Siena, for example, are acknowledged as masterpieces all over the world and attract huge numbers of visitors; in the tourist season they are full of people for most of the day, posing difficult problems of crowd control. Payment is required in Pisa (in the tourist season)[9] but not in Florence or Siena, though it is necessary to pay in order to enter the Baptistery in Florence. Rather less well known, but equally significant, are the museums attached to these buildings. These *Musei dell'Opera del Duomo* (Museums of the Works of the Cathedral) are institutions closely linked with the cathedral itself and with those who are responsible for both its fabric and its artistic heritage. The museum in Siena dates from 1869, that in Florence from 1891, and that in Pisa from 1986; all are housed in historic buildings adjacent to the cathedral itself. All three, moreover, contain exquisite masterpieces originally designed to be placed on or in the cathedral itself, not least the originals of medieval statues, now replaced by replicas in order to prevent erosion. Other priceless sculptures (for example Michelangelo's *Pietà* and Donatello's wooden *Magdalen*) have been moved to the museum in Florence for security reasons. As is to be expected, all three institutions charge for entry; they are considerably quieter (more serene) than the cathedrals themselves, even at the height of the season. Quite clearly they attract a different sort of public (this is the

---

[8] Interesting work has been done on the attitudes of Swedish people to church buildings; here an apparently secular population feels strongly about both the presence and the maintenance of church buildings, without which public life would be severely diminished. Attitudes towards the churchyard or burial ground were an important feature in these unexpectedly strong reactions (Bäckström and Bromander 1995).

[9] The closing of the Leaning Tower to the public has, it seems, cut off a significant source of income; hence the decision to charge entry for the cathedral and the baptistery.

world of high rather than popular culture), but a public which in many respects behaves *as if* it were still in the cathedral (Bourdieu and Darbel 1991).

So where, exactly, does the cathedral end and the museum begin? It is almost impossible to say.[10] The line, moreover, becomes all the more blurred in the case of the cathedral's treasury—in other words an historic, and often very valuable, collection of relics and reliquaries, vestments, silver, and manuscripts, built up over centuries as part of the cathedral's worshipping life and brought out for display on special occasions. In some places the treasury is still in the cathedral (more often than not with restricted access for security reasons), but in others it has been moved to an associated museum (this is certainly the case in the three cathedrals described above). Here it becomes part of a rather different collection, put together for its artistic merit rather than its functional attributes—the museum, moreover, is likely to add to its contents from a diversity of sources, seeking similar sorts of objects from different places rather than a collection associated with one institution with a continuous history. Much more positive, however, are the facilities that are offered: collections can be maintained and displayed in a modern museum to a higher standard than is possible in most cathedral buildings. One reason for this is the technology currently available (notably reinforced glass); a second is the money that comes from entrance fees.

But if the line between cathedrals and museums is so difficult to draw either in terms of content or in terms of atmosphere, why is it that more of the former do not charge entry for access—and to the cathedral itself, not simply to particular parts of it (the treasury or the tower for example)? It is at this stage that the debate becomes highly contentious, for there are many—not all of them overtly religious people—who feel that charging entry to a designated sacred place is simply not acceptable. Why this should be so in a modern and supposedly secular society is not easy to say, but a residual sense of the sacred is clearly a significant factor in the argument. An important corollary follows; namely that sacred space is in some way public space, even if it is not used by most people on a regular basis. If this is the case, the oversight and management of religious buildings must remain a public issue, counteracting growing, perhaps exaggerated, tendencies towards privatization in other aspects of religious life. Unpicking the strands in this controversial area will reveal layer upon layer of complexity, not only in relation to the public and the private in

---

[10] An interesting discussion of this distinction in an Anglican context can be found in Cathedrals Advisory Committee for England (1980), a collection of conference papers relating to the management of cathedrals, treasuries, and museums. The final quote from a conference participant is revealing: 'Personally I like use, and think emptiness leads to ruin; so to some extent the more activities a cathedral holds, the better I am pleased. Museums in adjoining buildings don't attract many visitors compared to the cathedral itself, either at home (Wells, Durham) or overseas (Florence, Rheims, Albi, Chartres).' (1980: 81).

modern European societies, but also in the conceptualization of the sacred. It is not a subject where rational judgements are likely to prevail.[11]

What is clear, however, is the capacity of the cathedrals cited above to attract a far more diverse public than their related museums.[12] A perceptive article in a special issue of the *Museums Journal* (Drakakis-Smith 1994) picks up this theme and examines in more detail the renewed popularity of European cathedrals in the late twentieth century and their relationship to the local community. The following quotation not only summarizes the article, but draws together many of the themes presented in this chapter so far:

in the past, in north western Europe, churches acted as the first museums and tourist centres. Their awe-inspiring buildings housed and safe-guarded precious, crafted artefacts—pictures, sculptures, stone and wood carvings, bronze and silver ware and textiles. They were repositories for books, manuscripts, documents, and records pertaining to the locality (births, baptisms, marriages and deaths) and centres of scholastic endeavour. Pilgrims came from afar to see these 'wonders'. Today visitor figures place cathedrals on a par with visitors for national and larger municipal museums and heritage attractions. (Drakakis-Smith 1994: 31)

The slippage in the vocabulary is clear enough, with important implications for management: the needs of the visitor (be they tourist, art lover, or pilgrim) need to be balanced against the regular worshipper if the cathedrals are to meet the demands placed on them.[13] In so doing they will, in fact, be rediscovering an earlier role: one far closer to the community that has been the norm since the seventeenth century (prior to this only the sanctuary was considered holy—the rest of the building was freely available to the population at large).

The relationship between the sacred and the museum, however, goes considerably further than this, for there are other types of religious museum in Europe. Careful attention should be paid in this respect to the museums of Judaism, in that they carry a particular and disturbing resonance for modern Europeans. Such museums vary in nature; some simply display the artefacts of Judaism and explain these and their uses to the public. Others embody the story of a particular community or family from its origins in different parts of Europe to the trauma of the Holocaust. Those in Central Europe (in Prague, Krakow, or Vilnius for example) have already been mentioned in a previous chapter; they are haunting places to visit. So too is the hugely popular Anne Frank Museum in Amsterdam, an understandable focus for school visits. It is

---

[11] In British society, paradoxically, there has been a similar debate about charging for state-owned museums and art galleries. The question of paying to enter cathedrals remains equally contentious, though it has been put into effect in some places.

[12] This is certainly not the case for all the museums in Florence; in the summer season visitors queue for considerable periods of time to get into the Uffizi Gallery.

[13] Simply placing a notice on the door indicating that a cathedral is not a museum (as they do in Cologne for example) indicates an awareness of the problem rather than a solution. Cathedrals are museums (undeniably), but they are not *only* museums; at least for the faithful, they embody the sacred as well as containing it.

rather more difficult to comprehend Hitler's bizarre plan for the museum that already existed in Prague; this he envisaged as an 'Exotic Museum of an Extinct Race'—a posthumous record of a religion which no longer existed.[14] Most disturbing of all, however, are the death camps themselves (notably Auschwitz-Birkenau), which carry the memory of the hundreds of thousands of Jews killed by the Nazis simply for being Jewish, a story replicated in the Holocaust Museum in Washington (assembled almost entirely from European materials). That the Jews who lost their lives and the communities they represent should not be forgotten is the explicit aim of these institutions; undoubtedly effective in fulfilling their goal, they are harrowing places for the visitor. Auschwitz-Birkenau remains, none the less, a contested site as the arguments continue concerning the presence of Carmelite nuns and the maintenance of Christian symbols on or near the site.

An innovative idea in Glasgow introduces a final example: the multi-cultural St Mungo's Museum of Religious Art and Life. A series of articles in a special issue of *Museums Journal* (February 1994) describes both the process and the problems of creating a museum of religion, setting these alongside the attitudes of the staff involved. The following comment reveals an inbuilt incompatibility in outlook:

If the aim was to communicate something of the meaning of the objects, we had to reverse the usual process in museums of draining them of their dangerous meanings to render them safely aesthetic, historical or anthropological. In the case of religion, 'meaning' has an emotional and spiritual dimension that can be described much more powerfully by those who experience it than those who have simply studied it. Some sort of consultation or collaboration with believers was therefore required. (O'Neill 1994: 28)

How this was carried out in order to achieve the right balance between the aims of a secular museum (with its own codes of practice) and a meaningful representation of the major world faiths is a story in itself; likewise the genesis of a multi-cultural museum in close proximity to St Mungo's Cathedral, whose Society of Friends originally envisaged a visitors' centre for the cathedral itself (Michel 1999). Reactions to the venture, whether from the religious constituencies, museum professionals, or the general public, vary from the enthusiastic to the sharply critical (Butler 1994; Clelland 1994). The concept, however, is an interesting one, not least the incorporation of feedback boards within the enterprise as a whole. The latter have proved an innovative source of sociological data, used by Michel (1999) to examine reactions to the museum at three levels: to the artefacts themselves, to the idea of multiculturalism that underpins the enterprise, and finally to the notion of religion itself. In introducing his monograph, moreover, Michel re-poses a central question of this chapter: how does the visitor locate him- or herself in a

---

[14] Over 200,000 items were gathered in the Nazi period, with synagogues in the surrounding communities obliged to make compulsory contributions to this unique source of documentation.

museum of religion? Is this public space? And if so, is it concerned with knowledge, with identity, or with faith itself? Quite clearly the ambiguities remain, neatly encapsulated in the following pair of quotations taken from the feedback board at St Mungo's: 'Glad to see religion consigned to a museum. Sadly it still lives', and, conversely, 'I came to visit a dead museum and found a living faith' (Michel 1999: 102).[15]

# Telling the Story

So far this chapter has concentrated more on the institutional level than the cultural. This imbalance will gradually be corrected as different ways of 'telling the story' are introduced. The first example, however, continues to reflect the ambiguities in location already underlined.

## Art and Architecture

The Scrovegni Chapel, in Padua, is accessed through the *Museo civico* (entry forms one part of an inclusive ticket); the numbers of visitors are strictly controlled and it is often necessary to wait some time before entering. The chapel itself was built for Enrico Scrovegni at the beginning of the fourteenth century, supposedly in expiation for his father's usury. It is a relatively small building and stands by itself, separate from the main museum building (the palace of which it was part was destroyed in the last century). Inside is the cycle of frescos painted by Giotto at the height of his power, a work described quite correctly as a profound theological statement. The double cycle of frescos is conceived as one element in a larger whole, depicting scenes from the life of the Virgin, followed by scenes from the life of Christ. Innovative in theology as well as artistic technique,[16] Giotto gives the biblical narrative a new and 'intensely human significance' (Macadam 1991: 318). Images from everyday life are drawn together into a powerful overall vision.

How, though, do both vision and details resonate at the end of the twentieth century? Almost all visitors arrive with either a guide or a guidebook, in order to pick out the various scenes in the narrative. The casual tourist would be unlikely to gain very much, though it is hard to avoid the impact of a graphic Last Judgement on the west wall, complete with usurers hung by their

[15] Interestingly, the *Museums Journal* returned to this theme in September 1999. Arthur (1999) examines the ethical and moral implications for museums which have introduced a religious dimension. The article is an extract from the initial chapter of an edited collection on religion and museums, which appeared as this book was in its final stages (Paine 2000). It is the first full-length study of this important topic and includes material on the complex relationship between museum and cathedral.

[16] The chapel is described in the guidebooks as 'a place of pilgrimage' (*sic*) for art lovers.

own purse-strings. Once started, however, the unfolding of the story of redemption is both clear and complete as it moves from the birth of the Virgin to the birth of Christ, and then through Christ's death, resurrection, and ascension, culminating in the giving of the Holy Spirit at Pentecost.

It is very much easier to follow, in fact, than a second, much more frequently quoted example of a medieval visual aid—the windows in Chartres Cathedral. Here, though, there is absolutely no ambiguity of place: entry to the main body of the cathedral is free, giving immediate access to the windows which form an integral part of the whole. Bearing this in mind, and remembering that the cathedral has a truly global reputation, there are surprisingly few aids to interpretation within the building itself; there is, in fact, considerably more information about the history of the Diocese of Chartres, its vicissitudes in the revolutionary period, and the contemporary functioning of the cathedral (not least as a place of pilgrimage).

Secondary sources are, however, widely available. Mâle, for example (1983: 170–2), looks in detail at selected examples of the windows, starting with a well-known biblical scene, the Good Samaritan. The initial panels depict the New Testament narrative straightforwardly enough, but later panels add elements from the story of creation and the murder of Abel. The latter provide a clue to the interpretation of the story by medieval theologians—the gospel account is reset into a larger narrative in which the traveller represents fallen humanity and the Samaritan is Christ himself (the priest and the Levite represent the failed attempts of the Law to effect salvation). The second of Mâle's windows describes the building of the cathedral itself and the role of the surrounding villagers in this undertaking. The third and fourth depict the lives of two very different saints—Germain l'Auxerrois and Julien l'Hospitalier—the first with evident supernatural qualities, the second offering a model for effective expiation of an earlier sin. The last window portrays scenes from the life of Charlemagne, even more difficult for a twentieth-century visitor to interpret in terms of Christian theology, but not without precedent in medieval buildings; the window is a replica of a similar one (now destroyed) at St-Denis on the northern edge of Paris. It is immediately clear from even the briefest description that the richness of each and every one of these windows requires specialist knowledge in order to be fully appreciated. This is true at two levels: first, to recognize the stories themselves (particularly the non-biblical ones), but second, to interpret their content within an appropriate theological context. Without such aids, the modern visitor is doubly disadvantaged.

Theological disputes of a different kind and in a different century surround an English account of story-telling in church windows. It illustrates an ongoing conflict between visual and textual narrative and is taken from 'A Poem, in defence of the decent Ornaments of Christ-Church, Oxon, occasioned by a Banbury brother, who called them Idolatries' (anonymous, 1656; reprinted in Grierson and Bullough 1934: 803–8). The first part of the poem defends the richness of art, music, and ornament in worship; the second is more specifically concerned with 'The Church-Windows' and their significance for Christian instruction. Two short extracts from the second part make the essential point:

> Cease then your railings and your dull complaints;
> To pull down Galleries and set up Saints
> Is no impiety: now we may well
> Say that our Church is truly visible:
> Those that before our glasse scaffolds prefer,
> Would turne our Temple to a Theatre.
> Windows are Pulpits now; though unlearned, one
> May read this Bible's new Edition.

> Hence then *Pauls* doctrine may seem more divine;
> As Amber through a Glasse does shine.
> Words passe away, as soon as heard are gone;
> We read in books what here we dwell upon,
> Thus then there's no more fault in Imag'ry
> Than there is in the Practice of piety,
> Both edifie: what is in letters there
> Is writ in plainer Hierogliphicks here.
> 'Tis not a new Religion we have chose;
> 'Tis the same body but in better clothes.

'Windows are Pulpits now' through which the 'unlearned' may access the narrative, provided he or she is sufficiently familiar with the stories to recognize their visual presentation. What, though, might these windows convey to the modern visitor—fully literate in one sense, but considerably less familiar with the stories displayed in the glass? It is this question that must be addressed in the following section.

## *From Words to Music*

Before doing so, it is appropriate to introduce an entirely different set of *aides-mémoire*—those that can be found in music rather than art or architecture. If we bear in mind the structure of this chapter, Sutter (1996) offers a useful frame of reference in this respect—one which brings together the religious and the aesthetic. Both, following Sutter, interrogate the place of the human being (or soul) in relation to other humans and to the universe itself, but do this in different ways. It is this perspective that Sutter uses to introduce a group of publications dealing with religiously motivated musicians; these range from the Catholic inspiration of Olivier Messiaen (former organist at Sainte-Trinité in Paris) to the Lutheranism of Bach and the musicianship of Luther himself. One particular theme repeats itself: is it possible to talk about 'religious music' as such or is it more accurate to talk simply about music that in itself conveys something of the sublime? Just like the movement between cathedral and museum, the language slips back and forth between the religious and the aesthetic, exemplified perhaps by Mozart, who could allow the same theme to appear in both his Coronation Mass and *The Marriage of Figaro*. The theme was first and foremost an inspired 'geste musical'—its appropriation by either religion or the theatre was secondary (Sutter 1996: 43). The musical settings of the Mass or the Passion contain similar ambiguities; it is not necessary to be a Christian to appreciate both their musical and dramatic power.

An interesting study of music at a more popular level can be found in a recent survey of hymns and hymn-singing in the Lutheran countries of Northern Europe.[17] These are populations which have very largely rejected the habit of regular churchgoing. None the less, the institutional churches remain the inspiration for a great deal of music-making at community level (whether this be religious or secular music). An *average* parish, for example, will have at least one and possibly two professional musicians—these are people who work full-time and are relatively well paid. And quite apart from what goes on in parishes, Nordic populations come together for communal occasions at particular moments in the year or in the life-cycle; the singing of hymns forms a central part of these events.

Ryokas (1998) offers empirical underpinning for such statements. Large numbers of Nordic people, for example, have a hymnbook in the house (over 80% of Danes and 90% of Finns) and many continue to associate the singing of hymns with churchgoing, even if the latter is an occasional rather than regular occurrence. The Danes, however, stand out as the nation who not only make this connection most strongly but cannot imagine Christmas without hymn-singing; over 90% responded positively to a question which linked the two. In interpreting this material, it is important to remember the significance of Nikolaí Grundtvig (1783–1872) in Danish life. Largely unknown outside Denmark, except through the criticisms of Kierkegaard, Grundtvig is universally recognized in his own country as the greatest single influence on the development of Danish society and culture in the last hundred years (Allchin 1994). Amongst many other achievements (as poet, scholar, and preacher), Grundtvig was responsible for about half of the hymns in the Danish hymnbook. With this in mind, it is hardly surprising that Danish people are acutely aware of their musical legacy, its significance in Danish life, and the need to appropriate such knowledge on a regular basis.

What, though, do the musical activities of Scandinavians signify from a religious point of view? It is clear, first of all, that relatively few 'hymn-singers' accept the doctrine or teaching contained in the hymns themselves. Less than half in Ryokas' study, for example, agree with the sentiments expressed in 'Ein' feste Burg ist unser Gott'; rather more, though, could assent to the children's hymns that praised creation. Hymn singing was not a teaching aid; it was

---

[17] This is a large-scale comparative study involving 3,700 respondents in the five Nordic countries (Denmark, Finland, Iceland, Norway, and Sweden). Some preliminary findings were presented at the Toulouse meeting of the International Society for the Sociology of Religion (1997) and at a invited colloquium on Religion in Europe in Göttingen (1998).

essentially expressive and in this capacity functioned at many levels of society. In terms of the perpetuation of a memory, moreover, it is clear that the Nordics wish these traditions to continue: even those who do not go to church or no longer consider themselves believers want children to learn the corpus of Lutheran hymns in school; such hymns are an important part of Nordic culture, quite apart from Nordic religion—the necessary knowledge must be passed to the next generation.

Up to a point the same has been true in Britain at least until the 1960s, a point which has already been discussed, albeit briefly, in connection with the media. There is also an educational resonance. To a very large extent and for understandable (if mistaken) pedagogical reasons, British schoolchildren are now taught religious songs—composed with a particular age-group in mind—rather than the traditional corpus of hymns. This, coupled with the decline in churchgoing in the post-war period, has brought about a marked change in the knowledge base of younger generations. Those born after 1960 simply do not know the hymns familiar to their parents and grandparents. In terms of the theme of this chapter, such shifts are bound to be significant. Those, for example, who absorbed the words of 'Once in Royal David's city' or 'There is a Green Hill Far Away' had in their heads, consciously or unconsciously, considerable sections of the Christian story. And though the evidence in Britain is far more impressionistic than that in the Nordic countries, it is likely to be the case that singing, as opposed to saying, the words of these hymns enhances one's memory of them—the more so if everyone sings together.

Musical cultures are not, however, universal even within one nation—a point nicely illustrated by anecdote. It is said that an experienced organist at a crematorium in Britain could, until very recently, choose suitable hymns for a funeral if he or she was informed about the address and the denomination of the deceased. In other words, with simple clues about the religious and social and economic background of the family in question, appropriate hymns followed. Hymn-singing, like so many other aspects of religious life, is socially patterned, a fact that was part and parcel of the professional life of an organist *de service*. To complete the picture, however, regional differences should also be taken into account, not least the markedly different cultures of Wales and Scotland. In the former, for example, hymn-singing not only persists as a significant carrier of Welsh non-conformist culture, it also involves far more men than in England through the medium of the male voice choir. In Scotland, by contrast, metrical settings of the psalms are more in tune with the austerities of Calvinist culture than the hymns from south of the border. Metrical psalms are also associated with the French Protestant community. Even more emblematic of the latter, however, is the chorale from Handel's *Judas Maccabaeus*. French Protestants, whether practising or not, will immediately recognize 'A toi la gloire' sung to this tune; it has acquired the status of an anthem.

The hymn-singing culture of most parts of Britain is in decline. Other forms of religious music prosper, however, and not only in Britain. Gregorian chant is one of them and in many ways brings the argument in this chapter full circle. Significant numbers of modern Europeans are looking for ways to escape the relentlessness of modern living. If time out to visit a pilgrimage site is one of these, the same sensation can be achieved for an hour or two with a well-chosen tape or compact disc. The emphasis, however, is on consumption: European individuals choose what they like from the rigours of monastic discipline; they rarely embrace the whole. The fact that the accumulation of such choices is sufficient to activate a powerful set of market forces simply reinforces the point. Gregorian chant competes on the market with other forms of popular music; its extraordinary success at the end of the twentieth century, however, invites a certain degree of reflection about the priorities of modern Europeans.[18]

## Aesthetic Memory: Art and its Audience

It is important at this point to connect this chapter with those that precede it. If it is clear, on the one hand, that the aesthetic or cultural memory associated with the Christian tradition is still very largely intact (the examples given above could be multiplied over and over again), it is much less clear that Europeans are able to access this memory in the way that might have been true for earlier generations, a point well illustrated by some, if not all, of the musical examples. It was, moreover, precisely this point that troubled the French head teacher quoted at length in Chapter 5. Even the most highly educated French students no longer had sufficient knowledge to appreciate, let alone understand, those parts of the artistic or literary heritage which draw on the Judaeo-Christian narrative. Henri Tincq (from *Le Monde*) made an additional, even more devastating comment: the teachers were almost as incapable as their students of making the necessary imaginative leaps. It follows that each generation will be more disadvantaged than the last in terms of their cultural heritage, quite apart from the point already made in Chapter 5 concerning the ability of younger generations to participate effectively in a religiously pluralist democracy.

A second way into the debate about accessibility also draws on French sources and more especially on the cross-cultural analyses of museum-going publics undertaken by Bourdieu and Darbel (1991). Museum-goers are predominantly middle-class people and represent the most culturally advantaged groups in European society. Across a wide range of European nations, level of education was by far the most salient variable in determining an individual's propensity to visit museums and to appreciate artistic objects. It follows that

---

[18] A rather similar example can be found in the marketing of selected goods through the retail outlets of French monasteries. Such goods are chosen for their 'purity' (both spiritual and ecological) and carry a distinctive trademark.

the love of art is culturally induced, a fact which is frequently denied in 'political' argument in that it implies an inadequacy in the education systems of the country in question. It is easier, from this point of view, to argue that the capacity to respond to works of art is innate rather than learned, for if this is the case, little need be done in terms of education or resources to improve the situation.[19] The implications of the political argument need not concern us here. What is important, however, is the evident need for knowledge in order that an individual may appreciate and understand what he or she is seeing.

Cultural memory, in other words, is interactive, not static; it is socially constructed and requires not only knowledge but training in order to continue as an effective resource or memory. The realization that this is so in a spiritual as well as aesthetic sense becomes increasingly clear as even the most elementary knowledge of both the Judaeo-Christian stories and their symbolic representation in art or architecture declines in the European population as a whole. An awareness of the possible consequences of this situation—together with a constructive attempt to do something about it—can be nicely illustrated in the aims of a French voluntary organization known as C.A.S.A. (Communautés d'Accueil dans les Sites Artistiques). C.A.S.A. was founded in 1967; each word in the organization's title has significance for the argument in this chapter:

- Communautés: these are communities whose members gather near a monument in order to discover its riches, to share with one another, and to welcome visitors.
- Accueil (welcome): the welcome comes from volunteers, especially during the tourist season; the aim is a free encounter between the visitor, the guide, and the work of art.
- Sites: the encounter takes place in an historic Christian site (all of these are in France).
- Artistiques: the sites are selected with reference to their historical, aesthetic, and spiritual importance.

The key phrase in the French version of the publicity leaflet is, however, the following:

The churches and monasteries of Europe are open to all, often without payment; these buildings are frequently visited throughout the summer. They stand as a witness to the faith and *savoir-faire* of those who built them and contain images and symbols which were eloquent for their contemporaries, *but which require rediscovery today*.

In order to respond to this need, the voluntary organization C.A.S.A., staffed entirely by volunteers, aims to welcome visitors in such a way that they move beyond the architectural and iconographic qualities of the building and are able to discover its spiritual dimensions. (C.A.S.A. 1998; translation and emphasis mine)

---

[19] Bourdieu takes this argument further still in asserting that the educated public are in fact using a *laissez-faire* policy to exclude a wider public, and to preserve the elite nature of the art world for themselves (1991: 108–13).

It should not be assumed, in other words, that this process is automatic. The modern visitor needs help in interpreting medieval symbols at both an aesthetic and spiritual level. Nor should it be assumed that C.A.S.A. itself has an evangelistic motive; anyone is free to join, Christian or otherwise, if they are in sympathy with the basic aims of the movement.

In 1998 one of the sites adopted by C.A.S.A. was the basilica of La Madeleine at Vézélay in Burgundy. The romanesque abbey and the community of which it is part epitomize many of the points made both in this chapter and the last. It was, first of all, the starting point of one of the four main pilgrimage routes across France, all of which converged in the western Pyrenees before making their way to Santiago in north-west Spain. Like many French churches, the fabric suffered considerably at the hands of both the Huguenots and the Revolutionaries. (It is important to bear in mind, however, that the behaviour of some abbots in the seventeenth and eighteenth centuries invited negative action.) The building itself was rescued by the great 'restorer' Viollet-le-Duc in the nineteenth century and has become in the twentieth a magnet for tourists of all kinds. A variety of spiritual resources await the visitor in a town that combines an interest in the New Age (but the most modern form of more ancient spiritualities in this locality) with more conventional expressions of religiousness. Just next to the abbey, for example, is the Magasin du Pélérin (Pilgrim's Shop), which advertises its goods under the title 'Tourisme Art Religion', with no punctuation between the words. A second emporium sells all the objects associated with the Catholic pilgrimage—Madonnas, rosaries, etc.—but alongside a table full of New Age merchandise including tarot cards. The whole is symptomatic of a consumer society: the indiscriminate gathering of spiritual goods for sale to the modern tourist/pilgrim, in shops which are set against the façade of an ancient and beautiful basilica, understandably sought after for both aesthetic and spiritual reasons.

# A Note on Liturgy

Whatever has been said so far, it is clear that by far the most explicit story-telling of all in European history resides in liturgy, which is quite literally a re-enactment of the dramas that sustain the memory in question. The fact that the Mass or Eucharist—the central act of Christian liturgy—has, at its core, the phrase 'Do this in remembrance of me' simply sharpens the perspective even further. Where the liturgy takes place and how it is enhanced by art or music have provided points of departure for this chapter; so, too, have the delicate overlapping between the religious and the aesthetic spheres and the capacities of Europeans to appreciate either or both of these elements. The question, finally, of who creates or enacts the liturgy on behalf of whom resets the debate within a sociological context and connects this chapter with those primarily concerned with the institutional churches. The complex relationships between active and passive church members were central elements in this discussion; looked at in a different way these same links provide a starting point for a more theoretical conclusion.

# TEN

# *Conclusion: The Memory Mutates*

THIS chapter reintroduces the framework of the book as a whole. In order to do this, the concept of memory itself becomes the central theme, with the sub-headings taken in the main from the titles of the previous chapters. In addition to these, however, a number of new ideas are also introduced; the concept of memory is pushed to its logical conclusions to reveal the full potential of this way of working. In so doing it becomes quite clear that there could have been significantly more substantive chapters in the book as a whole—what has been written so far is by no means an exhaustive analysis.

Two crucial questions underlie the whole endeavour. The first concerns the dominant Christian memory: how much of this is still intact in modern Europe? The answer, however, depends considerably on the variety of meanings that could be given to the word 'intact'. Does this mean that the memory still exists or does it mean that significant numbers of Europeans not only share the basic presuppositions of the memory, but could themselves articulate its principal features? 'Could they ever?' is a question which follows on, plus a certain latitude in what might be meant by *significant* numbers. One way of engaging these issues is to continue the discussion of liturgy initiated at the end of the previous chapter. Or to put the same point in a different way, to what extent does the key phrase, 'Do this in remembrance of me', have resonance for modern Europeans?

The second question concerns the gradual diversification of religion in modern Europe: European religion has become *de facto* the religions of Europe. Hence the attention given in previous chapters to alternative memories of various kinds and to innovation both inside and outside the main tradition. The balance between the two themes is, moreover, one of the most problematic questions to deal with in any assessment of the religious situation in Europe at the turn of the millennium. On the one hand it is difficult to give due weight to the historical tradition without appearing to exclude the other-faith communities, a variety of religious innovations, and the growing secular tradition. Conversely, over-attention to the diversity distorts the picture as a whole, especially if it gives the impression that the different faith communities compete as equals in Europe. They do not.

This rather sharp interjection needs a word of explanation before this chapter can proceed any further. As individuals, Europeans of different religious traditions are, of course, equal before the law and have every right to exercise their political, legal, and religious privileges. Such principles are part and parcel of a modern democracy and need not only to be respected but protected. Europeans should be vigilant in this respect. It is not the case, however, that the different faith traditions are equal from a cultural point of view. This is simply not possible given Europe's past—and, for the foreseeable future, cannot be. The point can be illustrated in terms of the keeping of time: the shape of both the European year and the European week is Christian and is likely to remain so. We may have arguments—indeed they can be heated ones—about the proper way to observe Sunday in a variety of European countries; we do not do the same in terms of Friday, though we may well (indeed we should) pay attention to the rights of particular Muslims, in order that they may have adequate time for their religious obligations on what is traditionally a working day in Europe.

## Vicarious Memory

A number of the points that have been raised in the introductory paragraphs have an immediate connection with the concept of vicarious religion—in other words with the notion that a relatively small number of people might be able to 'look after' the memory (and particularly the Christian memory) on behalf of others.[1] With respect, for example, to the intactness of the tradition, it is clear from this perspective that the Christian memory still exists and that a considerable, if diminishing, number of people are able to articulate its basic tenets. Who these people are and their positions in European society are questions that have been discussed in some detail in the early chapters of this book; they are more likely to be women than men, to come from older not younger generations and (in the West at least) from the educated and advantaged sections of the population rather than the disadvantaged. Particular attention has also been paid to the institutions that take *direct* responsibility for the maintenance of the historic tradition—they, too, are crucial in the understanding of vicarious memory.

Absolutely central, moreover, to the work of these institutions and to the professionals who staff them is the maintenance of the liturgical tradition. If they do nothing else, religious institutions must see that the liturgy is

[1] The notion of vicarious religion has been discussed at some length in the British context, but in ways that relate more to pastoral ministry than to theoretical understanding—see Reed (1978) for example.

properly carried out. Hence to a certain extent the efforts that are made to ensure that this is so, even when there are insufficient designated professionals to do the job themselves. An inescapable question immediately asserts itself: who does or does not have the right to conduct these liturgies? Given the argument of this chapter, the debate surrounding the ordination of women provides a pertinent illustration of this point, the more so given the centrality to this debate of the eucharistic prayer of consecration—i.e. the prayer which includes the words 'Do this in remembrance of me'. It is these words and the associated actions which lie at the heart of the Mass and its validity and from this perspective the answer to the question remains problematic. In most of the Protestant churches of Europe, women are able to consecrate the elements and form an increasingly significant section of the ordained ministry. In the Orthodox and Catholic traditions, they are not. Nor do any of these churches fully recognize each other's ministries (male or female), a necessarily damaging factor in the maintenance of a common memory. The Christian tradition remains, from this point of view at least, not only vicarious but profoundly divided (see below).

This is primarily a theological argument. Rather more central to the sociological discussion is the delicate balancing act between majorities and minorities implicit in the concept of vicariousness. Doing something on behalf of others must imply, surely, that the majority as well as the minority has some idea of what is going on; in other words that they are not entirely indifferent to the activities of the religious institutions even if they take no—or very little—part in them. It is this tacit understanding which is both the key to the whole enterprise and an impossibly difficult field to research; it is not amenable to anything but the most subtle of methodologies. It can, however, be approached in two ways, both of which have been referred to in Chapters 3 and 4. Chapter 3, for example, raised the question of the historic churches acting as the 'guardians of faith' in European societies whether that faith be Christian or otherwise. Chapter 4, on the other hand, was more concerned with the relationship of the European populations to the historic churches through their uptake of the occasional offices—which in many parts of Europe remains considerable.

In both respects the mainstream churches have a continuing role to play, albeit a very different one from that which they might have assumed in previous generations. In my view, moreover, the notion of vicariousness offers not only an innovative, but an empirically useful, approach to the notion of secularization as it is experienced in European society at the end of the twentieth century; a method of working considerably more subtle than those which are based simply or primarily on the numbers of regular churchgoers. Not everyone has to be able to articulate the memory for this (1) to continue in existence and (2) to have an appreciable effect upon the society in question—provided that certain conditions are met. Such conditions concern the viability as well as legality of the institutional churches, a statement requiring ongoing and careful scrutiny, and at different levels of society.

Three facts lead, I think, to a positive conclusion regarding the viability of the European churches at national level at the turn of the millennium. First, there is the evidence from Central and Eastern Europe in the early 1990s, where the need to reconstitute (rapidly) both the constitutional presence and public acceptability of the churches was immediately apparent (life without such institutions was not an option, though the particular form that they should take was not only much less clear but frequently disputed). Second are the attempts to extend the privileges of the historic churches on an equitable basis to the newly arrived religious communities in all parts of Europe. Religious communities both covet and compete for these privileges in Western Europe; they do not despise them. The final piece of evidence comes from the attitudes of significant numbers of non-churchgoers to both the 'guardians of faith' and the buildings for which they are responsible, exemplified (amongst other places) in the popular press and explored in some detail in Chapters 3 and 9. For substantial sections of the population, these are not attitudes of indifference but of vigilance; they imply that the churches of Europe (both East and West) have a job to do and standards (sometimes exacting ones) to meet. Europeans are not inattentive to religious institutions; they entrust to them very specific responsibilities and complain if these are inadequately ful-filled. It is for this reason, amongst others, that the future of these institutions and the law that surrounds them forms part of public rather than private debate.

And if this is true at national level, it is all the more the case with respect to local communities. Here the discussion forms part of the continuing debate about civil society, whether this be in societies previously dominated by com-munism or in those exposed to the rigours of the free market. What, the civil society advocates ask, are the most effective forms of organization to ensure a functioning democracy at all levels—a situation, that is, in which the state engages with a wide diversity of economic, social, political, and cultural organ-izations in order to create an effective and inclusive social agenda? Clearly the faith communities of modern Europe are crucial players in this sphere, repre-senting—directly or indirectly—a wide variety of interests, including some of the most disadvantaged sections of the population as a whole.[2] It is at this level, moreover, that the values embodied in the confessional parties of West Europe are most likely to gain their purchase. Like all political parties the con-fessional parties (notably Christian Democracy) have undergone a profound mutation in the closing years of the twentieth century, partially if not totally ceding their place to a multiplicity of pressure groups and social movements (Hanley 1994; van Kersbergen 1995). Some of these movements are overtly religious (those, for example, advancing or resisting liturgical change); others have a secular agenda but incorporate substantial sections of the religious

---

[2] An excellent example of analysis at this level can be found in Smith's work on the multiple faith communities in East London (Smith 1998).

constituency (those, for instance, who feel strongly for or against abortion or euthanasia); yet others (the green movement or aspects of the women's movement) can be analysed *as if* they were religions. Confessional parties as such may or may not cease to exist; the connections between the religious and the political sphere will continue. Working out these relationships at the intermediary level is central to the understanding of civil society.

## Precarious Memory

Looked at in a different way, however, *vicarious* memory is almost bound to be *precarious*, in that it depends by definition on someone else. Indeed there are those who argue that a memory held vicariously is necessarily a temporary phenomenon; it cannot endure indefinitely. Such a statement need careful unpicking, however, for there is more than one sense to the notion of 'precariousness' in terms of the religious memory or memories of modern Europe. Majority and minority religious groups, for example, are very differently placed in this respect. In terms of the former, the active participants are supported not only by the tacit acceptance of larger sections of the population, but by the cultural deposit of centuries. This is not so for most religious minorities, who have to find innovative modes of insertion into the religious life of modern Europe. Each of these categories (majority and minority) will be dealt with in turn.

For the historic churches, the notion of precariousness is at its most pertinent with respect to generational change. Both the chapter dealing with demography and that on the teaching of religion in the education systems of modern Europe underline the same point. It is abundantly clear (1) that the younger generations of Europe have effectively lost touch with the institutional churches in terms of anything approaching regular practice and (2) that the forms of religious instruction provided in the educational systems of modern Europe are moving away from a model based on catechesis to modes of teaching that offer information about rather than in religious beliefs. Given this state of affairs, it is hardly surprising that the knowledge base of younger people in terms of Bible stories, awareness of liturgy, and elementary church history is crumbling—there is very little to hold it in place. The notion of a shared language or grammar of belief based on the Judaeo-Christian tradition exists only in pockets among young people, for the most part among the children of active churchgoers or those involved in the youth movements run by the churches.[3]

[3] The situation has something in common with the precariousness of classical scholarship in almost all state schools in Britain. The teaching of Latin and Greek more or less disappeared as the grammar schools gave way to comprehensive education. One day Latin and Greek were taught in the state sector (albeit to a minority), the next they were not; a particular form of memory was lost. It is now held by a relatively small number of privately educated pupils.

This is not the whole story, however, for significant numbers of younger Europeans have shown themselves willing to engage the spiritual in rather different ways. If, for example, the definition of religion is widened to include questions about individual or social health, about the purpose of existence, the future of the planet, and the responsibilities of humanity both to fellow humans and to the earth itself (including the animal kingdom), a rather different formulation emerges. It seems that younger people may well respond to these profound moral and ethical (indeed religious) questions rather more positively than their elders. With this in mind it seems all the more important to distinguish between religious knowledge and religious sensibility; the two do not necessary move in the same direction. Generations which have lost the former do not necessarily lose the latter—indeed it is perfectly possible that openness to the spiritual may increase at precisely the same time that allegiance to and knowledge about the institutional churches declines. The associated collapse of discipline in itself encourages experimentation and innovative forms of spiritual encounter—the memory mutates. Sjödin (1995) offers interesting evidence from Sweden in this respect. Young people are not only rejecting the authority of the church; they are also questioning the assumptions of modern scientific enquiry. One result of this situation is an increasing acceptance of the paranormal by significant sections of the population.[4] Such views are held on an individual basis; they lie outside the realm of organized religion altogether.

In terms of precariousness, religious minorities face a very different set of issues. It is important, first of all, to acknowledge their economic and social vulnerabilty. Quite apart from any issues about culture or religion, Europe's religious minorities (with the partial exception of Judaism) are communities of the newly arrived, struggling for a foothold in terms of employment, housing, and education. For this reason alone, adherence to cultural or religious tradition becomes all the more important, for it is often these aspects of life which bind a community together in times of adversity. This is one reason why minorities (whether Christian or other-faith) tend to practise their religion with a greater degree of regularity than the majority; it is the focus of community life. Another reason lies in the absence of cultural support. Minorities are forced to be self-supporting in terms of religious life since nothing can be left to the designated professionals of the host community.

Generational patterns are a crucial factor in this process (just as they are for the majority), given that the relationship between the religious minority and the host society evolves over time. Younger generations of Muslims or Sikhs, for example, are offered choices unthinkable for their parents or grandparents. Exactly what happens in the second and third generation is not, however, always predictable. It is true that one possibility lies in the gradual dilution of

---

[4] The tendency towards unconventionality is, however, creeping up the age-range—it is no longer the sole preserve of younger age-groups. So far, however, the elderly (prewar generations) persist in their attachment to more conventional forms of religion.

the religious memory as elements of the host culture assert their dominance. An equally valid option can, though, be found in the *reinvention* of Muslim or Sikh identity, as the specificities of theology separate out from previous cultural packaging and become increasingly self-sufficient—a process which constitutes a form of religious innovation in itself (Babès 1995). Bearing the myriad of possibilities in mind, there is no alternative to careful observation in order to map the changes taking place; convincing patterns may indeed emerge, but they should be supported by empirical enquiry, not theoretical assumption.

Demography is a further factor to be taken into account, an area where the contrast between the Jewish minority and the more recently arrived religious communities is at its most evident. The discussion in Chapter 7 emphasized this point: Jewish populations of Europe—with the exception of the Sephardic constituency in France—are older than the average and family size is small. Muslims, Sikhs, and Hindus, in contrast, are relatively young communities in which birthrates remain for the time being (though probably not in the long term) higher than the European norm. In terms of precariousness, therefore, it is necessary to balance the relative prosperity of the Jewish population with its demographic vulnerability—up to a point the former compensates for the latter but not entirely.

It is, for example, in connection with the Jewish community that the possibility of an *extinguished memory* is at its most pertinent. This, certainly, is the view of Wasserstein (1996) though contradicted at least in part by Sacks (1999). There are two stages in Wasserstein's argument. In East and Central Europe the Jewish memory was to all intents and purposes extinguished during and immediately after the Second World War (this, after all, was Hitler's intention). A rich and distinctive culture effectively lost its resonance in Lithuania, Poland, the Czech Republic, and Hungary even if small communities continued to exist and in some places began to rebuild a communal life. This is also the case in the parts of West Europe most devastated by the Nazi policy of extermination, notably Austria and Germany. In other parts of West Europe, the Jewish communities re-established themselves after the war, only to face a different set of perils: threats to the future brought about by out-migration, assimilation, and intermarriage rather than persecution. Achieving their goal in one respect, the Jewish population becomes vulnerable in another—more so, probably, than any other faith community in modern Europe.

A longer-term historical perspective is, however, important in that chains of religious memory which have been *ruptured or broken* do, from time to time, reassert themselves. Jewish communities, for example, have experienced periods of expulsion from certain parts of Europe in previous centuries. They have none the less maintained themselves, re-emerging to play a highly significant role in the evolution of Europe's economic, cultural, and intellectual life; there is no reason why this process should not continue. Less dramatic but certainly significant from the point of view of the community concerned was the public eclipse of the Catholic memory in Britain for several centuries (see Chapter 2). The Catholic memory endured, however, allowing the Catholic community to make an important contribution to British life in the fullness of time. Recent scholarship has seen a further step in this evolution as the Reformation itself is reconsidered by British historians—resulting in a partial rehabilitation of Catholicism as an indigenous, rather than foreign, memory in late twentieth-century Britain.

Not unrelated to this renegotiation of Protestant and Catholic identities in Britain is the issue of Europe or Europeanness. The complexities are evident as an historically Protestant, and in some ways increasingly fragmented, group of nations seeks to come to terms with a primarily Catholic Europe. The rapid evolution of the Irish Republic (Britain's Catholic neighbour) within the European Union, involving not least a marked increase in material prosperity, simply compounds an already delicate issue. It is important to remember, however, that similar renegotiations are taking place all over the continent (not just in the British Isles), as the European Union begins gradually to assert its significance. Europe as a whole is invited to think again about what it has in common rather than what pulls it apart.

One way of responding to this question is to revive an older memory of Christendom (discarded for several centuries) and to use this to affirm European commonalities rather than difference, a point approached from a variety of perspectives in the useful collection of papers (some thematic, some more empirical) brought together by Bastian and Collange (1999). The association between Europeanness and new initiatives within the ecumenical movement is part and parcel of the same discussion; it was covered in some detail in Chapters 1 and 2. A third way into this crucially important debate can be found in the innovative analysis of nationhood elaborated by Hastings in the 1996 Wiles Lectures at the Queen's University in Belfast (Hastings 1997).[5] Following Hastings, the idea of 'nation' is not an invention of the eighteenth century but a far more ancient idea, embodied in the Old Testament understanding of a chosen people. This, however, is not the only strand in biblical teaching; it is countered by a New Testament emphasis on empire and universalism. The continuing tension between the particular and the universal has been a defining feature not only of subsequent theological reflection, but of European history itself.

It is hardly surprising, therefore, that the emergent commonalities of late twentieth-century Europe are to some extent threatened by an equally innovative range of alternatives or divisions, possibilities which are heavily mediated by a whole range of interested parties. These will be examined in some detail in the paragraphs that follow.

---

[5] In these lectures, Hastings substantially refutes the ideas of Eric Hobsbawm (the 1985 Wiles Lecturer) published in *Nations and Nationalism since 1780* (Hobsbawm 1990).

# Mediated Memory

Before doing so, it is necessary to rejoin the sequence of the book as a whole and to look again at mediated memory in the sense discussed in Chapter 6, a subject which provokes a rather different set of questions. If it is clear, on the one hand, that religious memory is, and always has been, mediated by something or by someone, it is frequently suggested that the 'mass media' of modern technological societies represent a quantum leap in this respect—with the strong implication that the manner in which the media become the message in late modernity is without precedent (a question which becomes all the more pertinent as the Web and the Internet become increasingly dominant forms of communication). Contrasting points of view are embedded in these assumptions. The first suggests that these exponentially powerful forms of communication not only transmit the message (or memory) but do so in ways that are necessarily distorting. The second is more moderate. These are indeed important innovations—different in some respects from their forebears but no more misleading in principle than earlier, but equally persuasive, forms of religious interaction.

A number of factors should be borne in mind in discussing these possibilities. First, modern forms of communication rely as much on the visual image as they do on the written or spoken word, a fact which has considerable potential for the enactment of a message, or set of messages, which is essentially dramatic. In this respect modern forms of media offer possibilities which have, in many parts of Europe, been put on one side for several centuries. A second factor reflects the nature of the electronic message: this is necessarily free-standing. It is watched or absorbed by choice, independent of community sanction or support. The modern media are unable to engender either the discipline or the pastoral care of a worshipping congregation. It follows that cultures of obligation inevitably give way to cultures of consumption as the cruising of multiple channels relieves the boredom of the overlong sermon, or interrupts the carefully planned liturgical event—so much so that mediated liturgy provokes an unprecedented set of theological questions, all of which may shift once again as interactive communication becomes the norm.

The interactive element is important. It is already possible to access, and (it follows) to criticize, sermons on the Internet.[6] Late-modern individuals, moreover, despite their physical isolation and lack of parish activity, can and do *re*-establish themselves in the form of virtual discussion groups, including religious ones. New communities form just as others disintegrate, formations which depend very largely on the instant exchange of information. Precisely the same facility (the instant exchange of information), can however, operate

[6] Through the Faculty of Theology in the Georg-August-Universität in Göttingen in Germany, for example. A programme of research relating to the users of this site is currently in progress.

in an entirely different manner, one that enhances rather than diminishes religious discipline. Communication is so rapid and so far-reaching that no misdemeanour (clerical or lay, theological or moral, near or far) can go unnoticed by the hierarchy. Paradoxically, organizational control is increased at the same time—and for the same reasons—that local communities are losing their capacity to enforce discipline. In some respects the memory is subject to greater restraint; in others it increasingly escapes the traditional boundaries.

## Alternative Memories

Whatever the case, media time (just like legal status or educational provision) is a coveted asset and sought after by a wide range of religious groups. Access has to be regulated, either by the market or by more consensual forms of decision-making, a process which reflects the growing diversity of religions in modern Europe and the need to find equitable ways of dealing with this—a subject that must now be considered in more detail. The first point is one of clarification: religious diversity can take a number of forms. It exists (1) within and between the Christian churches, (2) in the arrival of significant other-faith populations, and (3) in innovative forms of the sacred that lie outside the religious organizations altogether. Each of these presents a different set of issues.

The first, for instance, reflects the shift in the ecumenical movement away from the notion of organic unity towards the complementary contributions of different Christian churches, a change in emphasis particularly true of Europe's Protestant churches. Both the Orthodox and the Catholics have a rather different attitude, despite the metamorphosis in the latter at the time of the Second Vatican Council in terms of its relationships with other Christian communities. The Orthodox, moreover, have the capacity to maintain considerable diversity within the church itself—the same issue is engaged but in rather a different way. It should not be assumed, however, that greater co-operation between an acknowledged variety of Christian churches, even Protestant ones, has necessarily brought about unanimity. Far from it. What has emerged instead (or indeed in addition to denominational difference) are divisions that lie across rather than between the European churches as a whole. In all of these, for example, it is possible to find both individuals and groups who are particularly committed to the issues of 'Justice, peace, and a sustainable society' and those who resist what they feel to be meddling in worldly affairs. There are others who feel strongly about the under-representation of women in the leadership—if not the membership—of the Christian churches, together with their alter egos who resist the ordination of women. Yet others have strong views about liturgy and the advisability or otherwise of constant liturgical revision—a crucial element in the maintenance of a common memory. Most significant of all, perhaps, in terms of this chapter, is a point already mentioned: that is, the presence in all churches (and at all levels) of those who feel a strong sense of commonality on the European issue itself, and those who resist this—emphasizing instead the *national* significance of whatever church they may belong to. Each of these groups draws on a different version of the religious memory of Europe: the notion of Christendom competes with representations of national identity.

Ecumenical commitment in Europe has, however, reached a point unthinkable in the immediate post-war period. Or to say the same thing more directly, what is commonplace at the turn of the millennium was almost unimaginable fifty years earlier, a point that is often forgotten in the heat of continuing debate. In exactly the same period, however, the European religious scene has been transformed by *new* forms of diversity: the arrival of significant other-faith communities—notably Muslims, Sikhs, Hindus, and Buddhists (the Jewish population had, for the most part, arrived earlier). Interfaith relationships, moreover, raise altogether different issues from those between Christian churches, though it does seem to be the case that countries which are used to relative variety in the Christian sense are able (with some exceptions) to adapt more easily to new forms of pluralism than those accustomed to a virtual monopoly. Nowhere, however, are the issues that emerge simple or straightforward; unsurprisingly, in that they demand a transformation of assumptions embedded in the European consciousness for centuries. 'Live and let live' will not do, for the phrase implies in itself an attitude to religion not shared by many of those who are arriving. The kind of issues at stake were those discussed in Chapter 7. Paradoxically, moreover, the process is taking place at precisely the time when the historic churches of Europe are losing their dominance—in terms of religious discipline as much as secular influence. One result of the decline in institutional control is the emergence of increasing numbers of spiritual outlets beyond the reach of organized religion of whatever kind. The most talked-about manifestation of this tendency, the New Age, was dealt with in some detail in Chapter 8.

From a sociological point of view, a common thread ties together these very different manifestations of diversity—one, moreover, that connects very directly to the theoretical discussion of secularization introduced in Chapter 2. Until recently, most sociological thinkers had assumed that growing diversity and growing pluralism necessarily led to greater pressure on religious institutions and a tendency for faith as such to be undermined (truth cannot be relativized). Latterly, the line of reasoning has gradually begun to reverse itself in the sense that an increasing number of religious outlets, be they organized or not, simply stimulate the market—the take-up of religion (though not necessarily in its traditional forms) is likely to increase rather than decrease. It follows that one reason for the relatively low levels of religious activity in Europe has been the artificial restriction of the market, a process inevitably linked to the historical collusions between religion and power all over the continent. This, broadly speaking, is the view of the rational-choice theorists (see Chapter 2, note 5).

What, though, does this mean for the religious life of Europe at the end of the twentieth century? Will the growing diversity stimulate the market as it appears to have done elsewhere in the world or will this process simply not work in the European case? Responses vary. One argument suggests that key features of European religious life not only limited the market in the past, but will continue to do so in the future. Significant in this respect are the low levels of religious activity brought about by former restrictions: quite simply, churchgoing has sunk to a point beyond which it cannot reasonably be revived. This may indeed be so, in which case religious memories of all kinds will gradually fade away. Exactly the reverse process, however, is possible. New arrivals and new alternatives will stimulate demand, and all churches—at least all those perceptive to what is going on round them—can benefit. Theoretically possibly but unlikely, at least in the foreseeable future. A third line of argument lies somewhere between the two extremes. Europeans are not necessarily less religious than other late-modern populations but they are differently so, differences brought about by the specificities of their history. It follows that growing pluralism in this part of the world—the transformation of European religion to the religions of Europe—is also a special case. It will mutate within its own (empirically observable) parameters, not according to an abstract model. Only time will tell.[7]

## Conflicting Memories

A rather different aspect of the debate concerning the increasing pluralism of Europe's religious life relates to the relationship between alternative memories and *conflicting memories*. These are complex connections. Indeed the line from alternative to conflict (like that from mutation to alternative) is more of a continuum than a black-and-white distinction, just as some tensions are more creative than others. The tension, for example, between national loyalty and international obligation can take healthy as well as unhealthy forms; so, too, the awareness of regional difference within as well as between the different European nations. A sense of identity (national, regional, or other) that gives meaning to life is not necessarily a negative phenomenon even if it marks out one group of people from another. That the religious factor is an important feature in such differences can be seen all over Europe (see, for example, the Spanish case described in Chapter 8). It is, moreover, a central theme in Martin's forthcoming text on the socio-geographic patterning of religion in

[7] This is a line of argument which leads once again towards the notion of European exceptionalism. Another way of approaching the same question is to look at European religion from the *outside*, and to ask what forms of religion are widespread in the modern world, but do not exist (or exist only to a very limited extent) in Europe. (See Davie, forthcoming for a development of this argument.)

the history of Europe, within which Martin works through a whole range of spatial as well as sociological patterns as they impinge on Europe's past and present. These include centre and periphery (both within Europe as a whole and within each nation), capital and province, nation and region. The migration of critical poles of reference—whether these be religious (Rome and Geneva) or secular (Berlin and Paris)—forms an organizing theme. The axes around which European religions rotate are not immutable; they shift in the course of centuries, and at times far more rapidly.

It has to be acknowledged, however, that some religious differences—interacting as ever with a multiplicity of other factors—become not only enduring but violent confrontations. At the turn of the millennium the least tractable of these lie at the peripheries of the continent—in the Balkans and in Northern Ireland. The former conflict lay hidden for most of the post-war period under the pseudo-unity of the Yugoslav Republic; it broke out with extreme ferocity in the early 1990s, offering an alarming example of conflicting territorial claims (each legitimated by a different memory), which in turn justified levels of brutality not seen in Europe since 1945. It is easy to forget, in the aftermath of the 1990s, both the peaceable nature of Muslims in Albania and the reality of Sarajevo as a truly multicultural city for several generations. Northern Ireland in contrast simply grinds on. From time to time there are fresh initiatives, with the hope that the resulting lulls in the violence may become at least semi-permanent. One such occurred after the 1998 Good Friday agreements—the symbolism of a Christian festival being a significant factor in their signing. The basic conflict resides, however, in two incompatible versions of history which cannot be reconciled without compromise, and for some (how many, of course, is the critical factor) compromise is out of the question.[8]

Other, more ideological conflicts—for example the battle of the two Frances, one Catholic and one *laïque* (Poulat 1987) or the strongly pillarized nature of Dutch society (Goudsblom 1967)—have receded in the post-war period. These divisions (the French one horizontal, the Dutch vertical) formed the defining feature of political and cultural life for as long as most people could remember. Gradually, however, both the lines of division and the associated animosities have faded: quite simply they lost their *raison d'être*. A further penetrating question lurks, however, beneath the more amicable reformulations which emerge, one that echoes *both* the theoretical debate about secularization *and* the statements at the end of Chapter 7 concerning a tolerant and pluralist society. It can be summarized quite simply. Is it possible to achieve a greater sense of moderation in the religious life of Europe without losing sight of its significance altogether? Or, even more directly, is it necessarily the case that once Europeans cease to dispute the place of religion in

---

[8] The notion of the middle ground is central to the changes going on in Northern Ireland. Extremists on either side can only prosper given the tacit acceptance of larger numbers in the community.

modern societies, it ceases for the great majority to matter altogether? Holding the balance between these two extremes is not only essential to the maintenance of a healthy democracy, it forms the basis of courteous relations between different religions. Mutual respect between faith communities is just as difficult to achieve in a climate of indifference as it is in an atmosphere of hostility.

## Symbolic Memories

An interesting example of opinion veering from one extreme to another can be found in public discussion of the millennium. Indisputably a Christian anniversary, the marking of this event engendered extensive public controversy in different parts of Europe in view of the changing religious scene. There were those, first of all, who maintained that the absence of a Christian element in millennium activities was unthinkable, for without the Christian story there would be no sense of a millennium at all (two thousand years is a persuasive period of time). There are others who argued that a triumphalist celebration of the millennium—a necessarily Christian occasion—would be offensive to those of other faiths or of none, so it should be muted as far as possible. The attempts (in Britain) to create a 'Millennium Resolution' (*not* a prayer) avoiding any mention of God revealed, all too clearly, the pitfalls awaiting those who try to please both parties. Lowest common denominators do not work well in religion.

Rome—like the Holy Land—offers a natural focus for millennial activities, and welcomed a huge influx of pilgrims during the Jubilee Year of 2000, a moment anticipated by John Paul II for over half a decade. The apostolic letter *Tertio Millennio Adveniente* was published in November 1994 and set in motion a whole cycle of spiritual and practical preparations. The Vatican website provided extensive detail of the three-year preparatory phase, with its Trinitarian, theological, sacramental, and Marian dimensions. It also contained an outline history of the notion of Jubilee, and the full text of *Tertio Millennio Adveniente* and of the Bull of Indiction of the Great Jubilee of the Year 2000, *Incarnationis Mysterium* (all in several languages). Central to the whole endeavour was the call for the remission of international debt, a global issue guaranteed to catch public attention in secular as well as religious circles (a stroke of genius on the part of the Pope). A second theme—even more directly related to the argument of this chapter—can be found in the 'purification of memory' as the Great Jubilee approached; hence the apostolic letter contained a detailed review of European history including the violence associated with the Christian past. The reader was invited to question some very basic assumptions. The whole cycle of preparation came to a climax on Christmas Eve 1999 with the opening of the Holy Door in St Peter's (the goal of pilgrimage) and the public commencement of the Jubilee (which ends on 6 January 2001). The fact that these events followed hard on the heels of the tenth anniversary of the fall of the Berlin Wall only added to their significance for a Polish Pope committed to the defeat of communism in Central and Eastern Europe.

It is hardly surprising that the extensive preparations for the Great Jubilee became the focus of attention for Italian sociologists in the late 1990s, a group of scholars anxious above all to discern the great variety of elements that come together in such an event—centred in Rome but with an evident global significance. Martelli (1999), for example, analyses the Jubilee at three levels: the global, the organizational (i.e. the Catholic Church, the Italian state, the tourist sector etc.), and the individual. At each level, the categories become inextricably mixed, between the genuinely religious, the culturally inspired, and an ethic of consumption—itself ranging from 'big business' to the individual take-up of (virtual) 'faith'. The effect that such prolonged exposure by the media will have on the Catholic Church forms an additional theme. Macioti and Cipriani (1999) echo the mixing of categories. Pilgrimage has evolved through many centuries; in the modern period the spiritual and material become ever more difficult to disentangle. Such confusions are exemplified both in the hundreds of thousands of pilgrim-tourists who will arrive in Rome in the year of the Jubilee and in the attempts by the Roman authorities to accommodate their needs.

The millennium, however, is simply a well-hyped example of a wider phenomenon—the use of anniversaries (big and small) not only to prompt but to create a continuing sense of memory, whether religious or not. Some of these anniversaries are simply routine, the taken-for-granted nature of which reveals the dominance of the Christian tradition all over Europe. The cycle of the liturgical year, raised at the start of this chapter, is one such; it frames a great deal of European living. Christmas and Easter remain the major festivals around which holidays and festivities (of all kinds) are organized.[9] Significant numbers of Europeans, moreover, 'touch base' at this point—they attend church as part of their celebrations, taking part (literally) in the liturgies that re-enact the memory. Saints' days, particularly in Catholic countries, are similar; not only are they markers of time, but of space. These are local rather than national festivals and create a sense of belonging to this or that community; those who take responsibility for liturgy on these occasions are central characters in the drama.

Other anniversaries are more selective. Some are religious, others secular—still more are careful combinations of the two with an emphasis on inclusion rather than difference. They can, moreover, change over time in terms of the message or memory that they wish to endorse. The commemorations in France and elsewhere of the Edict of Nantes (1598) and its Revocation (1685)

---

[9]  The fact that the major Christian festivals themselves took over earlier celebrations (linked to the sun in the case of Christmas or the moon in the case of Easter) simply indicates their embeddedness in the habits of the region.

are excellent examples of this process. There is a marked contrast, for example, between the commemoration of the Revocation at the end of the nineteenth century with the equivalent event a hundred years later. In the 1880s, France was just emerging from the Franco–Pussian war and was deeply sensitive towards the overseas (and particularly the German) connections of its Protestant community. In some circles at least, there remained a sense that to be Protestant was not to be fully French. In consequence the anniversary belonged almost exclusively to the Protestant community. A century later, in an entirely different international climate, the global connections of French Protestantism were celebrated to the full, not only in terms of the growing unity within Europe but in relation also to Third World responsibilities; missionary links to the developing world became an asset rather than a liability. More problematic, in 1985, was the question of ecumenism: could the realities of the past be sufficiently acknowledged without reviving the hatred that went with them? (Davie 1987) In the end the principal event brought together not only Protestants, Catholics, and Orthodox, but representatives of the French Jewish and Muslim communities as well. In 1998, the anniversary of the Edict itself was widely observed, initiating a public debate on the nature of tolerance at the turn of the millennium. A flood of publications appeared throughout the year with a common theme: the careful documentation of the seeds of pluralism planted some four hundred years earlier, alongside the lessons to be learnt for the modern period.[10]

So much for the French Protestants. A distinctive—but disputatious—occasion for French Catholics was mentioned briefly in Chapter 6 in connection with the associated papal visit. In this chapter, it provides an initial step towards a conclusion in that it brings together a number of points concerning the changing place of religion in modern Europe. The fifteenth centenary of the baptism into the Catholic Church of Clovis, King of France, was a strange and recondite affair with little relevance to modern French people. The decision to combine its celebration with a visit of the Pope to France—recommended by Mitterrand himself (always an *aficionado* of anniversaries)—gave it the highest possible profile. By so doing it provided yet another trigger to the unresolved if diminishing debate about the place of religion in the public life of France. Predictably, and interesting for a discussion such as this, the visit also prompted a number of enquiries into the state of Catholicism in modern France (see, for example, *Le Point*, 14 Sept. 1996: 70–9). The statistics mirror those set out in Chapter 1; Catholicism remains the majority religion in France but the disciplines are eroding fast, both in terms of practice and belief. Despite such erosions the majority of French people (70 per cent), are likely— like their former President—to return to the church and to the familiar

---

[10] The most significant of the associated events—organized by the Fédération Protestante de France—took place (like its predecessor in 1985) at the UNESCO building in Paris. Jacques Chirac, the President of the Republic, was present. The national papers covered the event in some detail.

liturgies 'at the hour of our death' if not before. It is clear that memorialization of an individual (private as well as public) remains for most Europeans, not only the French, a primarily religious event.

A short paragraph on anniversaries in the other-faith communities provides a footnote to this section. Such events are far less visible than those so far described, especially for the newly arrived. Celebrated in particular localities, they do not catch the attention of the public at large. Herein lies the difference between religious currents that are supported by the mainstream and those that are not; in this sense there is, and will always be, an in-built imbalance to interfaith encounter insofar as it takes place in Europe. At a local level, however, the impact of a festival can be considerable: adolescents in a Church of England high school in the West of England were brought up short by the seriousness with which a young Muslim (almost the only one in the school) kept the rules of fasting through Ramadan in mid-summer. His friends elected to encourage him, knowing full well that none of them took their own religion sufficiently seriously to emulate his example.

## Mutating Memory—The Ongoing Reconstructions of European Religion

Mutation (see Chapter 8) concerns the adaptation of an organism to a changing environment in order better to ensure its survival. In the analysis of religion in modern Europe, too much emphasis has frequently been placed on one side of this equation—the adaptation (or the failure to adapt) of the organism in question; too little has been placed on the society of which the organism (the religious constituency) is part. A careful analysis of societal change reveals that in many aspects of their lives, religious organizations are simply operating in the same ways as many secular institutions as they come to terms with the transformations of late-modern societies, not least European ones. A second, rather more subtle, variation on the theme of one-sidedness also exists. It can be found in those analyses which do pay attention to the changing nature of society, but only in so far as the shifts from pre-industrial to industrial changes are taken into account. More space should be made for post-industrial changes—as populations move out of rather than into industrial cities and as identities develop in terms of consumption rather than production (Davie 1994).

A more rounded approach was suggested in Chapter 3: one which recognized that many of the problems of the historic churches have been brought about by their over-dependence historically on the 'centre' of West European society (in economic, political, and cultural terms) and as that centre itself becomes increasingly insecure, the churches have been correspondingly damaged. This is a long-term analysis which moves through several centuries well into the late-modern period. Churches in Central and East Europe present a slightly different case. Given the militantly secular nature of the centre in this part of Europe, religious institutions were necessarily pushed to the periphery—they became the focus (indeed the carriers) of an alternative rather than mainstream memory. With the partial exception of Poland, however, they face equally intractable problems in the form of drastically diminished resources (in money and buildings, but also in terms of people and experience). Rebuilding effectively once the possibility came has been an uphill task.

But what of the future? It is essential first of all to pay attention to the questions articulated at the beginning of this chapter and to make a careful distinction between the Christian churches (or Christian memory) as such and the provision for space in modern European societies where all faiths can flourish. The increasing demand for individualized forms of spirituality should also be taken into account. Difficulties will inevitably occur if these agendas become confused (a confusion well exemplified in the debates concerning religious education). There are times, clearly, when all faith communities can support one another in insisting that their mutual interests be taken seriously. But at other times their needs are incompatible and trying to do justice to everyone simply ends in pleasing no one. Interfaith worship is a particularly delicate area, frequently involving secular as well as religious organizations. The point reflects once again the central significance of liturgy in the maintenance of religious memory of whatever kind.

This is nicely illustrated by the world of higher education in Britain (Gilliat-Ray 1999). The first point to note is the marked expansion in higher education, brought about by economic necessity all over Europe (see Chapter 5). In order to meet this demand, a number of institutions in Britain have been upgraded to the status of 'university', acquiring in the course of this process new names and new charters. An increasingly popular marker of this 'elevation' has been some sort of religious service—far more so, in fact, than in the generation of universities established in the sixties, which were notably secular in their outlook. Finding an appropriate form of liturgy to mark such an occasion is, however, more difficult. This is hardly surprising given that inclusive worship raises, visibly and immediately, the central issue of an increasingly pluralist society. How far can those responsible for historic faith adapt to the new environment without compromising the principles of their own tradition? Or to put the same point in sociological rather than theological terms: is it possible to honour the integrity of the Christian mainstream without excluding from public celebrations a significant proportion of the community, notably in the major urban centres of modern European society? Civil religion (in the Durkheimian sense)—still in considerable demand—will have to mutate if it is to fulfil its binding function.

One particular possibility should, however, be mentioned in conclusion: the idea of a civil religion of Europe over and above its constituent nations. Indeed without some awareness of common identity and common heritage, it is unlikely that the European Union (or any other definition of the continent) can become an effective social, as opposed to economic, reality. The 'soul of Europe' cannot be left to chance (Bastian and Collange 1999). Careful attention should be paid to both its form and content in an increasingly pluralist society, bearing in mind external as well as internal relationships—the global context is crucial, as are the internal pressures of the continent. It is significant, moreover, that similar questions are posing themselves one after the other in different European nations. Their answers, as ever, will depend on particular national histories, on the specificities of church–state connections, on the nature of the institutions involved, and, undoubtedly, on the good will of the interested parties.[11] It is to everyone's advantage to find appropriate forms of religious life for the new millennium, in other words to affirm healthy mutations in Europe's religious heritage and discourage others. The understanding of religion as a form of collective memory should be considered in this light; it is, however, but one contribution to an urgent and very much wider task.

[11] Three brief examples demonstrate the range of possible responses. First, the lack of representation from the Muslim minority in Sweden in the memorial services following the nightclub tragedy in Gothenburg (autumn 1998) was noticeable; the more so given the fact that almost three-quarters of the deaths were from Muslim families (information from Anders Bäckström, Dec. 1998). Rather different in this respect is the increasingly public discussion of future Coronation services in Britain. Some sort of representation of the other-faith communities is considered likely; how it is to be effected and with what effect on liturgy is the crucial question. A third example can be found in the preparations for the Swiss Exposition in the year 2001. The directors, it seems, do not want to exclude religion from EXPO 01 but do want to 'manage' its public presentation themselves. The ambiguities that emerge from this situation may fascinate the sociologist of religion; they are rather more worrying for the churches (Campiche 1998).

# REFERENCES

Abbruzzese, S. (1989), *Communione e Liberazione*, Paris: Le Cerf.

Abela, A., Borowik, I., Dowling, T., Fulton, J., Marler, P., and Tomasi, L. (2000), *Young Catholics and the New Millennium: Private and Social Consciousness in Six Western Societies*, Dublin: University College Press.

Abrams, M., Gerard, D., and Timms, N. (1985) (eds.), *Values and Social Change in Britain*, Basingstoke: Macmillan.

Albert-Llorca, M. (1996), 'Renouveau de la religion locale en Espagne', in G. Davie and D. Hervieu-Léger (eds.), *Identités religieuses en Europe*. Paris: La Découverte, 235–52.

Allchin, A. M. (1994), 'Grundtvig and England: An Introduction', in A. M. Allchin, D. Jasper, J. H. Schjørring, and K. Stevenson (eds.), *Heritage and Prophecy: Grundtvig and the English-speaking World*, Norwich: Canterbury Press, 3–18.

Allieu, N. (1996), *Laïcité et culture religieuse à l'école*, Paris: ESF.

Arthur, C. (1993) (ed.), *Religion and the Media: An Introductory Reader*, Cardiff: University of Wales Press.

—— (1999), 'Curating the Creator', *Museums Journal*, Sept.: 41–5.

Arweck, E., and Clarke, P. (1997) (eds.), *New Religious Movements in Western Europe: An Annotated Bibliography*, Westport, Conn. and London: Greenwood Press.

Ashford, S., and Timms, N. (1992), *What Europe Thinks: A Study of West European Values*, Aldershot: Dartmouth.

Azria, R. (1996), *Le Judaïsme*, Paris: La Découverte.

Babès, L. (1995), 'Recompositions identitaires dans l'islam français', *Archives de Sciences Sociales des Religions*, 92: 35–47.

Bäckström, A., and Bromander, J. (1995), *Kyrkobyggnaden och det offentliga rummet*, Uppsala: Svenska Kyrkans Utredningar (contains an English summary).

Barker, D., Halman, L., and Vloet, A. (1992), *The European Values Study 1981–1990: Summary Report*, Aberdeen: Gordon Cook Foundation on behalf of the European Values Group.

Barker, E. (1997), 'But Who's Going to Win? National and Minority Religions in Post-Communist Societies', in I. Borowik and G. Babiński (eds.), *New Religious Phenomena in Central and Eastern Europe*, Krakow: Nomos, 25–62.

—— and Warburg, M. (1998) (eds.), *New Religions and New Religiosity*, Aarhus: Aarhus University Press.

Bastian, J.-P., and Collange, J.-F. (1999) (eds.), *L'Europe à la recherche de son âme*, Geneva: Labor et Fides.

Baubérot, J. (1990), *Vers un nouveau pacte laïque*, Paris: Le Seuil.

—— (1997), *La Morale laïque contre l'ordre moral*, Paris: Le Seuil.

—— (1998), 'La Laïcité française et ses mutations', *Social Compass*, 45: 175–87.

Bax, M. (1996), 'Making Holy in Medjugorje: The Politics of Meaning in a Bosnian Rural Community', *Journal of Mediterranean Studies*, 6: 219–32.

Beckford, J. (1985), *Cult Controversies*, London and New York: Tavistock Publications.

Beckford, J. (1986) (ed.), *New Religious Movements and Rapid Social Change*, London: Sage/UNESCO.

—— (1998), 'Secularization and Social Solidarity: A Social Constructionist View', in R. Laermans, B. Wilson, and J. Billiet (eds.), *Secularization and Social Integration*, Leuven: Leuven University Press, 141–58.

Bell, D. (1976), *The Cultural Contradictions of Capitalism*, London: Heinemann.

Berger, P. (1967), *The Sacred Canopy: Elements of a Sociological Theory of Religion*, New York: Doubleday.

—— (1992), *A Far Glory: The Quest for Faith in an Age of Credulity*, New York: Free Press.

—— (1999) (ed.), *The Desecularization of the World: Resurgent Religion and World Politics*, Grand Rapids, Mich.: Eerdmans Publishing Co.

Billiet, J. (1998), 'Social Capital, Religious-philosophical Involvement and Social Integration in Belgium: An Empirical Investigation', in R. Laermans, B. Wilson, and J. Billiet (eds.), *Secularization and Social Integration*, Leuven: Leuven University Press, 233–50.

Borowik, I., and Babiński, G. (1997) (eds.), *New Religious Phenomena in Central and Eastern Europe*, Krakow: Nomos.

Boulard, F. (1954), *Premiers itinéraires en sociologie religieuse*, Paris: Les Éditions Ouvrières.

—— and Rémy, J. (1968), *Pratique religieuse urbaine et régions culturelles*, Paris: Économie et Humanisme/Éditions Ouvrières.

Bourdieu, P., and Darbel, A., with Schnapper, D. (1991), *The Love of Art*, Cambridge: Polity Press.

Broch, H. (1984), *Hugo von Hofmannsthal and his Time: The European Imagination*, Chicago: University of Chicago Press.

Bruce, S. (1990), *Pray TV: Televangelism in America*, London: Routledge.

—— (1992) (ed.), *Religion and Modernization*, Oxford: Oxford University Press.

—— (1995), *Religion in Modern Britain*, Oxford: Oxford University Press.

—— (1996), *From Cathedrals to Cults: Religion in the Modern World*, Oxford: Oxford University Press.

Brückner, W. (1984), 'Fusswallfahrt heute: Frömmigkeitsformen im sozialen Wandel der letzen hundert Jahre', in L. Kriss-Rettenbeck and G. Möhler (eds.), *Wallfahrt kennt keine Grenzen*, Munich and Zürich: Schnell & Steiner, 101–13.

Bunting, M. (1996), 'God's Media Image', *The Tablet*, 16 Nov.: 1505–6.

Butler, B. (1994), 'Epiphanies', *Museums Journal*, Feb.: 29.

Byrnes, T. (1997), 'Church and Nation in the Slovak Republic', *Religion, State and Society*, 25: 281–92.

Campiche, R. (1995), *Quand les sectes affolent: Ordre du Temple Solaire, médias et fin de millénaire*, Geneva: Labor et Fides.

—— (1996), 'Religion, statut social et identité féminine', *Archives de Sciences Sociales des Religions*, 95: 69–94 (a special issue entitled 'La Religion: frein à l'égalité hommes/femmes?').

—— (1997a) (ed.), *Cultures jeunes et religions en Europe*, Paris: Le Cerf.

—— (1997b), 'Le Traitement du religieux par les médias', *Études théologiques et religieuses*, 72: 267–79.

—— (1998), 'De la Chapelle œcuménique aux "anges dans nos campagnes"', paper presented to 'Secularization and Social Integration', an international symposium to mark the retirement of Professor Karel Dobbelaere, Leuven, 10–11 Dec.

—— Dubach, A., Bovay, C., Kruggeler, M., and Voll, P. (1992), *Croire en Suisse:*

*Analyses des résultats de l'enquête menée en 1988/1989 sur la religion des Suisses*, Lausanne: Éditions l'Age d'Homme.

C.A.S.A. (Communautés d'Accueil dans les Sites Artistiques) (1998), 'CASA', unpaginated publicity leaflet, French-language version, Paris: C.A.S.A.

Casanova, J. (1994), *Public Religions in the Modern World*, Chicago: Chicago University Press.

Cathedrals Advisory Committee for England (1980), *Cathedral Treasuries and Museums*, London: Epic Publishing Ltd.

Champion, F. (1989), 'Les Sociologues de la post-modernité religieuse et la nébuleuse mystique-ésotérique', *Archives de Sciences Sociales des Religions*, 67: 155–69.

—— (1992), 'La Nébuleuse New Age', *Études*, Feb.: 233–42.

—— (1993), 'Religieux flottant, éclectisme et syncrétismes', in J. Delumeau (ed.), *Le Fait Religieux*, Paris: Fayard, 741–71.

—— and Cohen, M. (1996), 'Les Sociologues et le problème des dites sectes', *Archives de Sciences Sociales des Religions*, 96: 5–15.

Christian, W. (1972), *Person and God in a Spanish Valley*, New York: Seminar Press.

—— (1989), *Local Religion in Sixteenth Century Spain*, Princeton, NJ: Princeton University Press.

Clarke, P. (1988), 'Islam in Contemporary Europe', in S. Sutherland, S. Stewart, L. Houlden, P. Clarke, and F. Hardy (eds.), *The World's Religions*, London: Routledge, 498–519.

Clelland, D. (1994), 'Idol Work', *Museums Journal*, Feb.: 30.

Coleman, S. (2001), *The Globalization of Charismatic Christianity: Spreading the Gospel of Prosperity*, Cambridge: Cambridge University Press.

Collinson, P. (1994), 'Reformation or Deformation?', *The Tablet*, 22 Jan.: 74–5.

Cook, M., and Davie, G. (1999) (eds.), *Modern France: Society in Transition*, London: Routledge.

Copley, T. (1997), *Teaching Religion: Fifty Years of Religious Education in England and Wales*, Exeter: Exeter University Press.

Cottin, J., and Walbaum, R. (1997), *Dieu et la pub*, Geneva and Paris: Le Cerf.

Danchin, P. (forthcoming) (ed.), *The Protection of Religious Minorities in Europe*, New York: Columbia University Press.

Davie, G. (1987), 'The Changing Face of Protestantism in 20th Century France', *Proceedings of the Huguenot Society*, 24: 378–89.

—— (1994), *Religion in Britain since 1945: Believing without Belonging*, Oxford: Blackwell.

—— (1999a), 'Religion and Laïcité', in M. Cook and G. Davie (eds.), *Modern France: Society in Transition*, London: Routledge, 195–215.

—— (1999b), 'Europe: The Exception that Proves the Rule', in P. Berger (ed.), *The Desecularization of the World: Resurgent Religion and World Politics*, Grand Rapids, Mich.: Eerdmans Publishing Co., 65–83.

—— (2000), 'Religion in Modern Britain: Changing Sociological Assumptions', *Sociology*, 34: 113–28.

—— (forthcoming), 'Patterns of Religion in Western Europe: An Exceptional Case', in R. Fenn (ed.), *The Blackwell Companion to the Sociology of Religion*, Oxford: Blackwell.

—— and Hervieu-Léger, D. (1996) (eds.), *Identités religieuses en Europe*, Paris: La Découverte.

—— Kingsbury, R., and Bäckström, A. (1997), 'Building a Future: Report from the

Eleventh Anglo-Scandinavian Pastoral Conference in Tallinn 1996', unpub. report circulated to delegates.

Davie, G. and Martin, D. (1999), 'Liturgy and Music', in A. J. Walter (ed.), *The Week Diana Died*, London: Berg Publications, 187–98.

—— and Vincent, J. (1998), 'Progress Report: Religion and Old Age', *Ageing and Society*, 18: 101–10.

Davies, D. (1990), *Cremation Today and Tomorrow*, Bramcote, Notts.: Grove Books Ltd.

Davies, J., and Wollaston, I. (1993) (eds.), *The Sociology of Sacred Texts*, Sheffield: Sheffield Academic Press.

Dayan, D. (1990), 'Présentation du pape en voyageur: Télévision, expérience rituelle, dramaturgie politique', *Terrain*, 15 (Oct.): 13–28.

—— (1998), 'Les Grands Evénements médiatiques: Au miroir du rituel', paper presented to the Conference of the Association Française de Sociologie Religieuse on 'Médias et religion en miroir', Paris, 2–3 Feb.

De Antonelis, G. (1987), *Storia dell'Azione Cattolica*, Milan: Rizzoli.

Defois, G., and Tincq, H. (1997), *Les Médias et l'Église*, Paris: CFPJ.

DellaPergola, S. (1994), 'An Overview of the Demographic Trends of European Jewry', in J. Webber (ed.), *Jewish Identities in the New Europe*, London and Washington: Littman Library of Jewish Civilization, 57–73.

Dierkens, A. (1994) (ed.), *Pluralisme religieux et laïcités dans l'Union européenne*, Brussells: Éditions de l'Université de Bruxelles.

Dittgen, A. (1994), 'La Forme du marriage en Europe. Cérémonie civile, cérémonie religieuse: Panorama et évolution', *Population*, 2: 339–68.

—— (1997), 'Les Mariages civils en Europe: Histoires, contextes, chiffres', *Droit et Société*, 36/37: 309–29.

Dobbelaere, K. (1981), 'Secularization: A Multi-dimensional Concept', *Current Sociology*, 29(2): 1–216.

Drakakis-Smith, A. (1994), 'Church Times', *Museums Journal*, Feb.: 31–2.

Duffar, J. (1999), 'Les Nouveaux Mouvements religieux et le droit international', in European Consortium for Church–State Research, *New Religious Movements and the Law in the European Union*, Proceedings of the European Consortium for Church-State Research, 15: 365–89.

Duffy, E. (1992), *The Stripping of the Altars: Traditional Religion in England 1400–1580*, New Haven, Conn. and London: Yale University Press.

Elvy, P. (1986), *Buying Time: The Foundations of the Electronic Church*, Great Wakering, Essex: McCrimmons for the Jerusalem Trust.

—— (1990), *The Future of Christian Broadcasting in Europe*, Great Wakering, Essex: McCrimmons for the Jerusalem Trust.

Ester, P., Halman, L., and de Moor, R. (1994), *The Individualizing Society: Value Change in Europe and North America*, Tilburg: Tilburg University Press.

European Consortium for Church–State Research (1992), *Church and State in Europe: State Financial Support, Religion in Schools*, Proceedings of the European Consortium for Church–State Research, 20–1 Oct. 1989, Milan: Giuffré Editore.

—— (1999), *New Religious Movements and the Law in the European Union*, Proceedings of the European Consortium for Church–State Research, 15 Milan: Giuffré Editore.

Fane, R. (1997), 'A Sociological Analysis of Religion on Television', final-year BA dissertation, University of Exeter.

Fenn, R. (forthcoming) (ed.), *The Blackwell Companion to the Sociology of Religion*, Oxford: Blackwell.

Ferrari, S. (1996), 'State and Church in Italy', in G. Robbers (ed.), *State and Church in the European Union*, Baden-Baden: Nomos Verlagsgesellschaft, 169–90.

Flere, S. (1999), 'Church–State Relations in Slovenia in the Nineties', *Facta Universitatis, (series Philosophy and Sociology)*, 2(6): 23–6.

François, E. (1996), 'L'Allemagne du XVIe au XXe siècle', in G. Davie and D. Hervieu-Léger (eds.), *Identités religieuses en Europe*, Paris: La Découverte, 65–88.

Freysinnet-Dominjon, J. (1998), 'L'Image du religieux dans la publicité', paper presented to the Conference of the Association Française de Sociologie Religieuse on 'Médias et religion en miroir', Paris, 2–3 Feb.

Fulton, J. (1996), 'Young People and Religion in Britain and Ireland', in U. Nembach (ed.), *Jugend: 2000 Jahre nach Jesus*, Frankfurt: Peter Lang, 56–71.

—— and Gee, P. (1994) (eds.), *Religion in Contemporary Europe*, Lewiston, NY and Lampeter: Edwin Mellen Press.

Geaney, D. J. (1967), 'Catholic Action', in *New Catholic Encyclopaedia*, New York and London: McGraw-Hill, iii. 262–3.

Giarchi, G., and Abbott, P. (1997), 'Old Age in Europe', in T. Spybey (ed.), *Britain in Europe*, London: Routledge, 173–98.

Giddens, A. (1992), *The Transformation of Intimacy: Sexuality, Love and Eroticism in Modern Societies*. Cambridge: Polity Press.

Gill, R. (1992), *Moral Communities*, Exeter: Exeter University Press.

—— (1993), *The Myth of the Empty Church*, London: SPCK.

—— (1999), *Churchgoing and Christian Ethics*, Cambridge: Cambridge University Press.

Gill, S., D'Costa, G., and King, U. (1994) (eds.), *Religion in Europe: Contemporary Perspectives*, Kampen: Kok Pharos.

Gilliat-Ray, S. (1999), *Higher Education and Student Religious Identity*, London and Exeter: Department of Sociology, University of Exeter in association with the Inter Faith Network.

Giuriati, P., and Lanzi Arzenton, G. (1992), *Il senso del cammino: I pellegrinaggi mariani*, Padua: CRSR.

Goudsblom, J. (1967), *Dutch Society*, New York: Random House.

Gramunt, L. (1967), 'Opus Dei', in *New Catholic Encyclopaedia*, New York and London: McGraw-Hill, x, 709–10.

Grierson, H., and Bullough, G. (1934) (eds.), *The Oxford Book of Seventeenth-century Verse*, Oxford: Clarendon Press.

Gunter, B. and Viney, R. (1994), *Seeing is Believing: Religion and Television in the 1990s*, London: John Libbey & Co.

Gutwirth, J. (1998), *L'Église électronique: La Saga des télévangélistes*, Paris: Bayard.

Hadden, J. (1987), 'Religious Broadcasting and the Mobilization of the New Christian Right', *Journal for the Scientific Study of Religion*, 26: 1–24.

Halsey, A. H. (1985), 'On Methods and Morals', in M. Abrams, D. Gerard, and N. Timms (eds.), *Values and Social Change in Britain*, Basingstoke: Macmillan, 1–20.

Hanley, D. (1994) (ed.), *Christian Democracy in Europe: A Comparative Perspective*, London: Pinter.

Harding, S., and Phillips, D., with Fogarty, M. (1986), *Contrasting Values in Western Europe*, Basingstoke: Macmillan.

Harismendy, P. (1999), 'Age: The Life Course', in M. Cook and G. Davie (eds.), *Modern France: Society in Transition*, London: Routledge, 73–90.

Harris, M. (1998), *Organizing God's Work: Challenges for Churches and Synagogues*, Basingstoke: Macmillan.

Harris, R. (1999), *Lourdes: Body and Spirit in a Secular Age*, London: Allen Lane.

Hastings, A. (1986), *A History of English Christianity, 1929–1985*, London: Collins.

—— (1997), *The Construction of Nationhood: Ethnicity, Religion and Nationalism*, Cambridge: Cambridge University Press.

Heelas, P. (1996), *The New Age Movement*, Oxford: Blackwell.

Herbert, D. (forthcoming), 'Western European Experience and the Rights of Religious Minorities in Central and Eastern Europe', in P. Danchin (ed.), *The Protection of Religious Minorities in Europe*, New York: Columbia University Press.

Hervieu-Léger, D. (1986), *Vers un nouveau christianisme*, Paris: Le Cerf.

—— (1990) (ed.), *La Religion au lycée*, Paris: Le Cerf.

—— (1993), *La Religion pour mémoire*, Paris: Le Cerf.

—— (1994), 'Religion, Experience and the Pope: Memory and the Experience of French Youth', in J. Fulton and P. Gee (eds.), *Religion in Contemporary Europe*, Lewiston, NY and Lampeter: Edwin Mellen Press, 125–38.

—— (1996), '"Une messe est possible": Les Doubles Funérailles du Président', *Le Débat*, 91: 23–30.

—— (1998), 'The Past in the Present: Redefining *Laïcité* in Multicultural France', in P. Berger (ed.), *The Limits of Social Cohesion*, Boulder, Colo.: Westview Press, 38–83.

—— (1999*a*), *Le Pélérin et le converti: La Religion en mouvement*, Paris: Flammarion.

—— (1999*b*), '"Une messe est possible": Les Doubles Funérailles du Président', in J. Julliard (ed.), *La Mort du roi*, Paris: Gallimard, 89–109.

—— (2000), *Religion as a Chain of Memory*, tr. Simon Lee, Cambridge: Polity Press.

—— (forthcoming), 'Maurice Halbwachs (1877–1945)', in D. Hervieu-Léger and J.-P. Willaime (eds.), *Approches classiques en sociologie de religion*, Paris: Presses Universitaires de France.

—— and Champion, F. (1990), *De l'émotion en religion: Renouveaux et traditions*, Paris: Centurion.

Hobsbawm, E. J. (1990), *Nations and Nationalism since 1780*, Cambridge: Cambridge University Press.

Hoover, S. (1988), *Mass Media Religion: The Social Sources of the Electronic Church*, London: Sage.

—— (1998), *Religion in the News: Faith and Journalism in American Public Discourse*, London: Sage.

Introvigne, M. (1998*a*), 'Religious Liberty in Western Europe', A presentation to the Commission on Security and Cooperation in Europe and the House International Relations Committee, Washington DC, July 30, 1998.

—— (1998*b*), 'The Italian Supreme Court Decision on Scientology', English available at www.cesnur.org/testi/SCIE.HTM, full text (in Italian) available at www.cesnur.org/testi/Milano.htm.

*ITC Summary Report* (1994), London: John Libbey & Co.

Jupp, P. (1990), *From Dust to Ashes: The Replacement of Burial by Cremation in England 1840–1967*, The Congregational Lecture 1990, London: Congregational Memorial Hall Trust.

Kauppinen, J. (1992), *The St. Thomas Mass: Case Study of an Urban Church Service*, Tampere: Research Institute of the Lutheran Church in Finland.

Keleher, S. (1997), 'Orthodox Rivalry in the Twentieth Century: Moscow versus Constantinople', *Religion, State and Society*, 25: 125–38.

Kerkhofs, J. (1995) (ed.), *Europe without Priests*, London: SCM Press.

Knott, K. (1984), 'Media Portrayals of Religion and their Reception', final (unpub.) report of a project funded by the Christendom Trust from Jan. 1982 to June 1983. A shorter version of this report can be found in 'Conventional Religion and Common Religion in the Media', transcript of a talk given at the IBA Religious Broadcasting Consultation, Apr. 1983; Religious Research Papers 9, Department of Sociology, University of Leeds.

Kone-el-Adji, A. (1998), 'Le Bouddha cathodique: Construction d'une image du bouddhimse à la télévision française', paper presented to the Conference of the Association Française de Sociologie Religieuse on 'Médias et religion en miroir', Paris, 2–3 Feb.

Lash, S., and Urry, J. (1994), *Economies of Signs and Space*, London: Sage.

Leaman, O. (1989), 'Taking Religion Seriously', *The Times*, 6 Feb.: 18.

Le Bras, G. (1955), *Études de sociologie religieuses*, vol. 1: *Sociologie de la pratique religieuse dans les campagnes françaises*, Paris: Presses Universitaires de France.

—— (1956), *Études de sociologie religieuse*, vol. 2: *De la morphologie à la typologie*, Paris: Presses Universitaires de France.

—— (1976) *L'Église et le village*, Paris: Flammarion.

Lebrun, F. (1995), 'L'Histoire des religions au collège et au lycée', *Études*, July–Aug.: 90.

Ledanois, M. (1990), 'Introduction: La Religion à l'école', in D. Hervieu-Léger (ed.), *La Religion au lycée*, Paris: Le Cerf, 7–9.

Le Galès, P. (1999), 'The Regions', in M. Cook and G. Davie (eds.), *Modern France: Society in Transition*, London: Routledge, 91–112.

Lerman, A. (1989), *The Jewish Communities of the World*, Basingstoke: Macmillan.

Levitt, M. (1996), *Nice When They Are Young: Contemporary Christianity in Families and Schools*, Aldershot: Avebury.

Lewis, B., and Schnapper, D. (1994) (eds.), *Muslims and Europe*, London: Pinter.

Liederman, L. (1996), 'The Headscarf Affair: A Case Study of Religion, Society and Mass Media in Contemporary France', paper presented to the annual conference of the Association for the Sociology of Religion, New York, 15–17 Aug.

Linderman, A. (1993), *Religious Broadcasting in the United States and Sweden: A Comparative Analysis of the History of Religious Broadcasting with Emphasis on Religious Television*, Report No. 10, Lund Research Papers in Media and Communication Studies, Lund: University of Lund.

Lodge, D. (1980), *How Far Can You Go?*, Harmondsworth: Penguin.

Longley, C. (1991), *The Times Book of Clifford Longley*, London: HarperCollins.

Lotz, S. (forthcoming), 'National Identity, the State and Religious Education: A Comparative Study of Germany and Britain in the Context of European Integration', Ph.D. thesis in progress, University of Lancaster.

Lukatis, I. (1989), 'Church Meeting and Pilgrimage in Germany', *Social Compass*, 36: 201–18.

Luxmoore, J. (1995), 'Eastern Europe 1994: A Review of Religious Life in Bulgaria, Romania, Hungary, Slovakia, the Czech Republic and Poland', *Religion, State and Society*, 23: 213–18.

—— (1996), 'Eastern Europe 1995: A Review of Religious Life in Bulgaria, Romania, Hungary, Slovakia, the Czech Republic and Poland', *Religion, State and Society*, 24: 357–65.

—— (1997), 'Eastern Europe 1996: A Review of Religious Life in Albania, Bulgaria,

Romania, Hungary, Slovakia, the Czech Republic and Poland', *Religion, State and Society*, 25: 89–102.

Macadam, A. (1991), *Blue Guide. Northern Italy: From the Alps to Rome*, London: A & C Black.

Macioti, M., and Cipriani, R. (1999), 'Pilgrimages of Time: The Jubilee Nowadays', paper presented to the 1999 Conference of the International Society for the Sociology of Religion, Leuven, 26–30 July.

MacNeill, D. (1998*a*), 'Extending the Work of Halbwachs: Daniele Hervieu-Léger's Analysis of Contemporary Religion', *Durkheimian Studies*, 4: 73–86.

—— (1998*b*), 'Redefining French Identity? The Role of Religion in School', in K. Chadwick and P. Cooke (eds.), *Religion in Modern Contemporary France*, Working Papers on Contemporary France, 3, Portsmouth: University of Portsmouth, 47–57.

—— (forthcoming *a*), 'Religious Education and National Identity', *Social Compass*.

—— (forthcoming *b*), 'The Role of Religious Education in the Formation of National Identity in England, France and Germany', Ph.D. thesis in progress, University of Exeter.

Mâle, E. (1983), *Notre-Dame de Chartres*, Paris: Flammarion.

Martelli, F. (1999), 'Pèlerins: touristes ou consommateurs du bien religieux? L'Image de l'Année Sainte dans les médias en Italie', paper presented to the 1999 Conference of the International Society for the Sociology of Religion, Leuven, 26–30 July.

Martin, D. (1969), *The Religious and the Secular*, London: Routledge.

—— (1978), *A General Theory of Secularization*, Oxford: Blackwell.

—— (1990), *Tongues of Fire: The Explosion of Protestantism in Latin America*, Oxford: Blackwell.

—— (1991), 'The Secularization Issue: Prospect and Retrospect', *British Journal of Sociology*, 42: 465–74.

—— (1996*a*), *Forbidden Revolutions*, London: SPCK.

—— (1996*b*), 'Remise en question de la théorie de la sécularisation', in G. Davie and D. Hervieu-Léger (eds.), *Identités religieuses en Europe*, Paris: La Découverte, 25–42.

—— (forthcoming), 'Centre and Periphery: European Religion in Space and Time', unpub. typescript.

Marty, M., and Appleby, S. (1991) (eds.), *Fundamentalism Observed*, Chicago: Chicago University Press.

—— —— (1994) (eds.), *Accounting for Fundamentalisms: The Dynamic Character of Movements*, Chicago: Chicago University Press.

—— —— (1995) (eds.), *Fundamentalisms Comprehended*, Chicago: Chicago University Press.

Meldgaard, H., and Aagaard, J. (1997) (eds.), *New Religious Movements in Europe*, Aarhus: Aarhus University Press.

Messner, F. (1998), 'L'Accès des religions à la télévision dans les pays de l'Union européenne', paper presented to the Conference of the Association Française de Sociologie Religieuse on 'Médias et religion en miroir', Paris, 2–3 Feb.

Messner, F., and Woehrling, J.-M. (1996) (eds.), *Les Statuts de l'enseignement religieux*, Paris: Le Cerf.

Micewski, A. (1982), *Kardynał Wyszyński: Prymas i mąż stanu*, Paris: Éditions du Dialogue.

Michel, P. (1991), *Politics and Religion in Eastern Europe*, Cambridge: Polity Press.

—— (1996), 'Les Églises dans le monde post-communiste', *Cahiers d'Europe*, 1(1): 79–90 (special issue entitled 'Présence des religions').

—— (1999), *La Religion au musée*, Paris: l'Harmattan.

Mišovič, J. (1997), 'Religion in the Czech Republic of the 1990s in view of Sociological Research', in I. Borowik and G. Babiński (eds.), *New Religious Phenomena in Central and Eastern Europe*, Krakow: Nomos, 187–202.

Modood, T. (1997) (ed.), *Church, State and Religious Minorities*, London: Policy Studies Institute.

Monnot, P. (1996), 'L'Aménagement du temps scolaire au profit de l'enseignement religieux dans l'école primaire publique', in F. Messner and J.-M. Woehrling (eds.), *Les Statuts de l'enseignement religieux*, Paris: Le Cerf, 35–61.

Newport, J. P. (1998), *The New Age Movement and the Biblical Worldview*, Grand Rapids, Mich.: Eerdmans Publishing Co.

Nielsen, J. (1995), *Muslims and Western Europe*, Edinburgh: Edinburgh University Press.

Nonneman, G., Niblock, T., and Szajkowski, B. (1996) (eds.), *Muslim Communities in the New Europe*, Reading: Ithaca Press.

Nowicka, E. (1997), 'Roman Catholicism and the Content of "Polishness"', in I. Borowik and G. Babiński (eds.), *New Religious Phenomena in Central and Eastern Europe*, Krakow: Nomos, 81–92.

Obelkevich, J. (1976), *Religion and Rural Society*, Oxford: Oxford University Press.

O'Connell, J. (1991), *The Making of Modern Europe: Strengths, Constraints and Resolutions*, University of Bradford Peace Research Report No. 26, Bradford: University of Bradford.

O'Neill, M. (1994), 'Serious Earth', *Museums Journal*, Feb.: 28–31.

Østergaard, B. S. (1992) (ed.), *The Media and Western Europe: the Euromedia Handbook*, London: Sage.

Pace, E., and Guolo, R. (1998), *I fondamentalismo*, Rome and Bari: Editori Laterza.

Paine, C. (2000), *Godly Things: Museums, Objects and Religion*, London: Cassell.

Papastathis, C. (1996), 'State and Church in Greece', in G. Robbers (ed.), *State and Church in the European Union*, Baden-Baden: Nomos Verlagsgesellschaft, 75–92.

Peach, C. (1990), 'The Muslim Population of Great Britain', *Ethnic and Racial Studies*, 13: 414–19.

Peck, J. (1993), *The Gods of Televangelism: The Crisis of Meaning and the Appeal of Religious Television*, Creskill, NJ: Hampton Press.

Pérez Vilariño, J. (1997), 'The Catholic Commitment and Spanish Civil Society', *Social Compass*, 44: 595–610.

Postman, N. (1986), *Amusing Ourselves to Death*, Harmondsworth: Penguin.

Poulat, É. (1987), *Liberté, laïcité: La Guerre des deux Frances et le principe de la modernité*, Paris: Le Cerf.

Putnam, R., with Leonardi, R., and Nannetti, R. (1993), *Making Democracy Work: Civil Traditions in Modern Italy*, Princeton: Princeton University Press.

—— (1995), 'Bowling Alone', *Journal of Democracy*, 6(2): 65–78.

Quicke, A., and Quicke, J. (1992), *Hidden Agendas: The Politics of Religious Broadcasting in Britain 1987–91*, Virginia Beach, Va.: Dominion Kings Grant Publications.

Reed, B. (1978), *The Dynamics of Religion*, London: DLT.

Rémond, R. (1999), *Religion and Society in Modern Europe*, Oxford: Blackwell.

Richardson, J. (1995), 'Minority Religions, Religious Freedom, and the New

Pan-European Political and Judicial Institutions', *Journal of Church and State*, 37: 39–60.

Richardson, J. (1997), 'New Religions and Religious Freedom in Eastern and Central Europe: A Sociological Analysis', in I. Borowik and G. Babiński (eds.), *New Religious Phenomena in Central and Eastern Europe*, Krakow: Nomos, 257–82.

Robbers, G. (1996) (ed.), *Church and State in the European Union*, Baden-Baden: Nomos Verlagsgesellschaft.

Roof, W. C., Carroll, J., and Roozen, D. (1995) (eds.), *The Post-war Generation and Establishment Religion: Cross-Cultural Perspectives*, Boulder, Colo.: Westview Press.

Rygidzki, R. (1996), *In Pursuit of Europe*, Warsaw: ISP.

Ryokas, E. (1998), 'Warum Kirchenlieder? Nordische Forschung über Kirchenlieder untersucht die Funktion des Kirchenlieden', paper presented to an invited colloquium on 'Religion in Europe', Göttingen, 30 June–1 July.

Sacks, J. (1999), 'Judaism and Politics in the Modern World', in P. Berger (ed.), *The Desecularization of the World: Resurgent Religion and World Politics*, Grand Rapids, Mich.: Eerdmans Publishing Co., 51–63.

Sadowski, W. (1991) (ed.), *Directions of Change in Post-totalitarian Societies*, Warsaw: ISP.

—— (1997), *The Polish Paradox*, Warsaw: ISP.

Schmied, G. (1996), 'American Televangelism in German TV', *Journal of Contemporary Religion*, 11: 95–9.

Schött, R. (1996), 'State and Church in Sweden', in G. Robbers (ed.), *Church and State in the European Union*, Baden-Baden: Nomos Verlagsgesellschaft, 295–306.

Seward, D. (1993), *The Dancing Sun: Journeys to the Miracle Shrines*, Basingstoke: Macmillan.

Shahid, W., and van Koenigsveld, P. (1995), *Religious Freedom and the Position of Islam in Western Europe: Opportunities and Obstacles in the Acquisition of Equal Rights*, Kampen: Kok Pharos.

Sjödin, U. (1995), 'The Swedes and the Paranormal: An Exploratory Study of Belief in Paranormal Phenomena among Contemporary Swedes', paper presented to the International Conference on New Religious Movements, Rome, 10–12 May.

Smith, A. (1976), *The Wealth of Nations*, Chicago: University of Chicago Press.

Smith, G. (1998), 'Religious Belonging and Inter-faith Encounter: Some Survey Findings from East London', *Journal of Contemporary Religion*, 13: 333–51.

SOPEMI (1992), *Trends in International Migration: Continuous Reporting System on Migration*, Paris: Organization for Economic Co-operation and Development.

Spinder, H. (1992), *RE in Europe: A Guide to the Position of Religious Education in 15 European Countries*, Driebergen, Netherlands: Inter-European Commission on Church and School.

*Statistical Yearbook of the Netherlands* (1990), Netherlands Central Bureau of Statistics, The Hague: SDU Publishers, cbs publishers.

*Statistisches Jahrbuch der Schweiz* (1992), Basle: Birkhaüser.

Steggarda, M. (1993), 'Religion and the Social Positions of Women and Men', *Social Compass*, 40: 65–73.

—— (1994), 'The Social Location of Gender Differences in Religion', paper presented at the colloquium 'La Religion: Un frein à l'égalité?', Lausanne, 1–3 Dec.

Stoetzel, J. (1983), *Les Valeurs du temps présent*, Paris: Presses Universitaires de France.

Stout, D., and Buddenbaum, J. (1996) (eds.), *Religion and the Mass Media: Audiences and Adaptations*, London: Sage.

Sutter, J. (1996), 'Musique et religion: L'Emprise de l'esthétique', *Archives de Sciences Sociales des Religions*, 94: 19–44.

Thomas, K. (1971), *Religion and the Decline of Magic*, London: Weidenfeld and Nicolson.

Thompson, P. (1998), 'The Role of the Roman Catholic Church in Post–1989 Poland', final-year BA dissertation, University of Exeter.

Timms, N. (1992), *Family and Citizenship: Values in Contemporary Britain*, Aldershot: Dartmouth.

Toíbín, C. (1994), *The Sign of the Cross: Travels in Catholic Europe*, London: Jonathan Cape.

Tomka, M. (1992), 'Religion and Religiosity', in R. Andorka, I. Kolosi, and G. Vukovich (eds.), *Social Report*, Budapest: Tárki, 383–96.

—— (1993), 'The Contribution of the Churches in the Liberation from Below: On the Nature of Transition in East-Central Europe', in B. Schennink and B. Klein Goldewijk (eds.), *Liberation from Exclusion: Proceedings of a Conference on Liberation from Below in Latin America and Eastern Europe*, Oegstgeest: CEBEMO, Nijmegen: Peace Research Centre, and Utrecht: Pax Christi, 89–104.

—— (1997), 'Hungarian Post-World War II. Religious Development and the Present Challenge of New Churches and New Religious Movements', in I. Borowik and G. Babiński (eds.), *New Religious Phenomena in Central and Eastern Europe*, Krakow: Nomos, 203–35.

Towler, R. (1995) (ed.), *New Religious Movements and the New Europe*, Aarhus: Aarhus University Press.

Urry, J. (1990), *The Tourist Gaze: Leisure and Travel in Contemporary Societies*, London: Sage.

van Kersbergen, K. (1995), *Social Capitalism: A Study of Christian Democracy and the Welfare State*, London: Routledge.

Vertovec, S., and Peach, C. (1997a) (eds.), *Islam in Europe: The Politics of Religion and Community*, Basingstoke and Warwick: Macmillan in association with the CRER.

—— —— (1997b), 'Introduction: Islam in Europe and the Politics of Religion and Community', in S. Vertovec and C. Peach (eds.), *Islam in Europe: The Politics of Religion and Community*, Basingstoke and Warwick: Macmillan in association with the CRER, 3–47.

Vincent, G., and Willaime, J.-P. (1993) (eds.), *Religions et transformations en Europe*, Strasbourg: Presses Universitaires de Strasbourg.

Voyé, L. (1991), 'Les Jeunes et le mariage religieux: Une émancipation du sacré', *Social Compass*, 39: 405–16.

—— (1996), 'Crise de la civilisation paroissiale et recompositions du croire', in G. Davie and D. Hervieu-Léger (eds.), *Identités religieuses en Europe*, Paris: La Découverte, 195–214.

Wachtelaer, C. (1998), 'A Humanist Perspective', paper presented to the Europe of Neighbours Conference, arranged by the Edinburgh University Centre for Theology and Public Issues, Edinburgh, 6–8 Nov.

Wallis, R., and Bruce, S. (1986), *Sociological Theory, Religion and Collective Action*, Belfast: Queen's University.

Walsh, K. (1992), *Representation of the Past: Museums and Heritage in the Post-modern World*, London: Routledge.

Walsh, M. (1992), *Opus Dei*, San Francisco: Harper.

Walter, A. J. (1994), *The Revival of Death*, London: Routledge.

Walter, A. J. (1996) (ed.), *The Eclipse of Eternity*, Basingstoke: Macmillan.

—— (1998), *The Week Diana Died*, London: Berg.

—— and Davie, G. (1999), 'The Religiosity of Women in the Modern West', *British Journal of Sociology*, 49: 640–60.

Walters, P. (1988) (ed.), *World Christianity: Eastern Europe*, Eastbourne: Marc Europe.

Warburg, M. (1998), 'Restrictions and Privileges: Legal and Administrative Practice and Minority Religions in the USA and Denmark', in E. Barker and M. Warburg (eds.), *New Religions and New Religiosity*, Aarhus: Aarhus University Press, 262–75.

Wasserstein, B. (1996), *Vanishing Diaspora: The Jews in Europe since 1945*, London: Hamish Hamilton.

Webber, J. (1994*a*) (ed.), *Jewish Identities in the New Europe*, London and Washington, DC: Littman Library of Jewish Civilization.

—— (1994*b*), 'Modern Jewish Identities', in J. Webber (ed.), *Jewish Identities in the New Europe*, London and Washington, DC: Littman Library of Jewish Civilization, 74–85.

Weber, M. (1961), 'The Social Psychology of the World Religions', in H. Gerth and C. Wright Mills (eds.), *From Max Weber: Essays in Sociology*, London: Routledge and Kegan Paul, 267–301.

Webster, R. (1990), *A Brief History of Blasphemy: Liberalism, Censorship and 'The Satanic Verses'*, Southwold: Orwell Press.

Willaime, J.-P. (1990) (ed.), *Univers scolaires et religions*, Paris: Le Cerf.

—— (1991) (ed.), *Strasbourg, Jean-Paul II et l'Europe*, Paris: Le Cerf.

—— (1993*a*), 'Univers scolaires et religions en Europe', G. Vincent and J.-P. Willaime (eds.), *Religions et transformations en Europe*, Strasbourg: Presses Universitaires de Strasbourg, 381–95.

—— (1993*b*), 'La Religion civile à la française et ses métamorphoses', *Social Compass*, 40: 571–81.

—— (1996), 'Laïcité et religion en France', in G. Davie and D. Hervieu-Léger (eds.), *Identités religieuses en Europe*, Paris: La Découverte, 153–71.

Wilson, B. (1982), *Religion in Sociological Perspective*, Oxford: Oxford University Press.

Winter, J. (1995), *Sites of Memory, Sites of Mourning: The Great War in European Cultural History*, Cambridge: Cambridge University Press.

Winter, S. (1998), 'Quo Vadis? The Roman Catholic Church in the Czech Republic', *Religion, State and Society*, 26: 217–34.

Wuthnow, R. (1988), *The Restructuring of American Religion*, Princeton, NJ: Princeton University Press.

Young, L. (1997) (ed.), *Rational Choice Theory and Religion: Summary and Assessment*, New York and London: Routledge.

Zadra, D. (1994), 'Communione e Liberazione: A Fundamentalist Idea of Power', in M. Marty and S. Appleby (eds.), *Accounting for Fundamentalisms: The Dynamic Character of Movements*, Chicago: Chicago University Press, 124–48.

# INDEX